THE EMOTIONAL TIE

THE *Emotional* TIE

PSYCHOANALYSIS, MIMESIS, AND AFFECT

Mikkel Borch-Jacobsen

STANFORD UNIVERSITY PRESS   STANFORD, CALIFORNIA   1992

Stanford University Press
Stanford, California
© 1993 by the Board of Trustees of the
Leland Stanford Junior University
Printed in the United States of America
CIP data are at the end of the book

The Emotional Tie was originally published
in French in 1991 under the title
Le Lien affectif, © Aubier Montaigne.

For Charlotte, Sarah,
and Sophie

☞ *Acknowledgments*

The texts in this collection spring from a reading of psychoanalysis begun in *The Freudian Subject* (Mikkel Borch-Jacobsen, trans. Catherine Porter, Stanford University Press, 1988) and concluded more recently in *Lacan: The Absolute Master* (idem, trans. Douglas Brick, Stanford, 1990). Conceived and written as lectures, most often in response to an urgent request, these texts bear the marks of those circumstances: sometimes they take up the same themes, varying them according to the audience; sometimes the problematic changes without any real explanation offered. I have not tried to suppress these faults; to eliminate obvious repetitions and explain the silent ruptures would have required another book. As they appear here, these essays are merely signs along a path, like *snapshots* that decompose a gesture by freezing it in time. Apart from several changes in details, I have not modified these texts however much I have wanted to at times (this is especially true for the first section of "The Unconscious, Nonetheless" as well as most of the conclusions, too often written in haste). I have, however, added several notes in order to situate the context of these lectures and thus emphasize the (at least for me) dated nature of some of them.

I would like to add several names to these dates, names that, for me, make up part of the book's "mental landscape": Michel Henry, François Roustang, Léon Chertok, and Eric Michaud. What this book owes to their friendship, support, and occasionally pitiless critiques goes far beyond what I can acknowledge here. I hope that they will see some expression of my affectionate gratitude herein.

Most of the lectures reproduced in this book have already been published in English (sometimes in slightly different form compared to the "original" French version). "The Freudian Subject: From Politics to Ethics" appeared in *October* 39 (Winter 1986), copyright 1987 by the Massachusetts Institute of Technology and October Magazine, Ltd.; "Hypnosis in Psychoanalysis" appeared in *Representations* 27 (Summer 1989), copyright 1989 by the Regents of the University of California; "Analytic Speech: From Restricted to General Rhetoric" appeared in *The Ends of Rhetoric: History, Theory, Practice*, ed. John Bender and David E. Wellbery (Stanford, 1990), copyright 1990 by the Board of Trustees of the Leland Stanford Junior University; "Talking Cure" appeared in *The Oxford Literary Review* 12.1–2 (1990), copyright 1990 by *The Oxford Literary Review*; and "Mimetic Efficacity" and "The Unconscious, Nonetheless" appeared in the journal of Stanford University's Department of French and Italian, *Stanford Literature Review* 8.1–2 (Spring-Fall 1991) and 6.2 (Fall 1989), respectively, copyright 1991 and 1989 by Anma Libri & Co. I would like to thank the publishers for permission to republish these articles.

The translation of some of these articles was made possible by the generous support of the Department of Romance Languages and Literature of the University of Washington, Seattle, Washington. Special thanks are also due to Douglas Brick, Xavier Callahan, Angela Brewer, and Richard Miller for their excellent translations. "*Traduttore, traditore*": I could not wish to be better betrayed!

M.B.-J.

⌒ *Contents*

Freudian Politics

⤚ The Primal Band

So, haben Sie jetzt diese Bande gesehen?
—Freud to Binswanger concerning his disciples

"The Social Bond and Being a Psychoanalyst"—the title of this conference testifies to the fact that psychoanalysts are increasingly inquisitive about their *own* relationship to society and the political. This is something new; not, of course, that they have never tried to provide the psychoanalytic truth about society and politics: that attempt (or temptation), as we know, is as old as psychoanalysis itself. Then, however, it was a discourse delivered from an exterior, critical position, in relationship to a socio-political field unconditionally defined as illusion, alienation, or misrecognition of desire. The image has been prevalent, especially in France since the 1950's, of a psychoanalysis purified of any political aim, and thus of a depoliticizing and desocializing psychoanalysis. Hence the accusation of demobilizing apoliticism regularly brought against it: hence, too, the more recent fascination it held for all those whom the failings of socialism had discouraged about politics in general.

But it is precisely this position of extraterritoriality—and thus also of distant superiority—that psychoanalysts have now come to question. It is as if they could no longer speak of the social bond without returning to themselves, as if they could no longer speak of themselves without returning to what binds them together or, on the contrary, what unbinds and tears them apart. This is not unrelated to a certain institutional "crisis" or panic in psychoanalysis, in that this crisis brings to light, like an enormous symptom, practices that we believed were reserved for political bureaucracies. Psychoanalysts, sometimes with a certain astonishment, are noticing that the bonds uniting them within this or that association, society, or school of psychoanalysis are fundamentally no different from those described by Freud in relation to religious or military masses: the same blind fidelity to an all-powerful leader, the same totalitarian unanimity, the same unfurling of hate toward dissidents, the same panic when the chief retires. Reconstituting their history more rigorously than before (especially in François Roustang's remarkable work),[1] psychoanalysts also discover that this situation is not anything new, that if there is a "crisis," it coincides with the beginning of the psychoanalytic movement. If only for the rather brusquely summarized reasons just given, it has become very difficult for them to separate themselves from the question of the social bond: the question makes a massive comeback as one of psychoanalysis's *internal*, as well as *unresolved*, questions, which appears to leave psychoanalysts bewildered. Perhaps we can say that the "crisis" has become so *ripe* that it can no longer be considered an accident, an event coming from outside psychoanalysis. I recall this "situation of psychoanalysis in 1980" because it seems to weigh heavily on the problematic of this conference.

If we now turn toward Freud to ask the reason for this situation, we must first recognize that his relationship to politics is not one of criticism, as people too often believe. For there to be criticism, it would be necessary, for example, that he denounce politics itself as the alienation of the social bond's essence. But this somewhat Marxist gesture never tempts him. On the contrary, his first move is to reduce the social bond to a properly political one. Thus, in *Group Psychology and the Analysis of the Ego*, an ineluctable text with regard to the question at hand, the possibility of the social bond literally hangs on the existence of a beloved chief—that is, on the prior installation of the political. Like Gustave Le Bon, to whose analyses he owes more than he is ready to acknowledge, Freud places the chief at the beginning and the helm of the group, the *Masse*, understood as a homogenous, welded, assembled, *bonded* social body. Only the chief (only the *Führer*, since that is how Freud translates Le Bon's *meneur*) assures the cohesion of that mass. The proof is that the disappearance of the chief (a military or spiritual one, in Freud's examples) immediately provokes the general dissolution of social bonds, in the form of an "every man for himself" panic and of war of all against all. As Freud writes: "The mutual ties between the members of the group [*die gegenseitigen Bindungen der Massenindividuen*] disappear, as a rule, at the same time as the tie with their leader [*mit der Bindung an den Führer*]."[2]

Consequently, far from calling on some arbitrary liberation from the yoke of political bondage, Freud, in accordance with a very profound tradition, sees it as the condition of possibility, or essence, of the social bond. Hence we should not be surprised by passages like these from *Group Psychology*:

Man is . . . a horde animal, an individual creature in a horde led by a chief.[3]

The group still wishes to be governed by unrestricted force; it has an extreme passion for authority; in Le Bon's phrase, it has a thirst for obedience.[4]

And, thinking again of Roustang's analyses,[5] we should not be surprised that Freud founded the psychoanalytic community on the model of "a horde led by a chief." How could it be otherwise, since nothing in his theory of society furnishes the project of another model?

Someone may object that Freud unveiled the libidinal nature of the political as no one had before and that, in this sense, he irreparably undermined the ideology of power by exhibiting the love by which authority authorizes itself, the voluntary slavery that supports tyranny. Indeed, in *Group Psychology*, the bond that attaches the members of the mass to the chief is localized in the libidinal tie (*Libidobindung*) or in the love relation (*Liebesbeziehung*); and, as we also know, by virtue of this community of love for a single object taking the place of the ego ideal, the properly social bonds—designated as "emotional ties" or "bonds" (*Gefühlsbindungen*) of identification—are established. But, in the end, this only confirms, and even aggravates, Freud's own submission to the political model: To say that the political is fomented by love undoubtedly dismisses the illusion of a self-supporting power and dismantles the lure of mastery, but it also fuses libidinal economy to political economy by affirming that love is political—better yet (or worse), that love is the Political, as the unifying, binding power of society. In fact, how can we dissociate love from the political here? Power is not love's *other*. Instead, love opposes power to *itself* as *its* object, desiring submission, as Freud writes (and as others mindlessly repeat), and thus it submits *to itself of itself.*

I have been saying "love," but I could just as well have said "desire" or "the subject," for what binds and subjects itself is, obviously, the subject or, in the vocabulary of *Group Psychology*, the

"individual." That is also why Freud immediately rejects the opposition between group and individual psychology, saying that it "falls
wholly within the domain of individual psychology"[6]: sociality in-
scribes itself in the "individual," since it is inaugurated in the subject's love, in amorous self-binding. From the first libidinal tie,
from the first opening of the narcissistic monad to the other (to
the *Andere*), the political, power, and submission are *already there*.
Conversely, the political never goes beyond the limits of the subject
since the subject, too, institutes the political by amorously limiting
itself, by autoterminating and autodetermining itself. The subject is
the political and the political is the subject—this is the totally unavoidable proposition of the essay entitled, not by accident, *Group
Psychology and the Analysis of the Ego*. Thus there is no reason to look
for a nonexistent opposition between the subject of desire and the
political subject in Freud's "sociological" theory: by making libidinal *Bindung* into the political bond, as the social bond's foundation,
Freud actually equates the two, and this also means that libido theory
can simultaneously be read as political. This theory (i.e., psychoanalysis) engages itself as political, engages itself in, and is engaged
by, the political.

In this regard, the concept of *Bindung*, whose intervention in
Freud's reflections on the social and political bond is not fortuitous,
deserves careful attention. Indeed, it is one of the most decisive (and
problematic) notions in the Freudian apparatus, thus allowing us to
verify the complicity of the libidinal and the political over and above
the properly socio-political theses of *Group Psychology*. For Freud, in
fact, *Bindung* supplies the most general concept of union, understood
as the formation of coherent, homogenous, *massive* unities. Beginning with the *Project* of 1895, Freud makes the binding (*Bindung*) of
free or unbonded (*ungebändigt*) energy the condition for establishing stable unities with constant investment.[7] Thus, for example (but
not just any example), the ego is "a mass of neurones of this kind
which hold fast to their cathexis (which, that is, are in a bound condition), and this can only occur, no doubt, as a result of their mutual
influence."[8] Twenty-five years later, Freud takes up this same hypothesis in *Beyond the Pleasure Principle*, which invests *Bindung* with
a formidable role halfway between the "economic" and "biological" registers. First, it is the most "precocious" and "important"
function of the psychical apparatus, binding the destructive exter-

nal quantities of excitation in order to master them even before the intervention of the *Lustprinzip*, the tendency toward release of pleasure (*Lustentbindung*). More generally, *Bindung* is the means utilized by the life drives[9] (by Eros) in order to form new unities and maintain constancy or consistency of the living substance. By bonding in a "cellular State" (*Zellenstaat*) or by binding external excitations, single-celled organisms defer their own death drive. The same principle applies to higher organisms: by binding or bonding with the *other* or the *outside*, by uniting with it in a higher *Verbindung* or *Vereinigung*, different organisms neutralize the disbanding, lethal tendency that drives them to form an individual band, that is, to live and die alone—somewhat, Freud says, like "narcissistic" cancer cells. In this regard, there is no rupture between the speculation of *Beyond the Pleasure Principle* and the thesis proffered in *Group Psychology*. Freud returns to it several times in the latter work: the mass, social organism, or cellular super State, results from the *Bindung* of Eros, understood as the principle of organicity, of being fused together, of systematic assembly.

He writes that the tendency to form bands or masses is "a biological continuation [*eine biologische Fortführung*] of the multicellular character of all the higher organisms."[10] By bonding itself socially, the individual sacrifices its own particularity (its *Eigenart*) for that great individual, the mass, exactly *as* the single cell sacrifices itself for the cellular State, or *as* the narcissistic ego sacrifices its libido for the object—it being understood that this is an analogy of proportionality in which each organic unity is binding (vital) in relation to the unity of inferior degree, and potentially disbanding (lethal) in relation to the unity of superior degree, each one representing a specific binding or alloy of the life and death drives, of *Bindung* and *Entbindung*.

Such is the hypothesis, the *organicist* hypothesis, which, as is immediately obvious, implies an integrally political and—why not say it?—*totalitarian* conception of the social bond, since, from the beginning, it presupposes society to be one, united, unanimous, and undivided. This is already expressed in the term *mass*, which, as Hannah Arendt's work shows, is the principle term of modern totalitarianism.[11] From this point of view, the accent that Freud places on the figure of the chief is in no way fortuitous. In fact, only a *Führer* (which, in passing, is a term that Hitler, too, inherited from Le

Bon's *Psychologie des foules*) is capable of giving the mass an organic unity—that is, as Philippe Lacoue-Labarthe and Jean-Luc Nancy have strongly stated in a recent article, a unity of the subject.[12] Not that the chief *constrains* his subjects to political unity, since, as we have seen, his force comes solely from love; rather, and more fundamentally, the mass can erect itself as a subject only by erecting (and erecting *itself as*) the figure of the subject par excellence, the authoritarian chief who authorizes himself from himself alone. Therefore, in subjecting themselves to the organic figure of the subject, the subjects subject themselves to no one but themselves.

In this sense, *Bindung* is the subject's (or, if you will, the individual's, the ego's, the cell's) self-bonding, and the "sacrifice" that it implies is, after all, a very narcissistic one. Thus, when the cells bond themselves in the cellular State, they merely repeat the process by which they narcissistically bound themselves to themselves, already banding themselves to form a compact whole. And while the individuals of the mass amorously bond themselves to the chief and sacrifice their narcissistic autonomy to him, they still love themselves. Erotic *Bindung* does not, therefore, strangle the subject from outside. It comes *from the subject*, as a "biological continuation" of the subject, starting from the subject. The best model of this process is undoubtedly the one evoked in "On Narcissism" of "pseudopodia" emitted by the "narcissistic" protoplasm toward its "objects": that emission is an emission of self, and the subject never leaves its own limits (or *bounds*), even when it appears to overflow or unbind itself toward the other, toward the love object. On the contrary, in bonding itself to the other, it encloses the other in *its* limits to form a new subject, a new, banded, bonded ensemble, or (to speak German, this time) a new *Bund*: the *same*, therefore; always just as compact and absolute since it relates and bonds only to itself. Thus there is no opposition between *Bindung* and what it binds: the subject is not bound; it binds itself, and thus it remains master and subject of its own binding. The movement of Eros's *Bindung*, as self-binding of the living substance, is that of the reduction of opposition in general: conquering movement of the *autos*—that is, automovement of the Narcissus who self-opposes the object, self-objecting the other in order to be all the more itself once again in it, and thus to re-absorb it in itself. Eros, in other words, is a pseudopod of Narcissus. Thus the love of the members of the mass addresses itself to a chief, that is, as Freud explains in chapter 10 of *Group Psychology*, to an absolutely narcissistic subject who does not love anyone: Only in an absolute subject can the mass love itself narcissistically, bind itself to itself, in short, absolutize itself as subject. Here, as always, political absolutism is an ego absolutism, and Freud's politics must therefore be qualified as narcissistic. This, as you can see, must also be viewed as a certain ego narcissism on the part of Freud himself, as an I-the-autoanalyst-who-autoinstitutes-myself-as-me-the-analysis, me-the-psychoanalysts, as an I-who-leaves-my-ego-to-those-who-claim-to-descend-from-me, the-Freudian-cause.[13]

All this, which I have summarized rather bluntly, prevents an interpretation of Freud's politics as some slightly aberrant outgrowth of his psychoanalytic theory. In fact, his politics are firmly rooted in psychoanalytic theory, at a depth that, as it seems to me, is barely touched by the diverse attempts at institutional self-criticism occasionally launched from within psychoanalysis itself. Yet it is at this depth that, *despite everything*, Freud is held prisoner by the metaphysics of the Subject and, hence, by the Political in which that metaphysics has its end. This is not the time or place to support this contention as it should be supported. Therefore, leaving behind Freud's most explicit theses on the social bond, I would like to reverse the procedure in order to concentrate on the much more problematic gesture that simultaneously, mutely *disorganizes* that theory, prevents it from containing itself, and thus causes it to overflow the political framework in which Freud tries to hold it. Here again I will remain brief, limiting myself essentially to the argument developed in *Group Psychology and the Analysis of the Ego*.

In that text, Freud *tries* to affirm the precedence and preexcellence in the social order of the bond of love with the chief. But this can happen only under two conditions. On the one hand, the establishment of social bonds of identification, whose nonlibidinal, non-object-oriented character Freud recognizes, must depend on the prior establishment of the libidinal bond with the chief. This condition is amplified by what, to all intents and purposes, is an Oedipal theory, which would have the members of the mass identify with each other in a hysterical and triangular mode *because* of their communal love for the chief. On the other hand, and simultaneously, Freud must arbitrarily avoid and repress an enormous difficulty that

arises from the possibility of "bonds" that escape from the dictatorship of libidinal-political economy. This difficulty, which may be
shown to proliferate at every stage in Freud's argumentation, shows
up with peculiar insistence at two points in the text: first, at the
level of the analysis of panic and fratricidal hate, with the more or
less implicit but nevertheless readable appearance of the possibility
of nonlibidinal bonds *independent* of the bond of love with the chief;
and second, at the level of the analysis of identifications, when Freud
openly admits the possibility of a "primary" bond of identification
that is *anterior* and even *interior* to any libidinal bond. I would like
to suggest that these two possibilities indicate one and the same
impossibility of the mass in the sense intended by Freud.

First, let us consider the phenomena of panic and hate as they
are invoked in chapters 5 and 6 of *Group Psychology*. I will not restate
these well-known analyses but simply recall that Freud invokes panic
and hate as examples of *Entbindung*, of unbinding and disbanding,
in exact proportion to his intention to prove by a sort of reductio
ad absurdum that the bond with the chief is the only one capable of
establishing the social bond, the *Massenbindung*: without the chief,
the mass would return to the anarchic dispersion and violent egoism of Narcissi; the rupture of the libidinal-political bond would, in
other words, bring on the rupture of every bond, of every "altruistic" relation with the other, and the alternative would be decisive,
divisive, between political sociality and nonsociality.

Then, discussing William McDougall's theses on panic, Freud
tries to demonstrate that panic sets in as a result of the disappearance
of the chief, and not, as McDougall thought, as a result of anxiety
(*Angst*). As to panic's disbanding character, Freud apparently believes in it so completely that he reproaches McDougall, who saw it
as the perfect manifestation of the social tendency toward the "sympathetic induction of emotions," for having fallen into the paradox
(*Paradoxon*) of a disbanding bond or an asocial sociality. But it must
then be remarked that the paradox rebounds on Freud himself for,
very strangely, Freud does not deny that panic is a "sympathetic"
phenomenon—that is, as he had previously explained, a suggestive,
contagious, or mimetic one. His disagreement with McDougall is
aimed at the trigger mechanism of panic (fear *or* disappearance of
the chief), not at the process itself: "The contention that fear [*Angst*]
in a group is increased to enormous proportions through induction

(contagion) is not in the least contradicted by these remarks." [14] The paradox is this: since "sympathy" (i.e., co-feeling or suffering-with) truly constitutes the most immediate possible bond with others, the disappearance of the bond of love with the chief does not, as Freud wished it to, liberate the pure and simple disbanding of Narcissi. In a sense it does not liberate anything at all, and certainly not autarchic subjects (individuals), since panic is precisely an uncontrollable breaching of the ego by (the affects of) others, or, if you will, a mimetic, contagious, suggested narcissism.

What comes out in panic phenomena, I can note only in passing, is everything that Freud had violently rejected under the rubric of "suggestion" or "suggestibility," understood as the relation of immediate, "hypnotic" fusion with another. The important thing here is that Freud rediscovers this whole grouping in a phenomenon that hypothetically no longer arises from the libidinal-political economy and that henceforth confronts him with the paradox of a narcissistic bond. Indeed, panic actually bonds a band of Narcissi, and that is the whole problem. The acme of the "sympathetic" relationship with others is simultaneously the ultimate nonrelationship with others: each imitates the "every man for himself" of the others; here assimilation is strictly equivalent to a disassimilating dissimilation. The panic bond goes beyond the alternatives of bonding and disbanding, as well as each of the related oppositions manipulated by Freud. A disbanding band must be qualified as both narcissistic and nonnarcissistic, egoistic and altruistic, asocial and social. And if, as Freud would have it, panic designates the limit or breaking point of the mass, it nevertheless cannot be seen as external to that mass. That limit is a passage to the limit, an internal impossibility lodged at the very heart of the mass, like a cancer proliferating on the inside and using the paths of union to propagate disunion, narcissism, and death.

All this is necessarily related to the internal violence of "all against all," a second disbanding centered around the disappearance of the chief. In fact, Freud specifies in chapter 4 of *Group Psychology* that narcissism and hate make up one and the same absence of "altruistic" relationship with the other: hate is fundamentally narcissistic. Here Freud distinguishes two modalities of narcissistic hate, depending on whether or not they mix or bond with object love. The first possibility is an ambivalence that affects every relationship between people or social groups; in this case, as Freud had explained in chapter 3 concerning the mass, the hateful-narcissistic element is bound with or by love and displaced onto strangers. The second possibility is pure hate, not bonded, unbound, *narcissistic*, which thus corresponds exactly to what appears when the bond of love with the chief is broken:

> In the undisguised antipathies and aversions which people feel toward close strangers, we may recognize the expression of self-love—of narcissism. This self-love works for the preservation of the individual, and behaves as though the occurrence of any divergence from his own particular lines of development involved a criticism of them and a demand for their alteration. . . . In this whole connection men give evidence of a readiness for hatred, an aggressiveness, the source of which is unknown, and to which one is tempted to ascribe an elementary character.*

> *In a recently published study, *Beyond the Pleasure Principle* [1920], I have attempted to connect the polarity of love and hatred with a hypothetical opposition between instincts of life and death, and to establish the sexual instincts as the purest examples of the former, the instincts of life.[15]

Now, this narcissistic hate, which must therefore be conceived symmetrically as the purest delegate of the pure unbinding of the death drives, brings up exactly the same problem as the phenomenon of panic, for, in all rigor, how can one speak of unbinding with regard to hate? Even the coldest, least ambivalent hate still implies a relationship with the other, and it is no accident that Freud speaks here of *nahestehende Fremde*, of "close strangers" with whom one enters into contact: as he will state in *Inhibitions, Symptoms and Anxiety*, contact is "the immediate aim of the aggressive as well as the loving object cathexes."[16] Hate wants to *get its hands on* the other; it wants to touch even when it wants to destroy. The "narcissism" of hate must therefore be enclosed with the same quotation marks as the "narcissism" of panic; that absence of bond is still a bond, and vice versa, since the hateful bond is equal to the dissolution of every relationship: Alterity is immediately suppressed, assassinated, or reabsorbed by the assimilating violence of the Same. Thus we find ourselves confronted by the same "paradox" as before, that of an unbinding bind that can be classified neither as binding nor unbinding, or, again, as both at once (which allows us to emphasize, in passing, that this intractable double band is undoubtedly closely related to what is elsewhere called a "double bind," pragmatic paradox, logical undecidability, etc.). In other words, ambivalence is the law, and, according to Freud, it insists at the very point where a pure, elementary, unalloyed hate—namely, the absolute other of the bond, the unrelatedness of the death drive as such—should have appeared.

This is confirmed in an exemplary fashion by the passage from *Beyond the Pleasure Principle* alluded to in the note that I have just quoted, which carries the difficulty to the most general level of Freud's speculation on *Bindung* and *Entbindung*. In fact, his analysis of "the polarity of love and hate" intervenes in *Beyond the Pleasure Principle* at the moment when, having classed narcissism and the self-preservative drives on the side of Eros, Freud notes that with this hypothesis there would be "no other instincts whatever but the libidinal ones. . . . At all events there are none other visible." [17] In whatever direction we might look there would be nothing but erotic *Bindung*, and then, Freud objects, we risk falling back into Jung's libidinal monism. It is therefore absolutely necessary to find an example (*Beispiel*) of the death drive, that is, an example of what is without example, of that which works in silence and never appears. That example is sadistic hate. Sadism has long been recognized, Freud says, as a "component" of the sexual drive. "But," he adds (and the entire passage must be quoted),

how can the sadistic instinct, whose aim it is to injure the object, be derived from Eros, the preserver of life? Is it not plausible to suppose that this sadism is in fact a death instinct which, under the influence of the narcissistic libido, has been forced away from the ego and has consequently only emerged [*zum Vorschein kommt*] in relation to the object? It now enters the service of the sexual function. During the oral stage of organization of the libido, the act of obtaining erotic mastery over an object coincides with that object's destruction [*Vernichtung*]; later, the sadistic instinct separates off, and finally, at the stage of genital primacy, it takes on, for the purposes of reproduction, the function of overpowering the sexual object to the extent necessary for carrying out the sexual act. It might indeed be said that the sadism which has been forced out of the ego has pointed the way [*habe den Weg gezeigt*] for the libidinal components of the sexual instinct, and that these follow after it to the object. Wherever the original sadism has undergone no mitigation or intermixture, we find the familiar ambivalence of love and hate in erotic life.

If such an assumption as this is permissible, then we have met the demand that we should produce an example of a death instinct—though, it is true, a displaced one. [18]

Hence we must admit that the example of hate proves the death drive, proves the absolutely improbable. Yet hate is not an example of the death drive *itself* precisely because, as Freud recognized, it is a displaced drive, turned aside from its path, expelled from the ego toward objects, which is to say allied, bound to the life drives. Thus hate—the only, or at least the purest, most characteristic example— does not prove anything, except that there is no example of the death drive, or, what amounts to the same thing, that the death drive exists only as an example, impure, poorly expressed, mixed. Disbanding appears only *in* and *as* bonding. On the other hand, however, it does seem that hate furnishes the example par excellence of erotic *Bindung*, for Freud is not content to say that sadism is added to or mixed with an *already* established amorous bond. He adds—and this is undoubtedly the most inextricable proposition in his discourse on the intrication and disintrication of drives—that sadism points the way for the libido, *opens* the narcissistic ego to the object, *opens* the possibility of the object relation. Thus we learn that Eros is *nothing but* Thanatos (or Narcissus): aggression, the deferred death drive, inaugurates love and the libidinal bond. Far from simply entering "the service" of the sexual function, as Freud writes, aggression ini- tiates it as "mastery" of the object, and it does so in the mode of an ambivalence anterior to every composition, addition, or mixture. In the absolutely first, primary stage of oral incorporation, hate *is* love; the two are just as inseparable as ego and object, ego and other. Thus everything begins—or, rather, opens itself, and defers itself, repeats itself—in that consubstantiality of hate and love, that strange mur- derous intussusception which is the "narcissistic" incorporation of the "object" (maternal substance, foreign protoplasmic substance, etc.). In other words, everything begins and opens itself in that pri- mal double band which is doubly primal, since it is only in the amor- ous destruction of the "object," in the cannibal-like (non)relation with the other, that death *and* life are born.

All this is only an apparent detour from *Group Psychology*. First, this point is the opening of the possibility (or, better, the impos- sibility) of the bond in general and thus also of the social bond, whether the bond to the chief or the bonds of identification. Second, the political construction of *Group Psychology* is both founded on and ruined by that double bond of oral incorporation which intervenes in chapter 7, at the moment when Freud introduces the concept of primary identification. As is well known, Freud tries to think of primary identification as an "emotional," mimetic bond belonging to Oedipal prehistory (*Vorgeschichte*) and, above all *independent* of the libidinal-object bond. That value of independence, as I can only suggest here, is absolutely decisive in Freud's argumentation, for it is only on the condition of separating the bond of identification (to the father, in this instance) from the bond of love (to the mother) that he can engender the triangular identification of the Oedipus, which in turn furnishes the model for identifications within the mass: independent of love at the start, primary identification reinforces itself and becomes ambivalent *because* of love for the mother. But immediately after proposing this hypothesis (i.e., the Oedipal hypothesis, which amounts to making identification an effect of love), Freud continues, and this takes us back to the double band of incorporation:

Identification, in fact, is ambivalent from the very first; it can turn into an expression of tenderness as easily as into a wish for someone's removal. It behaves like a derivative of the first, *oral* phase of the organization of the libido, in which the object that we long for and prize is assimilated by eating and is in that way annihilated as such. The cannibal, as we know, has remained at this standpoint; he has a devouring affection for his enemies and only devours people of whom he is fond.[19]

Thus the Oedipal prehistory itself has a prehistory that goes back to the collective prehistory of humanity, to the cannibalism of primitive people, to the totemic meal, in short, to the whole great scene of the devouring community or communion described in "Totem and Taboo." And, most important for us, this prehistory inextricably mixes devouring identification, as an ego-formative process, with objectality, as the first bond with the other. At the origin of the origin, hateful identification and object love were one and the same thing, one and the same *assimilation* to and *of* the other. Being and having were one: "I am the breast," as the famous London note says. Narcissism, the ego—but, since we are now in the prehistory before all individual history, we must say instead it [*ça*]—is formed *with*[20] the other, *as* the other, by digesting it. Thus when Freud describes the Oedipal prehistory, bringing in three differentiated characters (an ego, a model, and an object) and two types of bonds (identification and love), he envisions a situation that is already very "historical," already very political. But anterior to that little triangular society,

and making it possible based on a socius older than every relationship of subject to subject, we must admit a sort of undifferentiated
mass, the Oedipal womb or matrix: something like, let us say, a
nonsubject that is initiating itself as an ego in a panicky disbanding
bond (which is anxiety and birth) with what is not yet either object
or subject, and that can be called "mother" only on the condition of
not confusing it with the maternal character in the Oedipus.

This is the point at which the Subject and the Political conjointly
open and collapse, for—and I would like to conclude on these very
elementary questions—if, as Freud says on several occasions, devouring identification constitutes "the earliest and original form of
emotional tie,"[21] if everything (subject *and* sociality) starts in that in-
dissociable double band, can we reconcile that with the affirmation
of a social bond that is originally political and amorous, assembling
the subjects in a beautiful, harmonious totality? Is the possibility of
hate and panic solely external to the bond of love? Or is it not, rather,
its internal condition of possibility, and thus its condition of impossibility—for example, the condition of impossibility of Oedipal
love and everything it is supposed to command? By placing love—
that is, the subject—in command of the mass, hasn't Freud passed
off as an essential law what is only a teleological, ethical, and political prescription, perhaps the oldest and most indestructible one: "Be
a subject"?

Translated by Douglas Brick

The Freudian Subject: From Politics to Ethics

> I have no conscience. The *Führer* is my conscience.
> —Hermann Goering

> When one has a sense of guilt after having committed a misdeed, and because of it, the feeling should more properly be called *remorse*. It relates only to a deed that has been done, and of course it presupposes that a *conscience*—the readiness to feel guilty—was already in existence before the deed took place. . . . But if the human sense of guilt goes back to the killing of the primal father, that was after all a case of "remorse." Are we to assume that at that time a sense of guilt was not, as we have presupposed, in existence before the deed? If not, where, in this case, did the remorse come from?
> —Sigmund Freud

It may seem strange that I should approach the notion of "the subject in psychoanalysis" from the angle of politics and Freudian ethics. After all, isn't the main subject with which and with whom psychoanalysis deals the individual, in all his remarkable resistance to the ethical and political prescriptions of society? Why, then, should we consider this implacably singular subjectivity from the perspective of what—as political power or moral taboo—most often oppresses it, shackles it, or censures it? And isn't the most intractable feature of the desiring subject precisely its tendency to balk at being reduced to what Freud called the social "ego," the political "ego ideal," the moral "superego"? Perhaps. But we may still wonder why Freud himself, after having set up this great antagonism between desiring subjectivity and the various "egoic" forms of repression, kept on trying to reduce it by rooting the ego in the id, by analyzing the libidinal structure of political submission's link to the Ego Ideal–Father–Leader, and even by uncovering the Oedipal origin of the moral superego. The question remains, in other words, of whether what we stubbornly persist in calling the *subject* of desire or the *subject* of the unconscious is really so easy to distinguish from what we no less stubbornly persist in thinking of as its *Other*—that is, in no particular order, the symbolic Father, Law, prohibition, society, power. . . .

We might as well start by saying that nothing seems more fragile than this distinction. Indeed, everything in the Freudian text combines to suggest the identity—the identification—between the desiring subject and this "Other" that, at first glance, seems to be opposed to it and to alienate it, divide it, or separate it from itself. In short, and at the risk of encroaching on what will be my conclusion, I would say that the Freudian subject *is* the other, is *the same as* the other. This equation is obviously ambiguous, and so we must understand it carefully, literally, and in all its senses. It involves two very different notions or "versions" of the subject, according to the emphasis we put on it. Thus, either we understand that the Other is *the same as the subject*, in which case the subject, always identical to itself, triumphantly assimilates or absorbs that otherness into itself—this is the dialectical (and, in Freud, the *political*) version of this equation—or we understand the subject to be *the same as the Other*, and at once the equation becomes more difficult to understand, at once we no longer know who or what this subject is that a moment ago seemed so obvious, nor do we know whether we are still dealing with a subject at all. Strictly speaking, I am not sure that we should even contrast this second "version" with the first. To do so would be to force it into the dialectical mode, whereas here it is only a question of a different emphasis on the *same* notion. But that notion does exist in Freud, where it indicates what I will call, for lack of a better term, an *ethical* "beyond" of the subject. That, at least, is what I would like to demonstrate, convinced as I am that here, in this infinitesimal, imperceptible difference of emphasis, is where Freud's notion of the subject is ultimately played out. This is also an opportunity for me to extend and reinflect certain of my own previously published analyses of the "Freudian subject."[1]

But even before we turn to the Freudian wavering between a "politics" and an "ethics" of the subject, we surely ought to reach some agreement on the significance and implications of that little word *subject*, apparently so obvious and so transparent. Nowadays we speak easily—and I've just been doing so myself—about the "subject of desire," the "subject of the unconscious," the "subject of fantasy." But are we really sure that we always know what we are talking about? For example, do we know the history, the origin, the genealogy of this term? In this connection, it may be useful to recall that the word *subject* appears only rarely in Freud, who preferred to speak of the "ego," the "id," the "superego," or of the "conscious" and the "unconscious." That is why it is best to recognize right away that the "subject" comes to us not from Freud himself but from a particular interpretation of his work: it is from Lacan and his "return to Freud," begun in the early 1950's, that we must date the intemperate use of the word *subject* by French psychoanalysts.

This word, as Jacques Lacan well knew, comes from philosophy. We could even say that it is the key term of Western metaphysics. The subject is not first of all the individual, much less the psychological ego to which we so often find it reduced today. Above all, the word *subject* designates the *hypokeimenon*, the "underlying" or "subjacent" goal of basic, founding philosophical inquiry, the quest for which is posed, supposed, and presupposed in Book VII of Aristotle's *Metaphysics*: τί τὸ ὄν, "What is being as being?" And, as Heidegger has shown, it is only to the extent that the ego, in the form of the Cartesian *cogito*, is heir to this ultimate basic position, the *ultimum subjectum*, that it becomes a "subject" in the strictly modern sense of the word. This should not be understood in the sense of an "egoist" or "subjectivist" determination of being, but rather in the sense that the whole of being is henceforth to be conceived on the initially Cartesian model of the autofoundation or autopositioning of a subject presenting itself to itself as consciousness, in representation or in the will, in labor or in desire, in the State or in the work of art.

Thus it was this modern (even strictly Cartesian, as we could show in some detail) concept of the subject that Lacan imported into psychoanalysis, with well-known success. Since others have already done so, I will not dwell here on the theoretical and institutional stakes of that operation, or on the complex conceptual "corruptions"[2] to which it has given rise. I would merely like to call attention, in a very preliminary way, to this operation's fundamentally equivocal character. No doubt this appeal to the philosopheme of the subject (as well as to several others: of "truth," "desire," "intersubjectivity," "dialectics," "alienation," and so on) permitted

18

the restoration of the Freudian text's trenchant quality by ridding it from the outset of all psychologism and biologism. But why, finally, keep the word—and hence also the concept—*subject*, particularly when it was simultaneously being invested with all the Heideggerian de(con)struction of the "metaphysics of subjectivity"? Wasn't what was at stake, as Lacan indicated in "The Mirror Stage as Formative of the Function of the I," the removal of the psychoanalytic experience of the I from "any philosophy directly issuing from the *Cogito*"[3]? In fact, would Freud have deserved even a moment's philosophical attention if he had not contributed, and more than anyone else, to a challenging of the notion of subject *qua* ego present to itself in consciousness, in representation, or in the will?

Nor is this a matter of overlooking the fact that the Lacanian subject is the originally divided, split subject of desire, the profoundly subjected subject of the signifier and of language—and therefore nothing like the transcendental and absolute subject of the philosophers, nothing like the strong, autonomous ego of the ego psychologists, its pale successor. Nevertheless, this infinitely decentered subject, reduced to the desire for that portion of itself that language simultaneously arouses and forbids it to rejoin, is still a subject. Lacan, in a very enigmatic way, retains the *word*—at least, that is, the pure position—of the subject. That this position, from the very fact of its being linguistic, is equivalent to a de-position or a disappearance makes little difference—and that much less difference if the subject's *fading* or *aphanisis* occurs through what we persist in describing as an autoenunciation. Emptied of substance, virtually null, the subject subsists in the *representation* of its lack, in the closed combinative of signifiers in which it stubbornly continues to represent itself, to present itself in front of itself, always disappearing but always reborn upon its disappearance.

It is not my intention here, however, to analyze this powerful ontology of the subject in any detail, this ontology that is all the more powerful for being presented in the guise of a kind of negative ego-logy eager to ambush the "imaginary ego" and the "subject supposed to know." If, getting ahead of analyses still to come, I have nevertheless referred briefly to this ontology, it is because it constitutes both the outer limit and the condition of possibility of any investigation into the "subject in psychoanalysis" today. Above all, I have referred to it because it seems to me that it functions as a veritable *symptom*. How, when we really think about it, are we to interpret this surprising resurfacing of the subject, right in the middle of a discourse devoted to a critique of the authority of consciousness and the illusions of the ego? Once Lacan's many conceptual "corruptions" of Freud's text had been taken into account, shouldn't we have asked what, even in Freud himself, had brought about this surreptitious restoration of the subject? Shouldn't we have suspected the radicality and depth of the break that Freud had made in the name of the unconscious? In short, shouldn't we indeed have returned to Freud, but to Freud's philosophical underpinnings, which alone hold the key to the confused fate of psychoanalysis in France?

That, it would be useless to deny, is what I attempted to do in *The Freudian Subject*. I thought that it might be timely, even urgent, to question whether, behind the apparently radical critique of consciousness and ego, the schema of the subject might not be silently continuing to govern the theory and the practice—which is also to say the politics—of psychoanalysis. In short, I wanted to know the extent to which the "fundamental concepts" of psychoanalysis might still be prisoners of, or might have escaped, the summons of their foundation—for that, in fact, is always what is involved in questions of "the subject."

And, indeed, once the question has been couched in these terms, isn't it obvious that by providing himself with an unconscious made up of "representations," "thoughts," "fantasies," "memory traces," Freud at the same time provided himself with a *subject* of representation, of imagination, of memory—in short, with the material for a new *cogito*, one simply conceived as more basic and more subjectival than the conscious ego? Let us not forget that the subject of the Moderns is first and foremost the subject of representation—we could even go so far as to say: subject *as* representation and representation *as* subject. Let us also remember that by representing itself, posing itself, in the mode of the *cogito me cogitare*, "with" all the representations it sets before itself, the Cartesian ego establishes itself as the basis of all possible truth, that is, as *subjectum* of the whole of being. Therefore, we must take care not to reduce the subject to the ego. In reality, the ego is nothing outside the *cogitatio* wherein it consciously presents itself to itself; and so it is the structure of representation as autorepresentation, rather than the ego, that actually should be called the true and ultimate subject.

In this sense, Freud, attempting to qualify this radical non-presence to the self that he called "the unconscious," could hardly have chosen a more unfortunate term than *representation* (*Vorstellung*).[4] To speak of unconscious "representations" was obviously to signal the existence of something beyond the subject, since I—I the ego—was thus supposed to have thoughts (*Gedanken*) that could think without me. But, through an inevitable countercoup, this was also to reinstate another ego (still the same one, of course) in that beyond, since there must be a spectator of that "other scene"—since such representations require a subject that represents them to *itself* and thus represents *itself* in them. It is this powerful constraint that caused Lacan, with respect to the "other scene" of language, to write that "the signifier is what represents *the subject* for another signifier."[5] It is also what obliged Freud to *substantize*—that is, to subjectivize—the unconsciousness with which he was dealing into an "unconscious," or into an "id." The various topographies erected since the "Project for a Scientific Psychology" are testimony to this constant substratification of the psychoanalytic subject, ever more fragmented and shattered, yet ever more deeply driven back down to its own primordiality. In this sense, the multiplication of topographic agencies and "characters" does much more to presume than to contradict the unity and identity of the subject: the subject can be divided only because it is first of all *one* subject. Finally, neither the theme of a "primal repression" nor even that of an *après-coup* (*Nachträglichkeit*) would have been enough to make Freud question the stubbornly maintained notion of an already given subject, already present to (already subjacent to, underlying) its representations. In this respect, we can guess that the idea so dear to Emmanuel Lévinas—that of a "trauma" predating and seizing subjectivity before any representation or any memory, and therefore also before any repression—would have seemed completely nonsensical to Freud. The unconscious, for Freud, *is* memory, a storehouse of traces, inscriptions, remembrances, fantasies. And this memory, traumatic and fractural though it may be, must be underlaid, re-membered, by a subject to whom and in whom it represents itself.

Does it change anything to call this eternal subject of representation "desire"? Probably not. Desire, whether understood as libido, drive, or fantasmatic wish, is always a subject's desire, at least to the extent that it is characterized as desire for an object. And although such an object may be defined as a fantasmatic or even "fundamentally lost" object, nothing can prevent its being presented, prosaically, as an object for a subject, before a subject. The object, for us Moderns, is always the object of a representing (that is, as the German language so aptly puts it, the object of a "setting-before," of a *Vorstellen*), and this notion is in no way challenged by our understanding the object as the object of a desire, a libido, or a drive. We need only wonder why, in Freud, the drive is inaccessible except through its objects: it is because Freud conceived of the drive only as *represented* to or before the psyche—that is, to or before the subject. The subject is necessarily presumed to underlie the object in which it presents its own pleasure or enjoyment before itself, and in which it simultaneously presents *itself* before itself. From this perspective, by conceiving of the object of desire as that "part" that language and representation deduct from the subject, Lacan merely confirmed the fundamentally autorepresentational structure of desire. The so-called object *a* eludes the subject so thoroughly only because the subject represented itself in it to begin with: thus the object subsists—breast or feces, gaze or voice—in the representation of its absence, of its lack-of-being-itself.

Therefore, this objectival conception of desire in Freud is not, I believe, where we should go looking for material to elaborate an in-depth schema of the subject. But that is not quite true for another, much more problematic aspect of Freud's theory of desire: the aspect that deals with the desire of the ego—and here we should take this possessive phrase in both its senses, the subjective and the objective. Indeed, we know that very early on Freud felt constrained to make room, alongside the desire for the object (the desire that he discerned in sexuality), for an "egoist" type of desire, a desire-to-be-oneself or desire-to-be-an-ego, which at first he called "egoistic" and later called "narcissistic," finally fusing it with the process of identification. Without retracing the various steps of Freud's discovery, through the themes of the "egoism" of dreams and fantasies, homosexuality, paranoia, or passionate love, I must stress this discovery's importance, for the implications of this shift in Freud's interest are often not fully appreciated. Indeed, to emphasize the violent passion that the ego devotes to itself (or that devotes the ego to itself) was not merely to overturn the initially objectival definition of desire by forever tilting all subsequent investigations toward the repressing "ego"—the ego that, as Freud admitted in a letter to Jung,[6] he had not studied enough. It was also—obscurely, problematically—to challenge the notion of the subject of desire, the same subject of desiring representation that had been so tenaciously presumed until then.

What is it all about, this desire that Freud called "egoist" or "narcissistic"? First of all, it is about being an "I," a "self"—that is, a subject: closed upon itself, free of all bonds, ab-solute in this sense. But if I *desire* to be (an) I, if I *desire* myself, then according to the most elementary logic, it must be because that is not what I am. Thus this singular desire is not, on the whole, the desire of any subject. When Freud wrote, for example, that the ideal of the narcissistic ego is "what we would like to be,"[7] or, with respect to identification, that it is an "emotional tie with another person" one desires *to be* (by contrast with the object one desires *to have*),[8] he was clearly emphasizing the abyssal nature of narcissistic passion. This ego-being (or ego-ness, as we could also call it, the essence and foundation of its *ego* identity) is not in me: it is elsewhere, in that other—always that *alter ego*—that fascinates me, in which I love myself, in which I kill myself. *Ergo*, I am that other: *ego sum alterum*. Or, better yet, a more Freudian version of this other and very different *cogito*: "I am the breast."[9]

By the strangest yet most logical of paradoxes, Freud's attention to the ego's narcissism led to the question of the other, of others. The question was to haunt him from that point on, all the more so in that this "other"—model or rival, homosexual figure or persecutor—seemed to be ever more identical to the ego, to the point where their opposition itself might disappear. That is probably why the major texts of the second topography inextricably blended "analysis of the ego" with analysis of culture and the social tie: when the other is no longer an object, an *Objekt*, there is a need to attend to nonerotic, "social," relationships with others; and, inversely, when the ego is no longer a subject, there is a need to inscribe this "sociality" into the ego itself, in the form of identification, superego, and so on. Thus, whether the ego was originally identified with others or others were first assimilated to the ego, everything converged, in many ways, to undermine the mutual posing of subject and object, which is also to say the posing of the subject of representation. And that is certainly the ultimate implication of the whole discourse on narcissism, on primary identification, and on primary incorporation: if I am the other, then *I no longer represent him to myself*, since the exteriority where he might have pro-posed himself to me, as model or object, as *Vor-bild* or *Ob-jekt*, has vanished into thin air. And, at the same time, I have become unable to *represent myself*, to present myself to myself in front of myself: the other that I am no longer exists, has never been in front of me, since I identified myself with him from the start, since I assimilated, consumed, incorporated him from the very beginning.

This—which is nothing other than what was formerly the "subject of desire"—is difficult to imagine, of course, and in any case is impossible to *represent*. But wasn't Freud moving in that direction, toward that unrepresentable "point of otherness," when he stated, for example, that the ego emerges through "primary identification," adding that this primitive relationship to the object is immediately equivalent to the incorporation that destroys it? Or when, using such various terms as "primary narcissism," "animism," "omnipotence of thought," and "magic," he attempted to describe a type of mental functioning that knows no distinction between ego and other, subject and object, desire and its fulfillment? And isn't it mainly here, in this fundamentally unrepresentable thought, this thought of no subject, that we ought to be seeking the ever-elusive "unconscious"?

But, as I have just said, this is difficult to imagine, and I must immediately add that Freud himself had great trouble confronting this difficulty. Freud most often interpreted this narcissism, this desire-to-be-oneself that so radically upset any idea of a "self," as a desire of oneself *by oneself*—in short, as a subject's autoaffirmation, auto-positioning, or circular autoconception. We need only recall the fascinating figures, entirely closed in on themselves, of the narcissistic Child and Woman in *On Narcissism: An Introduction*, or the theory of primary narcissism's secondary "granting" to and "withdrawal" from objects: everything originates from and returns to Narcissus, who loses himself in objects only to rediscover and represent himself in them as in a mirror, specularly, speculatively. It is this rediscovery of the narcissistic ego in the specular other that Lacan described with the term "imaginary," doing so, of course, in order to expose, virulently, the trap and the illusion. But by keeping the *image* of the ego, if not the ego itself, he too, with all the appearance of a reversal, allowed himself to be caught by the autorepresentative structure of narcissistic desire. Let the ego imagine itself outside itself, or image itself before itself in the mirror that the other holds up: in no way does this infringe on its autopositioning, since the domain of that auto-*ob*-positioning is precisely here. . . . As for branding the "alienation" of the narcissistic ego in the imaginary "small other," that merely helps confirm the deeply dialectical character of the process described in this way. The ego, in the Lacan of "The Mirror Stage" as in the Freud of *On Narcissism*, continues to *represent* itself—and therefore, inevitably, to represent *itself*—in the specular reflection wherein it loves and desires itself.

Therefore, I believe that these Freudian or Lacanian interpretations of narcissism must themselves be interpreted. They interpret narcissistic desire along the same lines as desire; they subscribe to a certain autointerpretation of desire, whereas desire is precisely a *desire to be a subject*, a desire to be oneself for oneself within an unalienated identity and an unalienated autonomy. In this sense, the proposition of narcissism does more than display, sometimes crudely and sometimes more subtly, the fascinated submission of psychoanalysts where the paradigm of the subject is concerned. It bears equal witness, as if reciprocally, to this paradigm's narcissistic character. Therefore, it is one and the same thing to say, as I have on various occasions, that psychoanalysis in its essence is deeply narcissistic and that it reinstates, sometimes in the form of a caricature, the old but always new question of the subject.

This reinstatement is probably most flagrant, most "massive," in Freud's so-called political or sociological texts. Moreover, this is all the more striking in that Freud's investigation into culture and the social tie corresponded at first, as I have said, to the constraining movement that tilted the question of the narcissistic ego toward the question of the other who inwardly haunts and obsesses it. In fact, the great 1921 "political" text *Group Psychology and the Analysis of the Ego* first appeared under the rubric of the *Andere* (the Other):

> In the individual's mental life, the other is invariably involved as a model, . . . as a helper, as an opponent; and from the very first, individual psychology . . . is at the same time social psychology as well.[10]

This admirable statement, by inscribing the other into the ego in this way, actually seems to contain, in embryo, a whole nonsubjectival

theory of the "subject" and of the "social relationship." Nevertheless, a reading of *Group Psychology* suffices to show that the theory
remains in embryonic form, stifled as it is by the whole question of
the political Subject.
Space does not permit a detailed description of the extraordinarily complex route traced by that essay, but we can say that Freud,
in his attempt to take account of the social relationship, ultimately
never stopped assuming a *subject* of the relationship, whether an
"individual" subject or a supra-individual, political subjectivity. Indeed, on the one hand, his analysis took desire as its point of departure, love or the libido of individuals, and these individuals were
consequently assumed to preexist the different erotico-objectival
relationships that link them to one another. And, on the other hand,
once Freud recognized the fundamental fact that all subjectivity and
all individual desire vanish in crowds, his analysis ended up with a
sort of political super-Subject, in the dual form of the narcissistic
Chief and the Mass bonded by love for this Chief. Society, Freud
said, is a unanimous "mass" whose members have all put the same
"object" (the "leader," the *Führer*) in the place of the ego ideal and
who identify with one another as a result.
   To say this is first of all to say that society—any society—is essentially political, since it is wholly dependent on the figure of a Chief,
of a sovereign head in which it represents itself and without which
it would simply fall apart. But we must then go on to say that society, any society, is fundamentally *totalitarian*—not, I hasten to add,
because state coercion or tyrannical violence are somehow essential
to this conception; these traits are in no way exclusive to totalitarian societies, and Freud clearly said that the reign of the *Führer* rests
above all on the fiction of his love. Rather, if society for Freud is
totalitarian in the strictest sense, it is because it presents itself as an
integrally political totality, as a *totale Staat*, knowing no divisions
except the one—minimal, and solely intended to relate the social
body to itself—between the beloved Chief and his loving subjects.
This is further borne out by the speculative biology underlying the
description in *Group Psychology* because, on the grounds of "union"
and erotic *Bindung*, it tends to turn society into an actual organism,
a real body politic. And, as Claude Lefort has shown, expanding
on work by Ernst Kantorowicz,[11] this is the totalitarian fantasy par
excellence. It is the profoundly narcissistic fantasy of a single, homo-

geneous body that knows no exteriority or alterity other than that of its own relationship to itself. It is therefore the fantasy, the auto-representation, of a subject: society, for Freud, is a compact mass, and this mass forms a complete *body* with the Chief-Subject that *incarnates* it.

There is certainly no point in saying that this description is false. History has confirmed it with too many examples for us to doubt its accuracy. Moreover, from this standpoint, I am completely prepared to recognize, with Serge Moscovici,[12] the exceptional importance of Freudian "group psychology" for any understanding of the political and social events of our time—but only if we also recognize that Freud did not so much analyze this totalitarian fantasy as subscribe to it. Contrary to what he is sometimes reported to have said (as in the thesis, or myth, of Lacan,[13] among others), Freud never *criticized* "group psychology" at all, convinced as he was that here was to be found the very essence of society. Nor did he ever question the primacy of the Chief, and he went so far as to write the following dreadful passage to Einstein:

One instance of the innate and ineradicable inequality of men is their tendency to fall into the two classes of leaders [*Führer*] and followers. The latter constitute the vast majority; they stand in need of an authority which will make decisions for them and to which they for the most part offer an unqualified submission.[14]

We must carefully examine what this exacerbation of the role of the mass's "leader" corresponds to, historically and theoretically. It corresponds—in Freud as in Gustave Le Bon or Gabriel Tarde, in the fascist ideologues as in the Georges Bataille of the 1930's—to the following observation, variously appreciated and exploited by these authors, but in the end always the same: modern man, the self-styled *Homo democraticus*, is in reality the man in the street, communal mass man, the man of the melting pot. And this anonymous man, brutally revealed by the retreat of the great transcendent political and religious systems, is no longer a subject: he is the "man without qualities," without his own identity, the deeply panicked, deindividualized, suggestible, hypnotizable (or "media-tized," as we might say today) being of the lonely crowd. From now on, only an absolute Chief—"prestigious" and "charismatic" for Le Bon and Max Weber, "sovereign" and "heterogeneous" for Bataille—can re-embody, give substantial consistency and subjective unity to, this magma of unanchored identifications or imitations. Thus the figure of the Chief-Subject, in theoretical texts as in the historical reality that they inspire, looms all the more brutally for its warding off of what is perceived as a radical desubjectification and alienation.

On this score, it is probably not enough to say, as we so readily do nowadays, that the totalitarianisms of the twentieth century have fulfilled the modern logic of the Subject in a political sense, filling in the outline of its total ab-solution and immanence. We must add that our century's totalitarianisms have fulfilled this logic all the more successfully for having lucidly and cynically confronted the de-liaison and dissolution of subjects that this outline implied all along. In short, the totalitarian Chief can impose the fiction or the figure of his absolute subjectivity all the more easily because he knows very well that it is a myth, and that before him is only a mass of non-subjects. In this connection, it is no accident that these totalitarianisms have seen the flourishing of so many "new mythologies" and "personality cults," or that Bataille and his friends dreamed, lucidly and naïvely, of opposing fascism with an *other*, "heterogeneous" and "headless," mythology. Once the masses have no identity of their own, only a myth can provide them with one, by offering them a fiction in which they can once again depict their unity—in which they can depict and present themselves as Subject. And *the Subject*, from now on, *is a myth* because we know very well that we are dealing with a fiction (with a deus ex machina), but also because in this fiction the subject is once again depicted and reinstated— "massively."

We find the same totalitarian myth of the Subject in *Group Psychology*, here again at the far reaches of an investigation into the nonpresence to oneself implied by being-in-society. Where social identifications are concerned, Freud, in the same way that he emphasized the radical alteration of so-called subjects assembled into crowds and stressed the primitive character of this "group psychology," also restored, reinstated in spite of everything, the primacy and principality of an absolute Subject. Recall that the investigation of *Group Psychology* concludes with an allusion to the "absolutely narcissistic" Father-Chief-Hypnotist. This theme of the Father's "narcissism" and jealous "egoism"[15] is decisive here, too, since it is very clear that only because the Chief allies himself with no one (with no "object," as Freud said) can he offer himself as the sole object of the admiring, terrified love of the tribe—in short, establish community where before there was only a chaos of reciprocal identifications and suggestions. In other words, everything becomes invested in this fascinating figure of a Narcissus or an Egocrat sprung up from no-where—and hence the difficult question of a social relationship or tie that predates the ego is freshly disposed of, in favor of a "scien-tific myth" that is simultaneously the myth of the Subject's origin and the myth of the founding of the Political. The Subject thereby proclaims itself Chief, and the Chief is self-engendered as Subject.

It goes without saying that we must still examine this myth, as much for its enigmatic resemblance to the totalitarian myth as for its strange reinstatement of the figure of the Subject. Does it suf-fice, however, to say that we are dealing here with a *myth*? I think not, and I want especially to emphasize this point because it was just such an exposure of the myth that preoccupied me in *The Freudian Subject*. The very crudeness, it seemed to me then, with which Freud proposed a Subject at the origin of the Political signaled the fail-ure of his attempt to establish a foundation, an *instauratio*. And, in a way, I enjoyed showing how he had failed: I was satisfied simply to draw attention to Freud's inability to establish the social tie—the relationship with others—except by assuming, in mythic form, a Subject founded in and by itself. In short, I was satisfied merely to bring up the unfounded, abyssal nature itself of this constant, circular assumption of a Subject-Foundation. But how, in that very abyss—the abyss of relationship—could one find the means for a non-"subjective" notion of the Political, a non-"political" notion of the Subject? Weren't we, in the deeply ambiguous gesture of our modernity, condemned to go sifting through lack-of-foundation, obliteration-of-subject, loss-of-origin, collapse-of-principle? And as for this "an-archy" of the masses that the myth of the Chief-Subject, as a last resort, was warding off, would it allow us a differ-ent, more essential understanding of "archy," of the beginnings, the commandment?

That, ultimately, is the formidable problem raised by the Freud-ian—and, more generally, the totalitarian—myth of the Chief-Subject. Once its mythic character has been noted, the source of its incredible *authority* remains to be understood. Like it or not, the myth works: everywhere, the masses gather around a Chief or a Party supposed to represent them, everywhere they convulsively sacrifice themselves at the altar of the Chief's or the Party's myth. And, as we have seen, this myth works all the better for assuming the radical absence of the same political subjectivity that it sets up. Where, then, does the myth get its terrible founding power? On what grounds does it authorize itself, since its authority does not come from a subject, since—and here, precisely, is totalitarianism's cynical lesson—the subject is a myth? Today, we can no longer avoid this question, especially because it is only through this question that we will be able—perhaps—to find the means of resisting what from now on will be the global domination of the "politics of the subject." Finally, *in the name of what* should we reject totalitarianism? In the name of what notion of the "subject" or of the "political," if it is now definitely impossible to speak either of the Individual arisen against the State or of the Rights of Man the Subject?

Perhaps, in spite of everything, we can find the beginnings of an answer to this question in the Freudian myth. But we cannot rely, as I have been doing up to this point, on the version of it that *Group Psychology* presents. That political version of the myth is already re-interpreting and reelaborating an older version, a more strictly *ethical* one, to which we must now return. We are familiar with this basic form of the myth: it is the fable of the primitive Father's murder, as set forth in *Totem and Taboo*. This fable, examined more closely, pictures a wholly different genesis of authority from the one found in *Group Psychology* (I use the term "authority" here so as not to have to say "power"). In *Totem and Taboo*, the primal authority is not the Father-Chief-Hypnotist, that "Superman" that Freud, following Nietzsche, alluded to before calling him, in *Moses and Monotheism*, the "great man." It is the *guilt-creating* Father, the Father able to create guilt because he is the *dead* Father. This is already tantamount to say-ing—but here lies the enigma—that this authority is the authority of no one, or anyway of no man, much less of an absolute Narcissus.

It is true that Freud was still speaking of the murder of a primitive *Father* and that in this he certainly seemed once again to be speaking the language of myth. That is what our whole disenchanted modern age, from Claude Lévi-Strauss to René Girard, has reproached him for: *Totem and Taboo*, by presupposing the Father's authority rather than deducing it, offers us nothing but another myth of origins, a myth of foundation. It happens, however, that this myth—which definitely is one, even in its autorepresentation *as* myth—is at the same time the myth of the origin of the myth of the Father (we would even have to say: the myth of the origin *of myth*). Freud was well aware that the dominating, jealous male of the Darwinian tribe is no Father, which is the whole reason why Freud in his narrative felt the need to have him finished off by his fellows: since his power resides in strength alone, he still holds no real paternal authority, and so sooner or later, in this logic of the natural state, he must be forcibly overthrown. Thus it is only *after* the murder, *after* having killed and devoured their tyrant, that his murderers submit to him, by virtue of a guilt and an obedience enigmatically described as "retrospective" (*nachträglich*). The "Father," in other words, appears only after the fact, in the remorse of those who for the first time in history become "brothers," and become "brothers" because they are guilty "sons." The "Father," then, in this strange Freudian myth, emerges only as myth—the myth of his own power, and the power of his own myth: "The dead," Freud wrote, "became stronger than the living had been." [16]

From our present perspective, this genesis of authority is extraordinarily interesting in that it defines the primal authority as "ethical," "moral" authority and not as political authority. What the members of the tribe submit to—and through which they form a community, ultimately a fraternal and human community—is in fact no power, since the holder of this power is now dead, perfectly impotent. Freud strongly emphasized that only in the feeling of guilt—in the feeling of a *moral* lapse—does there arise the terrifying figure of the one who will become the omnipotent Father and, later, God or the Chief. The feeling of guilt, as Freud said in *Civilization and Its Discontents*, is not social anxiety (*soziale Angst*), the ordinary fear of being punished by an external power or censor. It is moral anxiety (or anxiety of conscience, *Gewissenangst*) before an "internal" authority, as "imperative" as it is "categorical." This strange moral authority—all the stranger because the subject submits to it of his own accord, autonomously—is what Freud had described earlier as the "voice of conscience" (*Stimme des Gewissens*) and is what, from *Totem and Taboo* on, he called the "superego" or the "ego ideal." "In place of" that ego ideal he set up the *Führer* of *Group Psychology*, which finally amounted to saying that the essence of the community is ethical before it is political. What establishes the community is not principally the fusional, amorous partaking in a collective Super-Subject or "Superman" but rather the always singular summons of a Super*ego* that, strictly speaking, is no one.

This bears repeating: primal authority—ethical authority—belongs to no one, and especially not to the Father-Chief-Narcissus, whose myth appears only after the fact. That the murderers may have felt guilty with respect to a previously known and established law (which would bring us back to a situation of *soziale Angst*) is far from being the case; rather, it was in the feeling of guilt (in *Gewissenangst*) that they first came to know—inexplicably, terribly—the law of the Father: "They thus created," Freud wrote, careful to emphasize the paradox, "*out of their filial sense of guilt* the two fundamental taboos of totemism."[17] Freud did not say, then, that the murderers were anxious about having trangressed the taboos laid down by the Father. He said something much stranger: that the Father's taboos, and therefore human society, arise from anxiety—about what? About nothing, about no one. It is when the powerful male is dead and no longer there to prohibit anything at all that, in a perfectly disconcerting way, there emerge the alterity of duty and the debt of guilt, both of them all the more unbearable. The Father emerges from his own death, the law emerges from its own absence—quite literally ex nihilo. And that is why the Freudian myth, in spite of how it looks, is not a "myth of the twentieth century," a new myth nostalgically reinstating the lost transcendence of myth (the myth of the Father, of God, of the Chief). Freud did not lament the death of the Father, any more than he attempted to cure the resulting "discontents of civilization." On the contrary: rooting civilization in the "discontents" of an a priori guilt that precedes all Law and any Name of the Father, he offered us the myth of the *death* of myth—which is also to say the myth of its inexhaustible resurrection. After all, if the Father is dead (if his authority is purely mythic), then how is it that his murderers submit to him? And how does it happen that, if God is dead, we (for this is about ourselves, the "murderers of God") are so eager to reinstate Him at the center and base of our societies—socialist humanity prostrate before "Father" Stalin, the *Volk* or race fasciated behind its *Führer*?

It is because we feel guilty for having killed Him—that is Freud's answer, still a mythic one. But the question only rebounds: Why do we feel guilty, if there is no longer any Father—if there has never been one—to punish us? There lies the enigma of the myth—of the Freudian myth and of the mythic power that it describes. To solve the enigma, is it enough to mention love for the Father again? Freud wrote, in fact, that the murderers

hated their father, who presented such a formidable obstacle to their craving for power [*Machtbedürfnis*] and their sexual drives; but they loved and admired him too. After they had got rid of him, had satisfied their hatred and had put into effect their wish to identify themselves with him, the affection which had all this time been pushed under was bound to make itself felt.[18]

But this "love" for the Father is itself all too clearly part of the myth. It is only *after* having eliminated the hated rival, and under the influence of remorse, that the murderers began to love him as a Father and to be united in that love. To love him, then, they had to begin by killing him. Society, a community of love, rests on a crime and on remorse for that crime.

Thus it is not so much in "love" per se that we should be looking for the key to the son-brothers' "retrospective obedience" as in that love's ambivalent character, hateful and devouring from the very beginning. The members of the tribe, as the myth specifies, killed and *devoured* the jealous male. Why would they have done so, if this had been only a question of eliminating the monopolizer of the group's women? The myth spells it out: because his murderers "loved and *admired him.*" This peculiar "love" was an admiring, identifying, envious love, and so it necessarily led to the cannibalistic incorporation of the model. As the narrative has it:

The violent primal father had doubtless been the feared and envied model of each one of the company of brothers: and in the act of devouring him they accomplished their identification with him, and each one of them acquired a portion of his strength.[19]

"Model," "identification," "devouring," "appropriation"—this is quite clear. The myth is not telling us here about the love for an object but rather about an indissolubly narcissistic passion of identification: it is in order *to be* the Father—*to be (the) Subject*—that the members of the tribe kill and devour him, and not at all (or only incidentally) in order to *have* the women of the group. Freud, speaking of the "need for power" and the "desire to identify with the Father," put it aptly:

the stakes of the murder are not the possession of an object of love or of pleasure but rather the acquisition of an identity. The murder of the Father, in this case, is much less a brutish struggle than a Freudian version of Hegel's "struggle for pure prestige." If desire ends in murder and devouring, it is because it is the desire to appropriate the being of the other, the desire to assimilate his power (*Macht*), his potency (*Stärke*)—in a word, his mastery: his narcissistic autonomy. My being is in the other, and that is why I cannot become "myself," an ego, unless I devour him—here, in short, is what the Freudian myth is telling us, a myth ultimately much less mythic than it appears. What it deals with is the primitive relationship to others, taking it all the way back to the mythic origins of human community—"primitive" because it is the relationship of no ego to no other, of no subject to no object. Thus it is also a connection with no connection to others, an unbinding tie. I the ego am born by assimilating the other, by devouring him, incorporating him. Everything in so-called individual history, then, as in the history of society, begins with murderous, blind identification, all the blinder because there is still no ego to see anything or represent anything to itself at all, and because the "envied model" that it assimilates is immediately annihilated, eaten, engulfed: "I am the breast," "I am the Father"—that is, *no one*. In other words, everything begins with a subjectless identification—by which the Freudian myth corresponds exactly to the situation of the panicked, anarchic, headless masses without a Chief. The Father (who was actually not a Father, not even a brother, but only a counterpart) has been killed, and so there is no subject at the basis of the social tie, whether we mean loving subjects or a beloved Subject.

His myth arises at this very moment, however. The ghost of the Father-Subject assails the guilty conscience of the sons, who then attempt to redeem their sin through their love and submission. But where can this ghost be getting such vain, empty power? From the *failure* of this devouring identification. In a footnote, Freud gave what turned out to be his only explanation of the sons' "retrospective obedience":

This fresh emotional attitude must also have been assisted by the fact that the deed cannot have given complete satisfaction to those who did it. From one point of view it had been done in vain. Not one of the sons had in fact been able to put his original wish—of taking his father's place—into effect. And, as we know, failure is far more propitious for a moral reaction than satisfaction.[20]

As a result, none of the sons is able to become Subject and Chief by appropriating the identity and the glorious being of the Other. What, ultimately, is the irreducible alterity that causes the failure of this violent act of identification, this dialectical assimilation of the other? It can only be (to return to and reverse Hegel's term) the "absolute Master," death—death or *the dead one: der Tote*, for Freud. Empirically, there would be nothing to prevent one of the tribe's members from eliminating his rivals and taking the dominant male's place (in fact, Freud did conceive of this solution in other versions of the myth).[21] Therefore, we must be dealing here with something else entirely, something not at all empirical: the unoccupiable place of the dead one, since death sets the absolute limit on identification. The myth does not say this so clearly, of course, but there is no other way to understand the retrospective power of the dead one. *Der Tote* who is resurrected and lives on eternally in the guilty memory of the sons *represents* death, *represents* their own unrepresentable death to them. Indeed, at the myth's extreme, we must imagine that the murderers, having devoured the other in order to appropriate his being, suddenly found themselves once again facing "themselves"— that is, facing no one. The other was dead, *and so they themselves were dead.* The identifying act of incorporation confronted them—brutally, dizzyingly—with what is preeminently unassimilable: their own death, their own being-dead, the very thing that eludes all appropriation. That is why "the dead became stronger than the living had been" and also why the "sense of guilt" is born of the anxious apprehension of death "beside the dead body of the loved one," as Freud said in "Thoughts for the Times on War and Death."[22] "This dead man," his stupefied murderers must have said to themselves, "is myself—and yet he is infinitely other, since I cannot picture myself dead.[23] Being myself, he is all the more other. And this All-Other, this All-Mighty who has eluded my power—how will I now be able to appease His wrath?"

Attempting, like Freud, to represent the unrepresentable, attempting to represent to *myself* this other that I am, by once more setting that other in front of me, I have just been speaking the language of myth. It is a myth, of course, but the myth is unavoidable. That is precisely the power of myth: we cannot (but) represent the unrepresentable to ourselves, we cannot (but) present the unpresentable. That is why Freud, seeking to represent this abyssal withdrawal of the subject, could only write a new myth—powerful, like every other myth, and one that also founded a community. But this myth—the myth of the death of myth, the myth of the unavoidable power of myth—is no longer wholly a myth. Being the myth of the mythic emergence of the Subject, it is no longer wholly the myth of the Subject, which is why, lucidly confronting the vast power of the totalitarian myth, it allows us—perhaps—to elude it.

In the end, what does it tell us? In the first place, that we are submitting to nothing but ourselves—and here, of course, it merely repeats the totalitarian myth of the Subject: the State, the Law, the Chief, the *Führer*, the Other in general are all Me, always Me, always "His Majesty the Ego." And it is also quite true that Freud himself, in large part, believed in this myth and succumbed to its power. But by adding that this all-powerful Ego is "death," *our* death, he also told us something completely different, which can scarcely be uttered, and which he therefore put in mythic terms: "I am death and the dead one," "I am (the) other." In short: "I am not myself, I am not (a) subject." What the members of the murdering tribe submit to, what they gather to form a community around, is *nothing*—no Subject, no Father, no Chief—but their own mortality, their own finitude, their own inability to be Absolute Subjects, "absolute Narcissi."

And that, finally, is why Freud's enigmatic "retrospective obedience" is ethical respect before it is political submission, my respect for others before it is submission to myself. It is obedience to what, within the subject, transcends the subject, to what in me is above me, to the ego's superego. Or, to return to the Freudian myth and add *nothing* to it, "retrospective obedience" is obedience to what withdraws from the social body through its very incorporation, in this way—but only in this way—giving rise to the "body politic," to the "mystical body." "Here is my body. Behold here my death. Here behold your own."

Translated by Richard Miller and X. P. Callahan

From Psychoanalysis
to Hypnosis

⌒ Hypnosis in Psychoanalysis

Two statements by Freud constitute a useful point of departure for discussing hypnosis in psychoanalysis. The first one is taken from the nineteenth of the *Introductory Lectures to Psychoanalysis*:

I have been able to say that psychoanalysis proper [*die eigentliche Psychoanalyse*] began when I dispensed with the help of hypnosis.[1]

The second statement is in Freud's "Advice to Physicians on Psychoanalytic Treatment" (1912):

In practice . . . there is nothing to be said against a psychotherapist combining a certain amount of analysis with some suggestive influence in order to achieve a perceptible result in a shorter time. But one has a right to insist that he himself should be in no doubt about what he is doing and should know that his method is not that of true psychoanalysis.[2]

These two statements categorically define Freud's break with hypnosis: in the rejection of hypnosis—but also, and more generally, of all "suggestive" practices, even those limited to advice or exhortation—psychoanalysis *as such*, psychoanalysis "proper," "true" psychoanalysis is supposed to have been born. What was at stake around 1895, when Freud decided to abandon all hypnosuggestive practices in favor of the method known as "free association," was thus nothing other and nothing less than the very identity of psychoanalysis, in its supposedly total difference from all psychotherapy and indeed from all thaumaturgy. As a result, this decision involves all of psychoanalysis, applies to psychoanalysis as a whole; and, in fact, that is how this decision is ordinarily understood. The institutionalization of psychoanalysis has finally even lent this decision the features of actual psychoanalytic dogma. Jacques Lacan, for example, in *The Four Fundamental Concepts of Psychoanalysis*, says:

As everyone knows, it was by distinguishing itself from hypnosis that analysis became established.[3]

Thus "everyone knows," especially because it is finally on this "knowing" that (give or take a few differences on this point) the community of analysts is based. But does everyone know it *well*? As Hegel said, what is well known is badly known. And when we come across such phrases as "it is known that" or "quite obviously" or "clearly," the odds are that the evidence requires further investigation. We should be asking what is encompassed by the terms *hypnosis* and *suggestion* if we want to know *from what*, exactly, psychoanalysis has freed itself—if it has ever really done so.

Simply reading Freud is enough to show that on this point things are much more complex than they are ordinarily said to be. In the first place, when we consider Freud's statements that deal with the hypnotic unconscious (or *unconsciousness*), we must note that Freud never really dreamed of denying his indebtedness to research into the hypnotic unconscious—or, as people before Freud preferred to call it, hypnotic "automatism," the hypnotic "subconscious," or hypnotic "dual consciousness." Hypnosis, that slumbering of consciousness during which a subject paradoxically remains "awake," always seemed to Freud particularly revealing of an unconscious psychic activity not subject to the monitoring and control of the ego. How to explain, for example, that a subject carries out a posthypnotic suggestion—of which he no longer knows anything from any other source—if not by conceding the agency of nonconscious thought (that is, of ideas which the *I* does not "accompany," to use Kant's expression)? Thus we read in Freud's *Autobiographical Study*: "I received the profoundest impression of the possibility that there could be powerful mental processes which nevertheless remained hidden from the consciousness of men."[4] Moreover—whether in the sixth *Introductory Lecture*, in the "Note on the Unconscious," or in the article on "The Unconscious"—Freud invariably invokes hypnosis, as often as dreams, when he wants to "prove" or "illustrate" the fact of the unconscious:

Even before the time of psychoanalysis, hypnotic experiments, and especially posthypnotic suggestion, had tangibly demonstrated the existence and mode of operation of the mental unconscious.[5]

Again, in *The Ego and the Id*, hypnosis is elevated to the rank of paradigm of the unconscious, exactly on a par with dreams, and therefore also as a kind of second "royal road" of analysis:

> To most people who have been educated in philosophy the idea of anything psychical which is not also conscious is inconceivable. . . . I believe this is only because they have never studied the relevant phenomena of hypnosis and dreams, which—quite apart from pathological manifestations—necessitate this view. Their psychology of consciousness is incapable of solving the problems of dreams and hypnosis.[6]

These citations, of course, are far from exhaustive, but they are already sufficient to establish that, for Freud, the *fact* of hypnosis is certainly equivalent to the *fact* of the unconscious (the unique "object" of psychoanalysis).

This fact of hypnosis, this typical example of the unconscious, simultaneously represents a formidable "riddle" for psychoanalysis. This is "the riddle [*Rätsel*] of suggestive influence," the riddle of suggestion. After all, why is one susceptible, under hypnosis, to "an influence in the absence of all logical reason"? What is this strange emotional malleability of the hypnotized person, which causes him to feel, perceive, and sometimes even experience in his body everything that the hypnotist directs? How to explain this "paralysis" of the will, this radical disengagement of self, which is at the same time a radical engagement by another? In short, where do the extraordinary power of the hypnotist and the extraordinary docility of the hypnotized person come from?

This enigma, it must be stressed, is both the enigma of the unconscious and that of a certain relationship to others, perhaps even that of the unconscious *as* a relationship to others. It arises in *Group Psychology and the Analysis of the Ego* when Freud's investigation into the essence of the social tie—and, more generally, of what he calls the "emotional tie" (*Gefühlsbindung*) to others—provides the opportunity for a protracted debate with Gabriel Tarde, Gustave Le Bon, and Hyppolite Bernheim, all advocates of the theory of suggestion. Freud heartily rejects this theory in chapter 4: the notion of suggestion, supposed to explain everything, cannot explain itself, he says; it is only a "magic word" (*Zauberwort*) employed to explain, tautologically, "the magic of words." Freud therefore declines to explain hypnotic suggestion and related phenomena (such as "mental contagion" in a crowd, the "sympathetic inducement of emotions," *Einfühlung*, and so on) by the *theory* of suggestion—a theory based on the hypothesis of a kind of physical reflex (and, in this sense, unconscious) mimesis of others. But this refusal certainly does not remove the mystery that the very *fact* of suggestion still represents for him, for Freud himself has no alternative theory to propose: the one he attempts to put forward—the theory of the libido—ultimately fails when confronted with the phenomenon to be explained.

It is impossible to retrace here the extraordinarily complex route that leads, in *Group Psychology*, to the admission (or half-admission) of this failure. Here I shall only say, on the basis of previous analyses,[7] that Freud does attempt throughout this work to interpret the social or (and it comes to the same thing, in this context) "emotional" tie to others as a libidinal or erotic phenomenon, a phenomenon of love. Thus it is for love that someone would surrender to a hypnotist, for love that members of a crowd or a society would identify with one another, and again for love that they would submit themselves politically to the crowd's Father-Head-Ringleader. In other words, the libido, and not suggestion, is what would constitute the basis of the relationship to others (to "objects") in general. Nevertheless, a close reading of *Group Psychology* establishes that Freud himself was not satisfied with this answer—first of all because the whole problem of the "social" and "emotional" tie confronted him in many ways with the paradox of a "rapport *sans* rapport" with others, an identificatory relationship: ambivalent, preceding the ob-position of the ego and the object, and therefore also preceding any libidinal object or any erotic relationship. In short, just as the libidinal hypothesis was based on the idea of a monadic and substantial subject (desiring, instinctual, and so on) whom the relationship to others would affect only secondarily, so too did the whole problem of the social-emotional tie make it necessary to envisage a kind of original *alteration* (or *affection*) by others, well before any constitution of an "ego" and well before any Oedipal triangle. Thus Freud, having attempted at first to exploit the resources of the psychoanalytical concept of identification, ends by making *hypnosis*, in a striking reversal, the paradigm of the relationship to others. Hypnosis, he says, much more than love, most clearly shows the unfathomable "nature" or "essence" of the *Gefühlsbindung* to others.

This point warrants attention, given that psychoanalysts, with rare exceptions (such as Sandor Ferenczi and, more recently, Léon Chertok and François Roustang), have remained strangely deaf and blind to the question thus inherited from Freud. To assimilate *Gefühlsbindung* to hypnosis was not merely to challenge the libidinal presupposition of the analytical *Trieblehre*; it was also to rediscover the "emotional tie" to others, the object par excellence of psychoanalytical investigation, as a pure enigma. In chapter 8 of *Group Psychology*, shortly after saying, "It would be more to the point to explain being in love by means of hypnosis rather than the other way round," Freud goes on to remark:

Hypnosis would solve the riddle of the libidinal constitution of groups for us right away, if it were not that it itself exhibits some features which are not met by the rational explanation we have hitherto given of it as a state of being in love, with the directly sexual trends excluded. There is still a great deal in it which we must recognize as unexplained and mystical [or mysterious; *mystisch*].⁸

Hypnosis, he continues, is a "mysterious word" (*Rätselwort*), behind which hide the "uncomprehended" (*Unverstandene*), the "enigmatic" (*Geheimnisvolle*), the "positively uncanny" (*etwas direkt Unheimliches*).⁹ And this enigma is the "riddle of suggestion" (*das Rätsel der Suggestion*),¹⁰ the "riddle of suggestive influence" (*das Rätsel der suggestiven Einflusses*).¹¹

This impressive series of admissions of defeat is evidence that rejecting the theory of suggestion never eliminated the enigma of hypnotic suggestion for Freud. Moreover, this enigma managed to reappear *in* psychoanalysis as the enigma of its own foundation: with hypnosis—that is, with the unconscious and the "emotional tie"— psychoanalysis itself finally became the enigma for Freud. To put it another way, with hypnosis taken as paradigm of the relationship to others, psychoanalysis stumbled into the enigma of relationship *itself*, beyond the presupposed *subject* (desiring, in love, instinctual) of the relationship. But what does psychoanalysis deal with, then, if not with the *that* (*ça*; the id), which overwhelms and affects the subject beyond himself? What, if not with those archaic relations to others which are variously called "love," "hate," "anxiety," "guilt"?

It becomes difficult, at least, to maintain the thesis (authorized by Freud himself) of a pure and simple break between psychoanalysis, on the one hand, and hypnosis and suggestion, on the other. Psychoanalysis no doubt did found itself on the abandonment of hypnosis—but only, it must be recognized, to see hypnosis reappear, sometimes under other names or in other forms, at the crossroads of all questions; hence the importance of reconsidering this so-called abandonment, not so much to initiate a "return to hypnosis" as to examine, in light of the questions Freud was asking himself in his last phase, the reasons why in his first phase he had believed, rather too quickly, that these issues were settled. In other words, what is important is to reconsider what Freud called the "prehistory" of psychoanalysis, to return to it with the suspicion that this "prehistory" belongs to a certain future of psychoanalysis rather than to a long-dead past.

It is certainly with respect to everything touching on the transference that the "resurgence of hypnosis" (to quote the title of a recent book) [12] is most spectacular in Freud. And this is hardly surprising, if we reflect that the transference—that strange "rapport *sans* rapport" set up between patient and analyst—always represented for Freud a kind of blueprint or, better yet, a *repetition* of the "emotional tie" to others. Therefore it is only natural that the problems, both theoretical and practical, to which this *Gefühlsbindung* gave rise should have caused the whole problem of hypnotic "rapport" to reappear, with the crucial question now being to know how the transference relationship can finally be distinguished from the hypnotic tie, which analysis initially refused to mobilize in the cure.

It is this question that I would like to examine, by attempting to "repeat" (in Heidegger's but also Freud's possible meaning of this word) that part of history which runs from the discarding of hypnosis up to the definitive isolation of the transference as a distinct problem, and hoping that this journey will finally provide some insight into the "riddle" of the *Gefühlsbindung* to others.

To recall some historical facts, in December 1887, Freud told Wilhelm Fliess that he had immersed himself in "hypnotism" and that he had already obtained "all sorts of small but peculiar successes".[13] "Hypnotism" at that time meant "psychotherapy by suggestion," as practiced by Hippolyte Bernheim and the Nancy School. Briefly, here is what hypnosis consisted of. A verbal suggestion was given ("You are now in a deep sleep," and so on), followed by a further suggestion, still verbal, that the symptom or its immediate cause should disappear. This method, based on deliberate use of the "suggestibility" of the subjects and at the same time on what Freud was already calling the "magical power of words," is described favorably and at length in a series of articles written by Freud around 1890, mainly in his review of August Forel's *Hypnotism*, in the article "Hypnosis" in Anton Bum's dictionary, and in "Psychical Treatment."

In May 1889, Freud began the treatment of Emmy von N., in which he first used the "cathartic method" developed by Josef Breuer. This method still used hypnosis, but no longer for direct suggestion. Instead, hypnosis was used to reimmerse the patient into that "hypnoid" state during which a "traumatic" event supposedly had become embedded like an "internal foreign body" in the psychic mechanism, and thus to facilitate the recollection or reexperiencing of that event. According to this hypothesis, derived from Jean-Martin Charcot, hysterics "suffer[ed] from reminiscences"—that is, from nonabreacted ideas—and the symptoms would disappear when the patients were able to recount these "traumatic scenes" (the model of this "purgative narration" was still, of course, the "talking cure" invented by the hysterical *princeps* of analysis, Anna O.). What was emphasized was the patient's telling of his or her own story. Breuer and Freud called this narration "cathartic" because of the emotional purge it was supposed to bring about, and because they were no doubt thinking of the medical interpretation of Aristotelian *catharsis* provided by the uncle of Freud's wife, the philologist Jakob Bernaÿs. Be that as it may, we must note the strangeness of the process that led Breuer and Freud to call such narration "cathartic," since in true Aristotelian doctrine "catharsis" refers to dramatic rather than narrative imitation—or, as we might say with Plato, to *mimesis*, in which the speaker enacts a role, rather than to *diegesis*, in which the speaker recounts events.[14] If Freud and Breuer described the stories of their patients as cathartic, it is because these stories were in fact dramas that were played out, acted, mimed. To realize the truth of this proposition, one need only read the description of the cathartic procedure in the "Preliminary Communication" to *Studies on Hysteria*:

Recollection without affect [*affektloses Erinnern*] almost invariably produces no result. The psychical process which originally took place must be repeated as vividly as possible [*lebhaft* . . . *wiederholt*]; it must be brought back to its *status nascendi* and given verbal utterance.[15]

Thirty-two years later, in *An Autobiographical Study*, the cathartic cure is similarly characterized as "the tracing back of hysterical symptoms to events in the patient's life, and their removal by means of hypnotic reproduction *in statu nascendi*."[16] Now, repetition *in statu nascendi*, in the state of being born, is clearly not remembering; it is neither telling a story nor representing a past event *as past*. It is, as Freud and Breuer also write, reliving (*wiederdurchleben*) the event, with all the intensity of the first time, by repeating it *in the present*. If we add that the events thus enacted ("tragedized," says Breuer) were highly doubtful (as Freud realized later), and if we go on to say that these reexperienced events and their corresponding emotions occurred under hypnosis (that is, in a state of absence from self), then we can understand that Freud's and Breuer's hysterics remembered nothing, had nothing to tell; they were playing, living, and acting roles, not so much by means of fantasy representation (*Vorstellung*) as by "acting out" (*Agieren*). To be more precise, they were miming the affects, body and soul—perhaps the only way to feel or "experience" an emotion if, as Freud later suggests in several ways, there is no emotion except through identification with others. But this affective mimesis, which Freud and Breuer describe perfectly, they simultaneously theorize as a diegesis, as the "verbalization" of a recollection. And here arises constant ambiguity, seen clearly in the confusion maintained throughout the *Studies* between the reexperiencing of a traumatic event under hypnosis and insight (*prise de conscience*) into the event. This ambiguity was pointed out by Lacan, in a passage of "The Function and Field of Speech and Language in Psychoanalysis" worth quoting here:

If this event [which is "the pathogenic event dubbed the traumatic experience"] was recognized as being the cause of the symptom, it was because the putting into words of the event (in the patient's "stories") determined the lifting of the symptoms. Here the term *"prise de conscience,"* borrowed from the psychological theory that was constructed on this fact, retains a prestige that merits a healthy distrust of explanations that do office as self-evident truths. The psychological prejudices of Freud's day were opposed to acknowledging in verbalization as such any reality other than its own *flatus vocis*. The fact remains that in the hypnotic state verbalization is dissociated from the *prise de conscience*, and this fact alone is enough to require a revision of that conception of its effects.[17]

How, then, Lacan wonders, could Breuer and Freud have attributed the dispelling of hysterical symptoms to a *prise de conscience*, to insight, to conscious recollection of the traumatic event, since in hypnosis recollection operates far more in a state of absence, unconsciousness, forgetfulness of self? This point is far from incidental, for in cutting through this ambiguity—in maintaining only the one aspect, that of conscious recollection—Freud founded psychoanalysis proper, *die eigentliche Psychoanalyse*.

In the fall of 1892, Freud began to use the method called "free association," from which all suggestive or hypnotic elements were gradually purged, until the definitive abandonment of hypnosis around 1896. But why was hypnosis abandoned? Why was there this shift toward a purely narrative, demimeticized, deemotionalized therapeutic method? We know that the reasons Freud gave later on were quite diverse: hypnosis would provide only temporary remission of symptoms, it was apparently powerless to overcome the "resistance" (Freud also says the "autocratism") of certain subjects, or (and here is an apparent contradiction) it would prevent analysis of this "resistance" by suppressing it artificially.

On closer examination, however, we observe that the divorce between analysis and hypnosis occurred essentially over the issue of remembering. The initial idea, in fact, was that one could just as well obtain the patient's recollections without hypnosis. This idea had been supplied by certain experiments of Bernheim, who showed that it was possible to dispel posthypnotic amnesia merely by applying light pressure on the patient's forehead once the patient was awake. It was this *Druckmethode*, significantly qualified as "light hypnosis," that Freud began to use, although finally he trusted the patient's speech alone, speech free to say anything (so long as *everything* was said). Thus if hypnosis was abandoned, it was first of all in its capacity as a simple *technical procedure* designed to bring about the recollection of "scenes," whether real or, later on, in fantasy. From this remembering, this recollection of "forgotten" ideas, Freud continued to expect the relief of symptoms, and this is why hypnosis was rejected in favor of a therapy using language alone—specifically, *narration*. Indeed, rather than being invited to reexperience or mime the pathogenic "scene," with its accompanying affects, the patient now had to narrate, recount a story passed on to a physician who was not supposed to intervene in the story at all. The analyst, as we know, is not a true interlocutor. He does not answer, he listens; and if he does speak, it is only to fill in the gaps in the autobiographical account of the patient with interpretations and constructions. One could even say (referring to what would have been the "ideal" analytical method of the 1900's) that the analyst is simply an auxiliary of the patient's autobiography and self-analysis. In the more modern version of the same "ideal," the analyst is the addressee, the silent respondent who returns to the subject his own message or history in an inverted form.

This shift toward narration raises a number of problems, if only from a strictly therapeutic standpoint. Indeed, we may wonder whether Freud, by rejecting hypnosis in favor of a method more suitable for evoking recollections, did not actually reject the very source of those spectacular hysterical "recoveries." After all, what caused the relief of symptoms in the first hysterical patients? Was it recollection, insight? We have already seen, with Lacan, that this could not have been true, since the so-called *prise de conscience* occurred in a state of hypnotic unconsciousness. Then was it the *verbalization*, in a hypnotic state, of the traumatic event? At first sight, this solution is seductive, to the extent that it refutes the opposition that is often observed between a hypnotic method considered to be entirely nonverbal and a psychoanalytical method supposed to have finally enabled the patient to speak. Yet this dogmatic representation of hypnosis as an infralinguistic and therefore simply irrational process oversimplifies a far more complex situation: there was in fact no less "verbalization" (or, as Lacan also says, "full speech" [*parole pleine*]) in the cathartic method than in the method of free association. Of course, it is still necessary to understand what is meant by "verbalization" and *parole pleine*. As we know, Lacan defined the latter as "the assumption by the subject of his own history, insofar as it is constituted by the speech addressed to the other." [18] With respect to the alleged "hypnotic recall," Lacan asks:

Why is it that the staunch advocates of the behaviorist *Aufhebung* do not use this as their example to show that they do not have to know whether the subject has remembered anything whatever from the past? He has simply *recounted* the event. But I would say that he has verbalized it . . . that he has made it pass into the *verbe* or, more precisely, into the *epos* by which he brings back into present time the origins of his own person. And he does this in a language that allows his discourse to be understood by his contemporaries, and which furthermore presupposes their present discourse. Thus it happens that the recitation of the *epos* may include a discourse of earlier days in its own archaic, even foreign language, *or may even pursue its course in the present tense with all the animation of the actor*; but it is like an indirect discourse, isolated between quotation marks within the thread of the narration, and, if the discourse is played out, it is on a stage implying the presence not only of the chorus, but also of spectators.

Hypnotic recollection is, no doubt, a reproduction of the past, but it is above all a spoken representation—and as such implies all sorts of presences [emphasis added].¹⁹

It is notable that "verbalization," supposed to bring about the relief of symptoms, is defined here by two traits: (1) it is *speech*— that is, a discourse addressed to an *other* and through which the subject is supposed to recognize *himself* in his own truth; and (2) it is a *narrative* (Lacan also calls it an *epos*, no doubt thinking of the "mixed diegesis" of Plato), since even when the subject presents his story "in the present tense with all the animation of the actor," this mimesis is held to constitute a kind of quotation "in the thread of the narration" addressed to the physician.

Yet this idea of hysterical "verbalization," no doubt valid for the classical analytical situation, causes major problems if, with Lacan, we transpose it onto the hypnotic situation. Indeed, the least we can say is that in this case there is not an *I* facing the *you* and therefore no *parole pleine* either, no symbolic mediation, no "intersubjectivity," no dialectic of recognition wherein the subject receives his own message in inverted form. The other, in hypnosis, does not appear *as other*, and if the subject does recognize himself in the other, it is rather by totally *identifying* with him.

To grasp this, we have only to think of hypnosis by verbal suggestion, as Freud described it, for example, in "Psychical Treatment." The hypnotist says, "You are falling asleep," and *voilà*, *I* fall asleep. He says, "You are smelling a flower," and *I* smell the fragrance. He says, "You see a snake," and *I* see the reptile, *I* am afraid, and *I* cry out. It would be totally false to claim that an *I* is submitting or responding to another here. In reality, "I" am *spoken by* the other,

I come into the place of the other—who, by the same token, is no longer an *other* but rather "myself" in my undecidable identity of somnambulistic ego. Thus the other disappears from the awareness of the hypnotized subject at the very moment when the other provides the subject's consciousness with ideas, perceptions, volitions, and so on. We could even say, as Freud did in the "Note on the Unconscious," that the other remains "unconscious," so long as we understand that this withdrawal of the other person from consciousness precedes any *idea* of the other person and likewise any remembering and repression. In this sense, hypnotic suggestion may well be defined, in the terms Freud used in the preface to his translation of Bernheim, as "a conscious idea which has been introduced into the brain of the hypnotized subject by an external influence, and which has been accepted by the subject as if it had arisen spontaneously." [20] This very singular hypnotic "spontaneity" is here the effect of a radical *forgetting of the other*—a forgetting inaccessible to any recollection (and very close, by the way, to the "forgetting" of which Heidegger and Maurice Blanchot speak, each in his own fashion).

The preceding description, which applies to direct hypnotic suggestion, applies equally to the kind of somnambulism experienced by Anna O., wherein the hypnotized person seems to enjoy a somewhat greater autonomy toward the hypnotist, since the latter's intervention is limited to the suggestion of hypnotic "sleep." Here the somnambulist allows herself to be permeated, or entranced, not by the hypnotist but by another identity, another role, or even (to borrow one of Anna O.'s expressions, which condenses the whole question) "another me." We should recall that one of the characteristics of the hysterics treated by Breuer and Freud was their oscillation, under hypnosis, among several "personalities" ("I am a woman from the last century," Emmy von N. said). Therefore, in every case, the basic phenomenon of hypnotic "verbalization" was that the "subjects," far from *speaking to* another, let themselves *be spoken by* another, while miming the other. If we add that this hypnotic "miming" was enacted *in the present*, "with all the animation of the actor" and in a kind of identification with or mimesis of another person, we see that characterizing hypnotic "verbalization" as narrative is just as inadequate as describing it as speech addressed to another.

And so we are confronted once again with the question of knowing what could have brought about the relief of symptoms in these hysterical patients. Once we are dealing with neither a question of recollection (as Freud thought) nor one of narrative speech (as Lacan would have it), should we not attribute the healing process, if not to hypnosis proper, at least to the mimesis that characterized it? Wasn't it this trance, this forceful invasion of the "subject" by another identity, that was decisive? If so, this would mean that from the outset Freud led analytical therapy down the wrong path by basing it on recollection and narration. This idea is actually not so surprising if we bear in mind that the "psychotherapies" (or, better yet, the "sociotherapies") that preceded psychoanalysis—from shamanistic techniques to "animal magnetism," not to mention exorcism of the possessed—have always included, in one form or another, an element of trance or disappearance of self. From this standpoint, isn't Octave Mannoni correct to say that the transference, as it is handled in analysis, "is what is left to us of possession"? "Eliminate the devil," Mannoni says, "and people with convulsions remain. Eliminate relics, and Mesmer's 'magnetized subjects' remain. Eliminate hypnosis, and what remains? The transference. Thus the question of the transference touches on basic issues, which we might call 'anthropological,' given the special meaning this adjective may have for an analyst."[21] But rather than go into this vast and fascinating prehistory of psychoanalysis, or consider the enormous question of knowing whether the kinds of therapies just mentioned may still have any effectiveness in our symbolic system,[22] it would be more useful to examine the resurgence of this prehistory in analysis itself, under the name—the new name, among so many others—of "transference."

Almost immediately, transference came to disturb the ideally narrative method of analysis. Very early, in fact, Freud realized that the person of the analyst regularly intervened in the associations of patients. This development had not been foreseen. It meant that the purely autobiographical narrative of the patient tended to transform itself yet again into a current relationship, one that was acted out (not to say mimed) with the analyst. This phenomenon, which Freud noticed as early as the *Studies in Hysteria*, he first explained as one more resistance among others, simply as a displacement (the terms *Verschiebung* and *Übertragung* were at that time almost synonymous).

In this regard, it is instructive to consider the passage of the *Studies* where the concept of transference first appears. In that passage, Freud proposes a theory that consists of interpreting the patient's present demand (his *discourse*, as Emile Benveniste might say) as a *narrative in disguise*—that is, as a resistance to the remembering required by the analyst. Thus, referring to a hysterical patient who threw her arms around his neck in the middle of a session, Freud immediately explains that the patient's desire was not addressed to him but to another, a "third person." Behind the *you* stated in the current situation, one should hear a *he* narrated in the past:

> The content of the wish had appeared first of all in the patient's consciousness without any memories of the surrounding circumstances which would have assigned it to a past time. The wish which was present was then, owing to the compulsion to associate which was dominant in the consciousness, linked to my person. . . . Since I have discovered this, I have been able, whenever I have been similarly involved personally, to presume that a transference [*Übertragung*] and a false connection [*falsche Verknüpfung*] have once more taken place.[23]

Hence there appeared (Freud continues) a resistance to the treatment, since the patients broke off their associations at the point where certain personal relations seemed to come into play, and where a third person (*dritte Person*) blended with the person of the physician.[24] Freud offers the same explanation a bit later, in *Dora*, and he also calls on it to explain hypnotic phenomena. Transferences (the plural is used) are new editions or facsimiles of the impulses and fantasies that are to be aroused and made conscious during the analysis, but their characteristic peculiarity is to replace some earlier person with the person of the physician. In other words, a whole series of psychological experiences is revived *"not as belonging to the past, but as applying to the person of the physician at the present moment."*[25] Further on, Freud says:

> Hysteria may be said to be cured not by the method but by the physician, and . . . there is usually a sort of blind dependence and a permanent bond between a patient and the physician who has removed his symptoms by hypnotic suggestion [what is meant here is, in Pierre Janet's beautiful phrase, "somnambulistic passion"], but the scientific explanation of all these facts is to be found in the existence of *transferences* such as are regularly directed by patients onto their physicians.[26]

Thus we find (1) that the phenomenon of transference is, as Freud himself admitted, nothing other than the reemergence, within analysis, of the characteristic relationship ("rapport") of hypnosis (dependence, submission, and even, as "Psychical Treatment" says, *Alleinschätzung*, the attaching of exclusive importance to the person of the physician); and (2) that this singular "rapport" with another person, as soon as it is recognized, is immediately interpreted *in analytical terms*, in that the patient's current relationship with the analyst is understood (and at the same time derealized) as the displaced representation or reproduction of an earlier "emotional tie" to a loved and / or hated *dritte Person*. The emotional scene that the patient plays out to the analyst supposedly conceals a narrative and makes a past memory present ("with all the animation of the actor," to repeat Lacan's phrase). The patient, Freud said later and very significantly in the *The Question of Lay Analysis*, is "obliged to stage a revival" of an old play; he reproduces it "tangibly, as if it were actually happening, instead of remembering it." [27]

This hypothesis is decisive, since it establishes the supposedly irreducible difference between the analyst and the hypnotist. Indeed, to respond to the somnambulistic affect of the patient, as Freud untiringly explains, would be to swing into the orbit of hypnotic suggestion. It would confuse the ostensible *you* of the emotional impulse with the *he*, the *dritte Person*, and thus would lock the patient into the "perpetual attachment" that binds the subject to that third person, when the point is precisely to expose this bond for what it is and free the patient from it. In this sense, an analyst is an analyst only if he does not respond to the affects and demands of the patient, thus forcing him to move from acting to telling, from repeating to remembering, from the present to the past. In fact, the abstinence and impassibility (or, perhaps more accurately, the apathy and disaffection) that Freud demands of the analyst correspond to this strategy or policy of enunciation. The analyst must not open himself to the actions or affects of the patient, which by their very nature are always in the present, active, acted out (mimed, we might say), and therefore "resistant" to the narration required by analysis.

This definitive hypothesis notwithstanding, things did get complicated when Freud realized that the transference, far from being only one resistance among others, really constituted *the* major resistance to analysis. The harder the analyst tried to obtain the patient's recollection, the more the patient tended to forget himself, as it were, in the analyst's arms, so that all the other resistances seemed to revolve around that particular "amnesia." As a result, analysis of resistances increasingly became analysis of the transference or, in other words, analysis of the analytical relationship itself, as if the transference were both the obstacle to and the mainspring of the cure. Freud made this point in 1912, in the article on "The Dynamics of Transference," and it means among other things that it was becoming more and more difficult, even impossible, to distinguish between the mechanics of analysis and those of hypnosis, even though hypnosis was supposed to have been discarded once and for all. If the transference tends to dominate the whole analytical situation, and if the analyst's silence, rather than keeping the transference at bay, actually provokes it, then one can no longer oppose, as Freud had done earlier, the pure interpretative listening of the analyst to the direct suggestion of the hypnotist, or the interventionism of the hypnotist to the abstentionism of the analyst. This is what Roustang has pointed out: whether the analyst speaks or not, uses suggestion or not, is relatively unimportant because suggestibility (or passivity) appears in the patient anyway, taking the form of what Freud calls "positive" transference.[28] Instead of talking about his past loves, the patient "loves" his analyst, thinks only of him, submits compliantly to his advice, accepts all his interpretations and constructions, believes blindly in psychoanalytical theory, and so on. We might go so far as to say that the whole analytical process moves once again toward the establishment of a hypnotic type of "rapport," in which the subject speaks and thinks like another, and even toward an actual state of trance (as Ferenczi was forced to acknowledge, calling it "neocatharsis").

It is futile to object that this "transference love" is still very different from the intense mimetic-emotional relationship seen in hypnotic trance. Bernheim had already said that suggestibility, which he also called *crédivité*, is found at least as much in the waking state as in deep hypnosis, the latter being on the whole an especially spectacular manifestation of suggestibility. Freud certainly knew this, especially since the term *Gläubigkeit*, which he uses constantly to describe positive transference (that is, *believing, credulous* transference), is the same term he used in "Psychical Treatment" to render Bernheim's *crédivité* in German. Positive transference, in this sense, is none other than *gläubige Erwartung*, the "credulous" or "confident expectancy" that Freud at the time considered to be the basis of effective therapeutic suggestion. Thus, in almost all the "technical writings" he produced from that time on, and with remarkable honesty and consistency, Freud recognized that what analysis rediscovers in the transference is suggestibility on the patient's side and suggestion (even if unintentional) on the analyst's. For example, we read in the *Autobiographical Study*:

In every analytical treatment there arises without the physician's agency, an intense emotional relationship [*eine intensive Gefühlsbeziehung*] between the patient and the analyst which is not to be accounted for by the actual situation. . . . We can easily recognize it as the same dynamic factor which the hypnotists have called "suggestibility," which is the agent of hypnotic "rapport" [*des hypnotischen Rapports*] and whose incalculable behaviour led to difficulties with the cathartic method as well.[29]

We also find the following statement at the beginning of chapter 3 in *Beyond the Pleasure Principle*:

Psychoanalysis was then first and foremost an art of interpreting. Since this did not solve the therapeutic problem, a further aim quickly came into view: to oblige the patient to confirm the analyst's construction from his own memory. In that endeavour the chief emphasis lay upon the patient's resistances: the art consisted now in uncovering these as quickly as possible, in pointing them out to the patient and in inducing him by human influence— *this was where suggestion operating as "transference" played its part*—to abandon his resistances [emphasis added].[30]

We immediately perceive the problem that statements like these cannot help raising: if "transference" is only a new name for "suggestibility," how can analysis be distinguished from suggestion and even from hypnosis? For example, how is it possible to guarantee that the analyst's interpretations and constructions are correct, if the patient's conviction is extorted by "suggestion operating as transference"? How can we know that the patient's memories are not pseudomemories, *memories for the sake of love*, somewhat like the fantastic "reminiscences" of Anna O. and Emmy von N.? In other words, how can we ensure that the results of an analysis do not owe more to hypnotransferential "rapport" than to interpretation of and insight into repressed material? All these questions, which periodically came up in his works, Freud generally answered by invoking the "dissolving" (*Auflösung*) of the transference. Analysis, in provoking "transference neurosis," also revived hypnotic "rapport," but for Freud this rapport was revived the better to be destroyed in being consigned to the patient's past. In the *Autobiographical Study*, we read:

It is perfectly true that psycho-analysis, like other psycho-therapeutic methods, employs the instrument of suggestion (or transference). But the difference is this: that in analysis it is not allowed to play the decisive part in determining the therapeutic results. The transference is made conscious to the patient by the analyst, and it is resolved by convincing him that in his transference attitude he is *re-experiencing* [*wiedererleben*] emotional relations which had their origin in his earliest object attachments during the repressed period of his childhood.[31]

In the twenty-eighth *Introductory Lecture*, where all these issues are discussed at length, Freud says again that in analysis the transference is dissolved:

It is this last characteristic which is the fundamental distinction between analytic and purely suggestive therapy and which frees the results of analysis from the suspicion of being successes due to suggestion. In every other kind of suggestive treatment the transference is carefully preserved and left untouched; in analysis it is itself subjected to treatment and is dissected in all the shapes in which it appears. At the end of an analytic treatment the transference itself must be cleaned away; and if success is then obtained or continues, it rests, not on suggestion but on the achievement by its means of an overcoming of internal resistances.[32]

Thus the difference between analytical treatment and hypnosuggestive treatment lies uniquely in the dissolution of the transference, alias "suggestibility," alias hypnotic "rapport." This should not be surprising, since it is only to say once more that the practice of analysis differs from that of its predecessor on the basis of the enunciation (or, as Lacan writes, the "verbalization") required in analysis. And what, indeed, is "dissolving" the transference, if not getting the patient to tell his story and remember, whereas hypnosis keeps him stuck in the repetitive enactment of an "I love / I hate you" addressed to the physician? But we also see that the difference between analysis and hypnosis, or between analysis and suggestion, is far from being as clear as it was in the early days of psychoanalysis, since now psychoanalysis also appears to be a kind of *internal* exit from hypnosis. The *eigentliche Psychoanalyse*, just as before, is supposed to begin where hypnosis leaves off—but now it is through hypnosis, *through* the transference. Thus one issue—the beginning of "true" analysis—now becomes another, distressing one: the end of analysis. Is there an end to analysis, after all? Is analysis "terminable"? Can hypnotic transference be "dissolved"? Or is it instead the part of analysis that cannot be analyzed, of which the patient cannot be cured, any more than of repetition?

This question—absolutely crucial for psychoanalysis, since what is at stake is its "identity" and its "singularity"—has really never been settled. In the end, is psychoanalysis, to use Roustang's expression, "long-drawn-out suggestion"? There is certainly no way to decide on the basis of the facts. Indeed, can we ever determine whether an analysis is really over, whether the transference is really gone? It is more useful to ask what the transference *is*—that is, to ask (as we know now) what *hypnosis* is—if we want to know whether the transference can truly be eliminated. This last question rapidly brings us back to the original "enigma," that of the *Gefühlsbindung*, the "emotional tie," the "rapport *sans* rapport" with another, for it is this rapport that Freud found in the transference, and perhaps it was simply pointless to try to dissolve it. It is constituent of the "subject" and, as such, unrecollectible, untellable, unrepresentable—indissoluble.

What, then, *is* the transference—or hypnosis? Freud answers that it is a resistance. But to what? To remembering. To remembering what? It is a resistance to remembering "some portion of infantile life," says chapter 3 of *Beyond the Pleasure Principle*, "of the Oedipus complex, that is, and its derivatives."[33] Therefore, transference is a resistance to remembering a libidinal object-tie that, because of a conflict, has succumbed to repression.

Yet how does the transference rapport resist remembering? By concealing the "emotional tie" it is supposed to reproduce? Quite the contrary. "These reproductions," we find in the same passage of *Beyond the Pleasure Principle*, "emerge with . . . unwished-for exactitude."[34] But why, then, speak of "resistance" if the unconscious is, as it were, nakedly exhibited in the transference? The answer is that the unconscious is, paradoxically, exhibited *unconsciously*, in a kind of absence from self that excludes all remembering and all representation. This is what Freud explains at the end of "The Dynamics of Transference," using terms that cannot help recalling the hypnoid "reliving" of experiences, as reported in the first hysterical patients:

In the process of seeking out the libido which has escaped from the patient's conscious we have penetrated into the realm of the unconscious. . . . The unconscious impulses do not want to be remembered in the way the treatment desires them to be, but endeavour to reproduce themselves in accordance with the timelessness [*Zeitlosigkeit*] of the unconscious and its capacity for hallucination. Just as happens in dreams, the patient regards the products of the awakening of his unconscious impulses as contemporaneous [*Gegenwärtig*] and real; he seeks to act out his passions [*seine Leidenschaften agieren*] without taking any account of the real situation.[35]

Three points are worth noting here. First, it is "passions" or "impulses"—in other words, *affects*—that elude recollection. If the transference "resists" being remembered, this is because it is "transference of affect," and affect, as Freud says elsewhere, is always perceived in the present, unlike representations. In other words, the affect in transference is experienced *in statu nascendi*, with all the intensity of the first time. This first point, of course, accords with what Freud says in *Studies in Hysteria* about the "abreaction" of affects under hypnosis.

Second, and at the same time, the transference is "timeless." "Timelessness" means here, as it always does in Freud, complete disregard of the past and the future in sole favor of the present. The transference *makes present* the "fragment of infantile life," and this actualization Freud designates by two terms, equivalent for him: "acting out" (*Agieren*) and "repeating" (*Wiederholung*). (Freud uses these two terms from 1914 on; they first appear in *Recollecting, Repeating, Working Through*.) What is decisive about the notion of *Agieren* is not so much acting out, or nonverbal enactment, as actualization. Affect, in transferential repetition, is acted out in the present; it is unremembered and unrepresented; thus, in the transference, gestures accompany speech and thought immediately becomes act, rather than the reverse.

The third point is doubtless the most enigmatic: the transference is governed by primary unconscious processes. As Lacan says, although with completely different intentions, the transference is "the enactment of the reality of the unconscious."[36] This idea hardly accords with the concept of transference as resistance, nor can it be reconciled with an unconscious theorized as made up of repressed *representations*. The unconscious does manifest itself in the transference as affect, as an "emotional tie," but it is scarcely conceivable that the transference would resist its own dis-covery, since it *is* this very dis-covery. That is why Freud was obliged to say more explicitly, in *Beyond the Pleasure Principle* and in *Inhibitions, Symptoms and Anxiety*, that transferential repetition is not so much resistance *to* the unconscious as resistance *of* the unconscious.[37] Repetition in the transference is finally less a resistance to the recollection of the unconscious than *the unconscious as resistance to recollection*, as "devilish" persistence in amnesia. Thus one is ultimately reduced to asking whether the wish to obtain a recollection of the unconscious makes any sense at all. Chapter 3 of *Beyond the Pleasure Principle* makes this point:

> It is certain that much of the ego is itself unconscious. . . . We can say that the patient's resistances arise from his ego, and we then at once perceive that the compulsion to repeat *must be ascribed to the unconscious repressed*. It seems probable that the compulsion can only express itself after the work of treatment has gone half way to meet it and has loosened the repression [emphasis added].[38]

Freud's footnote to this passage, added in 1923, not only completes the fusion of these three notions—"transference," "repetition," and "the unconscious"—but also links this group of terms to suggestion (in other words, to hypnotic "rapport"):

> I have argued elsewhere that what thus comes to the help of the compulsion to repeat is the factor of "suggestion" in the treatment—that is, the patient's submissiveness to the physician which has its roots deep in his unconscious parental complex.[39]

But all this information, enigmatic in itself, does not tell us whether the hypnotransferential tie to another person can rightly be "dissolved," untied. Is it possible to dispel the amnesia that belongs to the unconscious? Or (really the fundamental question) can affect be narrated, *abreagiert* in the narrative mode? These questions are meaningful only in relation to an at least possible recollection. It is because Freud continues to think that the unconscious is made up of representations (and not affects), of repressed memories or fantasies (and not enactments), that he can state his objective as the undoing of the transference, conceived as blind repetition of an earlier "emotional tie" to an object of love and / or hate. But can this *Gefühlsbindung* really be remembered? For such remembering to be possible, this "emotional tie" would have to be presented to the subject (to his conscious or unconscious, it really does not matter) as a *representation* (a perception or a fantasy; again, it does not matter), so that it could be kept present in a memory and possibly be recollected as a memory. This hypothesis presents no problems so long as we hold to the idea that the transference repeats "some portion of the Oedipus complex," as Freud says. With the Oedipus complex, in fact, we are dealing with an already formed subject or "ego" that maintains diverse emotional relationships with differentiated others (love for the maternal *object*; admiration of and hateful rivalry with the paternal *model*); therefore, the hypothesis of repressed representations, transferred affects, and so on still seems quite plausible.

The hypothesis of recollection nevertheless does grow problematic when Freud informs us—essentially in *Group Psychology*, but also in *The Ego and the Id*, and, more generally, in all the texts of the second "topography"—that Oedipal ties in turn reflect, because they repeat it, a more archaic "emotional tie" that Freud variously calls "primary identification" or "incorporation," and that he continually describes as a deep emotional ambivalence (*Gefühlsambivalenz*). Yet this "emotional tie," which certainly remains very close to the hypnotic "tie," still cannot be represented or remembered, if only because it precedes the ego, the subject-of-the-representation. "Identification," Freud says in *Group Psychology*, "is the original form of emotional tie with an object,"[40] and this means that the ego forms itself or *is born* in this devouring identification with the other. Thus there is no ego, no subject to form a representation of the object and / or of the identificatory model, since it is precisely in the singular "event" of the appropriation (of this *Ereignis*, we could say with Heidegger) that the ego as such emerges. The "other" whose identity is thus incorporated sinks into an oblivion that precedes memory and representation, never having presented itself to any subject—and it is "myself," the unutterable affect of my birth. As Freud suggested in connection with anxiety, birth is the primordial affect, and we might add that this is so because it is identification, mimetic *Gefühlsbindung*. Because "I *am* the breast" (in Freud's famous phrase), because I am nothing before this earliest identification and because such is my birth, affect comes about—in other words, my being affected (*affection*) by an otherness (*altérité*) that is my identity or my "selfness" itself.

This first "emotional tie" to another, which is also the unrepresentable event of my "own" birth, can never be remembered, never be recalled to memory. This is also why it can never be "dissolved," as Freud would have it. But (and this is what happens all the time, if it happens) it can be *repeated*—for example, in hypnotic trance, or in the oblivion of the transference. In the end, in this strange rite of passage that today we call "psychoanalysis," perhaps the only stake is this: repeating, repeating the other in oneself, dying to oneself— to be reborn, perhaps, *other*.

Translated by Angela Brewer and X. P. Callahan

Analytic Speech: From Restricted to General Rhetoric

Has rhetoric ended? Or can we today still make it serve some end? Is it still the productive, influential *techné* of which the ancients spoke? Is it dead, "dried up" (as Martin Heidegger says of the flowers of rhetoric),[1] or is it "living" (as Paul Ricoeur says of metaphor)?[2]

All depends on what is meant by "rhetoric." Defined as the theory of tropes or of figures of speech, rhetoric undoubtedly died in the mid-nineteenth century. Roland Barthes, Gérard Genette, Ricoeur, and Tzvetan Todorov have all variously written out its death certificate by imputing what they see as rhetoric's two-thousand-year decline to a progressive restriction of its range and objectives: "natural eloquence" was reduced to a codification of probable argumentation; the great edifice of oratorical eloquence then shrank to the study of literary and poetic *elocutio*; *elocutio* subsequently diminished to a theory of tropes; tropes were limited to metaphor and metonymy; and, to end it all, the whole of rhetoric was defined as metaphor alone.[3] Thus, in their accounts, the history of rhetoric is a lethal "generalized restriction."[4]

To say that rhetoric is dead by restriction, however, is also to say that only restricted rhetoric is dead. Nothing prevents one part or another of ancient rhetoric-in-general from surviving, reviving, or simply prospering under another name. How could it be otherwise? The *techné rhétoriké* dealt with language that allows effective action on another; thus its vast "empire"[5] comprised almost all aspects of language taken as an act of communication: *inventio, dispositio, elocutio, actio, memoria*. It would be very surprising if we had not kept or recaptured something of this domain, albeit unknowingly. To discover present-day relatives of ancient rhetoric, we need not invoke specialized research on "speech acts" or on the "pragmatics of communication," both attentive to the active and operant value of language. It suffices to think of the modern techniques of mass communication, whether advertising or political propaganda. Our "media-tized" societies, however different from Sicilian or Athenian democracies, are nonetheless similarly regulated by a rhetorical politics centered on the persuasive power of the probable and of popular opinion, of *eikos* and *endoxa*. Given the phenomenon of the mass media, how can we doubt that rhetoric is alive and well in the heart of our societies? Our very lives, both public and private, tend to turn (or to return) to rhetoric, to pure "commonplace."

Therefore it may be retrospective illusion to speak of the "end" or "death" of rhetoric. The history of rhetoric is not the continuous and closed story of its progressive restriction but the discontinuous and indefinite one of a permanent tension between two uses of the term: one of extreme generality (and therefore extreme vagueness), which makes it an art of persuasion (this is its oratorical, pragmatic, or "impressive" pole, corresponding roughly to what G. A. Kennedy calls "primary rhetoric");[6] the other of more restricted scope, which makes it an art of speaking well (this is its literary, poetic, ornamental, or "expressive" pole, corresponding roughly to what Kennedy calls "secondary rhetoric" and V. Florescu *letteraturizzazione*).[7] Between these two poles there is a constant oscillation punctuated by "deaths" and "renaissances" of rhetoric. That "secondary rhetoric" has regularly tended to replace "primary rhetoric" does not exclude (but, on the contrary, explains) the latter's having no less regularly reasserted its rights each time that historic conditions made the need of return to a persuasive or "impressive" use of language felt. No doubt today we are witnessing a resurgence of "primary rhetoric": the very fact that we ask ourselves about the "ends" of rhetoric testifies that we are living the nth chapter of that tension between a taxonomy of the figures of speaking well and a pragmatics (or politics) of effective speaking.

Conforming to the old probationary technique of the exemplum, in the interest of persuasive effectiveness, I propose to illustrate this "chapter" with a limited case, psychoanalytic rhetoric, or rather— for it is necessary to qualify immediately—what is *conventionally* called psychoanalytic "rhetoric."

The assimilation of dream work, slips of the tongue, and symptoms to the figures of rhetoric has become one of the most insistent topoi of our linguistico-psychoanalytic culture since Emile Benveniste, Roman Jakobson, and Jacques Lacan first advanced it in a series of famous articles that appeared in 1956–57.[8] Benveniste, in a rather vague and prudent manner, outlined a comparison between the oneiric processes described by Freud and the stylistic figures of speech: metaphor, metonymy, synecdoche, but also euphemism, allusion, antiphrasis, litotes, ellipsis, and so on. Jakobson, more precisely (or more audaciously), proposed assimilating displacement and condensation to metonymy, identification and symbolism to metaphor—these two rhetorical figures being themselves reduced, by a perilous leap, to the two properly linguistic operations of syntagmatic combination and paradigmatic selection. Lacan, extending the hypotheses of Jakobson, with no less temerity suggested identifying condensation and symptom with metaphor, displacement and desire with metonymy, thus promoting a linguistic interpretation of the unconscious. These formulations, however different, agree that there is a "figurality" of desire, a "rhetoric of Freud," a "rhetoric of denial," and even a catachrestical "anasemy" of psychoanalytic conceptuality.[9]

Is this "rhetorical" interpretation of the unconscious legitimate—beyond the objections that can be made to details touching such and such a more or less improper (more or less metaphoric) displacement of concepts? The principal reproach I would make is not that such an interpretation reduces the unconscious and its manifestations to rhetorical processes. Many passages in Freud's work can support such a reading, and I will return to them in a moment. Rather, I would point out that this interpretation restricts the operations of the unconscious to a rhetoric that is itself restricted, whether the restriction takes the extreme form of an integral reabsorption of rhetoric into linguistics (as in the works of Jakobson and Lacan) or the inverse form of a boundless generalization to simple figural displacement (as in the Jean-François Lyotard of *Discours, figure*). Psychoanalytic "rhetoric," as it has been understood and practiced in France for nearly thirty years, is in reality *restricted* rhetoric, rhetoric restricted to the figures of speaking well (or, in this case, the impossibility of speaking well), and also, therefore, to a language amputated from its effective, pragmatic, or persuasive dimension.

We should recall that the inverse of such amputation—an examination of the persuasive power of language—was Freud's initial point of departure. Moreover, this point of departure is also, I will show, Freud's point of arrival: a pure question mark. To examine this is to explore the understanding that we today can have of psychoanalysis, of rhetoric, and of their common power.

The psychoanalytic "talking cure" is historically rooted in the practice of hypnosis, more precisely in what Hippolyte Bernheim, in his 1886 *De la suggestion et de ses applications à la thérapeutique*, called "suggestive psychotherapy." But what is "suggestive psychotherapy" or "psychical treatment," as Freud, who translated the work in 1888, preferred to call it? In the article "Psychical Treatment," a "defense and illustration" of psychotherapy published by Freud in 1890, we find the following definition:

"Psychical treatment" [*Seelenbehandlung*] denotes treatment taking its start in the mind [*Behandlung von der Seele aus*], treatment (whether of mental or psychical disorders) by measures which operate in the first instance and immediately upon the human mind. Foremost among such measures is the use of words; and words are the essential tool of mental treatment.[10]

Contrary to modern medicine, which treats body and soul by means of the body, psychical treatment treats soul and body by means of the soul, by utilizing the word. Freud concedes, however, anticipating certain developments in *Totem and Taboo*, that this attributes a quasi-magical power to words:

A layman . . . will feel that he is being asked to believe in magic. And he will not be so very wrong, for the words which we use in our everyday speech are nothing other than watered-down magic.[11]

This will necessitate, he adds, "a roundabout path in order to explain how science sets about restoring to words a part at least of their former magical power."[12]

The goal of this roundabout path—which, as we will see, is the detour by hypnosis—is clear. Science (here medical science) must recuperate, to its profit, the power of language abandoned to magicians, preachers, and healers. That power—of which Freud remarks in passing that it is all the more effective in that it is employed in isolation from the discourse of science, in the domain of religious faith and popular prejudice—that properly miraculous power of the word is persuasion, *Einreden*. In brief, it is the rhetorical *dunamis*, the power of enchantment stigmatized by Plato under the name of *goétèia*,[13] of which Nietzsche said, anticipating Freud, that it "does not intend to instruct, but to transmit to others a subjective emotion and apprehension."[14] How, in fact, does the soul act on the body? Essentially by the intermediary of affects that "are characterized," says Freud, "by a quite special connection with somatic processes": grief, terror, anguish, joy, enthusiasm, or *gläubige Erwartung*, "confident expectation" vis-à-vis the therapist. It is by language that a person can communicate an affect to another person, can influence him, convince him, move him, and so forth. (One will have recognized in passing the two objectives of rhetorical *inventio*: *fidem facere et animos impellere*.) Freud's provisional conclusion is:

Words are the most important media by which one man seeks to bring his influence to bear on another; words are a good method of producing mental changes in the person to whom they are addressed. So that there is no longer anything puzzling in the assertion that the magic of words can remove the symptoms of illness.[15]

But this is not all. The affective power of the word would remain abandoned to chance and empiricism (that is, would remain "magic") if science did not have at its disposal a *techné* capable not only of provoking such and such an affect, but also of inducing *patheia* as such, a "mental compliance," or what Freud calls, after Bernheim, "suggestibility."[16] That technique (that "specific therapeutic method")[17] is hypnotism, with which, Freud tells us, "modern mental treatment has taken its start."[18] In effect, he explains, playing on the word *Ein-reden*, one can "talk" the patient "into" a special state of "mental compliance" in which he becomes "obedient and credulous" vis-à-vis the hypnotist, submits himself to the hypnotist's injunctions, models his "mental life" on the hypnotist's, and so on.[19] In brief, by a fabulous process (which would have been the dream of the ancient rhetoricians) one can persuade the listener to be "persuadable," "affectable." Suggestion (which is, says Freud, the technical name of the "words spoken by the hypnotist which have [these] magical results")[20] possesses the remarkable property of annulling (at least for the hypnotized person) the distance between locutor and listener, emitter and receiver. It does not communicate a message (information, or even an order); it communicates a state of faith (*Gläubigkeit*)—that is to say, both a receptivity to the message and an identification with the emitter. Freud wrote in his preface to the German edition of Bernheim's book:

What distinguishes a suggestion from other kinds of psychical influence, such as a command or the giving of a piece of information or instruction, is that in the case of a suggestion an idea is aroused in another person's brain which is not examined in regard to its origin but is accepted just as though it had arisen spontaneously in that brain.[21]

Hence its affective (pathogenic or, contrarily, cathartic) power, since the listener completely appropriates for himself this discourse of the other; hence also its contaminating, contagious power, since the listener identifies with and mimics it. As Freud says, "Words have once more regained their magic"[22]—that is, their mimetic magic, their mimologic omnipotence, described (and condemned) by Plato in Books 3 and 10 of the *Republic*.

This reading of "Psychical Treatment" could take us far toward what Freud later called the "magical omnipotence of thoughts" and the absence of doubt and negation proper to unconscious "primary processes"[23]: the singular "logic" of the unconscious is, undoubtedly, the mimo-patho-logic of hypnotic suggestion. That is to say, it is the rhetorical mimo-patho-logic understood as the "art of conducting souls by words" (which is Socrates' definition in *Phaedrus*).[24] If the effectiveness of the psychoanalytic cure rests entirely on the power of speech, as Lacan has repeated many times, this power was originally, in Freud's work, that of "suggestive," affective, and impressive—in brief, persuasive—speech. What Freud rediscovered, around 1890, in Bernheim's, Joseph Delboeuf's, or Pierre Janet's researches on verbal suggestion, was at base a new version (with scientific and experimental pretensions) of the "pathic" part of ancient rhetoric, as we know it in its codification by Aristotle in Book 2 of the *Rhetoric*.[25] How can we not see that the project outlined in "Psychical Treatment" is a sort of medical rhetoric, fallen away from its relation with scientific medicine and yet, nevertheless, sufficiently "technical" (thanks to hypnotism) to escape from empiricism and from the magic of healers? It is the project—halfway between *épistémé* and *empeiria*—of a *patho-logy*, in the double sense of an affecting discourse (capable of provoking certain *pathé*) and of a discourse *on* affects (of an *Affektivitätslehre*, as Freud would later say).

One might object that this patho-logical *techné* has exactly nothing to do with psychoanalysis and that Freud quickly abandoned it in favor of the technique of "free association" (by the patient) and an "art of interpreting"[26] (by the therapist). The hypnosuggestive technique was expressly rejected by Freud (even in its "cathartic" form) for a very simple reason, which is, at bottom, reason itself. The patho-logy understood as discourse *on* affects (thus as theoretical discourse) can only compete with, and finally eliminate, the pathology understood as affective, persuasive discourse, for how is one to say the truth about this false power, this *pseudologos* that makes one believe in no-matter-what and that causes, according to Socrates, "that which is small to appear large, and that which is large, small"? As Plato says in *Phaedrus*, the rhetoricians do not know what they are saying (that is to say, what they are doing): they speak *to* the soul of their listeners, but not *of* the soul in its relation with speech, and therefore they cannot produce the truth of their own psychagogic discourse.[27]

Beginning in 1895, Freud directed just such a reproach against suggestion, and that reproach is a sign of a forceful return in his discourse to the values of truth and scientificity in the very place where the hypnosuggestive *techné* was only interested in therapeutic effectiveness. Freud does not object to the effectiveness of suggestion (on the contrary, here and there Freud even regrets its loss),[28] but rather to its irrational, "mysterious,"[29] and thus unmanageable and "uncheckable" character.[30] This critique is made explicit in chapter 4 of *Group Psychology*: Suggestion—which is supposed to explain everything—cannot even explain itself; a word for the "magic of words," it would itself be a "magic word," a *Zauberwort*, incapable of resolving the enigma (*Rätsel*) of an "influence without adequate logical foundation."[31] In brief, it designates a power which is not that of the truth, not a knowledge; hence, of course, its condemnation as "violence" and as a hold exercised on another, a condemnation that is itself very violent (indeed "magic") and that evokes Plato's expulsion of rhetoric from the philosophical *logos*. Psychoanalytic dialogue has often been compared to Platonic dialectic,[32] and here this comparison is more pertinent than ever: the passage from suggestive technique to analytic "talking cure" corresponds almost point for point with the Platonic passage from rhetorical argumentation, in which the stakes are persuasive "probability," to the "true rhetoric" or *dialèk-tikè*, in which the stakes are "the truth about the subject that you speak . . . about."[33]

The "thing of which one speaks" in the analytical *dialegesthai* and about which one is to arrive at a consensus or *homologia* is here the speaking subject himself, however. (In this the psychoanalytic cure is already much closer, as Lacan has noted, to dialectic in its modern Hegelian form.) [34] The post-Cartesian Freud conceives of truth as certitude, as the self-knowledge of consciousness. This attitude explains, beyond historical vicissitude, why "psychical treatment" passes from the persuasive setup of hypnosis, where it is the other who *ein-redet* the subject (in a state of unconsciousness), to the autoenunciative setup of psychoanalysis, where the subject speaks of himself to another who is now only the mediator of his certainty (of the *Erinnerung*, the "realization" of the repressed). The treatment continues to be a treatment by words and by affects, though now in the sense that the words of the subject must adequately express (and thus "abreact," as Freud says) [35] an affect that has been detached from its proper representation because of repression. As for the therapist, he no longer speaks (or he speaks very little); moreover, he becomes himself one of the "transferential" forms in which the subject fallaciously expresses his affect. In a word, he becomes a *figure* of the subject and of his autoenunciative discourse.

It is here that Benveniste, Jakobson, and Lacan have, more or less legitimately, grafted on the rhetorico-linguistic interpretation. Once one admits that the subject's discourse (which includes his dreams and symptoms) is the indirect expression of an affect that cannot be directly expressed because of repression and censorship, then the different operations of symbolization located by Freud can all be described as the distance between a proper sense and a transposed or tropic sense (one need only think of *Übertragung*, which exactly translates Aristotle's *metaphora*). By radicalizing certain Freudian themes (for example, the necessary inaccessibility of the unconscious apart from its "translation" to consciousness, [36] or the figural character of the analytic *Bildersprache*), [37] one easily arrives at Lacan's thesis: the subject can only signify himself by metaphorizing himself in the signifier by which he expresses himself, and therefore he cannot signify himself except by losing himself as subject of the enunciation, in accordance with a metaphoricity without proper sense (or a *signifiance* without signified), which makes the whole structure of the unconscious like language and the "discourse of the Other."

This interpretation, however, continues to make the analytic setup into a setup of autoenunciation (even if this is declared impossible) and the "rhetoric" of the unconscious into a rhetoric restricted to the figures of discourse (even if these are defined in terms of signifying substitution and no longer as figures of sense). The Lacanian subject cannot properly express himself, since his discourse is always-already that of the other—but that is exactly his most proper truth (which says, "I, truth, speak" and which, as we know, must be taken "literally"),[38] and the "discourse of the Other" has nothing to do with some "persuasive" or "suggestive" discourse of the analyst. Lacan's whole enterprise is expressly directed against an interpretation of the analytic cure as persuasion or suggestion, which he always denounces in the name of "Freudian truth" as "imaginary identification with the analyst" and "alienation" into the specular "small other." Freudian rhetoric is perhaps that of the "metaphor of the subject,"[39] but it should definitely not be that of the persuasion of the subject, according to Lacan.

Such an interpretation would be unproblematic if Freud had kept to his initial rejection of verbal suggestion and of the persuasive dimension of words. But that is not the case, and on this point the "truth" or "the letter of Freud" is much less univocal (in any case, much less appropriable) than Lacan says. Suggestion—more precisely, the *question* of suggestion—returned in many ways to the center of Freud's preoccupations, above all in the practice of the cure itself, under the form of the transference. Freud realized very early on that the analyst's abandonment of all forms of suggestion or verbal persuasion did not prevent the "spontaneous" reappearance in the patient of the suggestibility that is characteristic of hypnosis. On the contrary—this is the phenomenon of transference called "positive"—the more silent and reserved the analyst remains, the greater the patient's passion for him: the subject "loves" his analyst, thinks only of him, submits to his "influence," has faith in his interpretations, and so on. All these traits being those of the hypnotic "rapport," Freud could not miss making the connection. To quote the *Selbstdarstellung*, one among many analogous passages:

In every analytic treatment there arises, without the physician's agency, an intense emotional relationship between the patient and the analyst which is not to be accounted for by the actual situation. . . . We can easily recognize it as the same dynamic factor which the hypnotists have named "suggestibility," which is the agent of hypnotic *rapport*.[40]

This affirmation has many implications (for instance, for the henceforth problematic "objectivity" of analytic interpretations, or for the no less problematic possibility of a final "dissolution" of the transference). Here I will simply note that the connection between transference and suggestibility causes an inevitable resurgence in reverse, so to speak, of the whole problem of the pathology, understood as affective power, and of the "magic" of language. At bottom, what is transference as described by Freud if not hypnosis without a hypnotist, persuasion without a rhetorician, since it is produced in the absence of any direct suggestion? Paradoxically, the phenomenon of transference reveals that the influence of the hypnotist and / or analyst is based not on a particular technique or power, but rather on an a priori affectability (a "spontaneous receptivity") in the patient— that is to say, on the "rhetoricity" of the affect *as such*, a rhetoricity anterior to any verbal persuasion and also to any metaphoric expression of passions. The analytic pathology in its ensemble, now understood as *Affektivitätslehre* and the theory of drives, thus finds itself concerned with the problem of rhetoric and its power. Why does another affect me? Why am I affectable, suggestible, persuadable by the discourse of the other—even, and especially, when he says nothing? Is it because I feel an affect in his regard (because I love him, or the unconscious personage that he represents "transferentially")? Or does he affect me with "my" affect, because I have no affect of my own?

This is the question of the "affective tie" with another, alias the "enigma of suggestive influence." This last question appears (or reappears) in *Group Psychology and the Analysis of the Ego*, in a detour made in an inquiry on the nature of the social tie. Why there rather than elsewhere? Because Freud, in conformity with the analyses of Gustave Le Bon (and also Gabriel Tarde and William McDougall), understands the essence of social being on the model of the crowd (or *Masse*) dominated by a leader (or *Führer*). This model is that of collective hypnosis, as the characteristics of "group psychology" enumerated by Freud, following Le Bon, can testify: disappearance of any individual will or personality, affective contagion, suggestibility, hypnotic submission to a "prestigious" leader, and finally, the "magic power of words." Freud writes:

The crowd is extremely credulous and open to influence . . . the improbable does not exist for it. It thinks in images . . . whose agreement with reality is never checked by any reasonable agency. . . . . A group, further, is subject to the truly magical power of words; they can evoke the most formidable tempests in the group mind, and are also capable of stilling them. . . . And, finally, groups have never thirsted after truth.[41]

This dramatic picture is not an aberrant or pathological phenomenon. It is the very image of our media societies that I invoked earlier. It is also the vision that the fascist ideologues, great readers of Le Bon (if not of Freud), made into a historical reality in the 1930's with the terrifying efficiency that we all know. And it is, finally, almost to the last detail, the picture accusingly painted by Plato of the listeners enchanted by poets and orators. Here we arrive at the common root of the patho-logic, of rhetoric, and of politics.

Significantly, Freud, while subscribing unreservedly to this description of "group psychology," refuses the hypnosuggestive theory that underlies it in the work of Le Bon. (It is in *Group Psychology* that Freud's virulent critique of suggestion as *Zauberwort* is to be found.) If the individuals assembled in a mass are so easily persuaded by another, it is not, he explains, by virtue of a mysterious "suggestibility," but because of *love* for the leader. More precisely, if the social tie is really a mimetico-affective tie—an identificatory *Gefühlsbindung*, according to Freud—it is because the members of the mass identify with each other in the mode of hysteria (here a collective one) as a function of their love for a common "object," the *Führer.* Far from being a mass affective contagion, the social tie indirectly expresses the affects of individuals: the identification is a sort of libidinal metaphor (a comparison on the base of an "analogy"),[42] and the *Führer* takes his power from being a transferential figure of desire just like the analyst or hypnotist: exit, consequently, the phantom of suggestion and of the "magic of words."

In *Group Psychology*, however, this official doctrine of the social tie is paralleled by a different, much more problematic doctrine, which returns us to the "enigma of suggestive influence," for the affective tie with the *Führer*, Freud had to concede, is not a libidinal tie. It is a perfectly "desexualized" tie of submission, analogous if not identical, he says, to the "mysterious" hypnotic rapport; he proposes to assimilate it to the tie with the narcissistic ego ideal. Now this tie, Freud had expressly established in chapter 7, is really just identification understood as the "earliest and original form of emotional tie,"[43] anterior to any libidinal-erotic investment:

Identification is known to psychoanalysis as the earliest expression of an emotional tie with another person. . . . A little boy will exhibit a special interest in his father; he would like to grow like him and be like him, and take his place everywhere. We may say simply that he takes his father as his ideal.[44]

To summarize briefly, the affective social tie—that is, the whole domain of suggestion, mimetico-affective contagion, the magical power of words, and so on—reposes on the equally hypnotic tie with the *Führer*-Ego-Ideal, itself reduced to the affective tie of "primary identification."[45] This solution to the "enigma of suggestive influence"—and therefore to the *Einreden*, the power of rhetoric—is merely *that enigma itself*, brought back to the vanished ground of the "subject," for what is the identificatory *Gefühlsbindung* if not another word for stating (or restating) openness to influence, passiveness in regard to another, or depropriation of the affect? To affirm that "the earliest emotional tie with another person" is identification is, in effect, to assert that affect as such is identificatory, mimetic, and that there is no "proper" affect except on the condition of a prior "affection" of the ego by another. Another does not affect me because I feel such and such an affect in regard to him, nor even because he succeeds in communicating an affect to me by way of words. He affects me because "I" *am* that "other," following an identification that is my affection, the strangest alteration of my proper autoaffection. My identity is a passion. And reciprocally, my passions are always identificatory.

Here, therefore, is the enigma—the renewed enigma of rhetoric—and I do not believe that it can be resolved. This enigma hides nothing, dissimulates nothing—or only *the* nothing, the absence of any ground, of every *subjectum* and every subject. It is the irrevealable enigma of a *mimesis* that is all the more effective and "technical" because it has nothing of its own, and because it creates from nothing. Thus there is absolutely nothing to say about it unless it be to repeat, following Freud and so many others, that this enigma is not that of truth. This does not render it any less powerful, as those who have tried to silence rhetoric have always recognized. For, as rhetoric herself says, through the mouth of Socrates in *Phaedrus*: "Why do

you extraordinary people talk such nonsense? I never insist on ignorance of the truth on the part of one who would learn to speak; on
the contrary, if my advice goes for anything, it is that he should only
resort to me after he has come into possession of truth: what I do,
however, pride myself on is that without my aid knowledge of what
is true will get a man no nearer to mastering the art of persuasion."[46]

Translated by Douglas Brick

~ *Talking Cure*

How does psychoanalysis cure (when it cures)? By speech, it is said. Right from its "cathartic" beginnings, psychoanalysis was (as Anna O. baptized it) a "talking cure," which at once approaches magic, exorcism, and more generally, all those historically precedent techniques that cure by speech. In this regard Maurice Blanchot writes,

What faith in reason, what confidence in the liberating power of language. What virtue accorded to the simplest relation: a man who speaks to another man who listens. And here, not only spirits are cured, but bodies. This is admirable, this now goes beyond reason. To avoid any grossly magic interpretation of this marvelous phenomenon, Freud had to make a stubborn effort at elucidation, all the more necessary since his method had an impure origin, having started very close to magnetism, hypnosis, and suggestion.[1]

Freud knew it well: psychoanalysis, in its curative effectiveness, never does anything but return to the ancient "magic power of words." Defining in 1890 what he then called "psychical treatment" (*Seelenbehandlung*), he wrote:

"Psychical treatment" denotes . . . treatment taking its start in the mind [*Seele*, "soul"], treatment (whether of mental or physical disorders) by measures which operate in the first instance and immediately upon the human mind. Foremost among such measures is the use of words; and words are the essential tool of mental treatment. A layman will no doubt find it hard to understand how pathological disorders of the body and mind can be eliminated by "mere" words. He will feel that he is being asked to believe in magic. And he will not be so very wrong, for the words which we use in our everyday speech are nothing other than watered-down magic.[2]

It might be objected that Freud is here speaking of a specific technique, that of Hippolyte Bernheim's "suggestive psychotherapy," which later will be purposely abandoned. But in 1926 he uses exactly the same terms, in *The Question of Lay Analysis*, this time speaking of psychoanalysis:

Nothing takes place between them [the patient and the analyst] except that they talk to each other. . . . The analyst agrees upon a fixed regular hour with the patient, gets him to talk, listens to him, talks to him in his turn, and gets him to listen.

To which Freud immediately objects, through the mouth of an "Impartial Person": "Nothing more than that? Words, words, words, as Prince Hamlet says. . . . So it is a kind of magic . . . you talk and blow away his ailments." To which Freud's own response is: "Quite true. It *would* be magic if it worked rather quicker. . . . And incidentally do not let us despise the *word* . . . originally the word was magic— a magical act; and it has retained much of its ancient power."[3]

This should in no way be understood as a temptation to obscurantism. As Blanchot indicates, it is, on the contrary, a profession of faith in the "God Logos." If, in Freud's eyes, psychoanalysis is close to magic, it is in the precise sense of providing it with its truth, its completely rational truth. Admittedly curing by speech, it cures, in effect, *only* by speech—by disenchanted speech, purified of all ceremonial, all fascination, all influence, and finally brought to its pure and simple essence (in this, notes Blanchot once again, it is very close to properly philosophic dialogue and dialectic).[4] In short, it cures by *logos*, by reason: psychoanalysis extracts the "rational kernel" from magical speech by removing it from its "mystical shell" (notably hypnotic). And that kernel is speech, *all* speech, and *nothing but* speech of the patient.

It is well known that this thesis (in fact much more finely nuanced by Freud himself than I have suggested here) was radicalized in the 1950's by Jacques Lacan in his effort to "return" to what he deemed to be the sense of Freud's discovery. Psychoanalysis, in the "purified" version proposed by Lacan, is neither a manipulation of transferential and countertransferential affects, nor a strategy destined to dissolve the subject's resistances, nor a technique of identificatory reconstruction of the ego. To adopt one of these methods would truly be a return to the maneuvers of suggestion—in short, to the whole impure magic of speech that Freud deprived himself of right from the start by rejecting hypnosis (*Ecrits: A Selection*, p. 49).[5] In reality, psychoanalysis has no other "means" than "those of speech," no other "domain" than "that of concrete discourse, in so far as this is the field of the transindividual reality of the subject" (ibid.):

Whether it sees itself as an instrument of healing, of training, or of exploration in depth, psychoanalysis has only a single medium: the patient's speech. (ibid., p. 40)

And it is the

assumption of his history by the subject, in so far as it is constituted by the speech addressed to the other, that constitutes the ground of the new method that Freud called psychoanalysis. (ibid., p. 48)

It is this famous thesis that I would like to reexamine, modifying it a bit, but holding myself essentially to the formulation Lacan gave it in his 1953 "Rome Discourse" ("The Function and Field of Speech and Language in Psychoanalysis," ibid., pp. 30–113) and other texts of the period. Not, I hasten to add, that I want to dispute that the "means" of psychoanalysis are those of speech. But I would like to ask *which* speech cures and, especially, *how* it cures (when it cures). After all, "how does it happen that by the operation of the signifier people are cured?" Lacan asked himself the same question at the end of his life, during a conference organized by the Ecole Freudienne de Paris in 1979. And he added: "Despite everything I may have said on occasion, I don't know anything about it. It's a question of *truquage.*"[6] It is this enigmatic "operation of the signifier," this *"truquage"* surging forth from the middle of the most rational discourse, that I would like to question. Is the effectiveness of *pure* analytic speech (Lévi-Strauss's famous "effectiveness of symbols") finally just as mysterious as the *impure* speech of ritual, magic, and hypnotism? Does the "rational shell" of psychoanalysis hide a "mystical kernel"?

That the analytic cure rests solely upon speech is what Lacan affirmed in 1936 in his article "Beyond the Reality Principle," at a moment when, nevertheless, his interests were essentially centered on the theory of the "mirror-stage" and the imaginary-paranoiac constitution of the *ego*. This is all the more interesting in that it allows us to better grasp the continuity of his thought on this point, beyond the rupture introduced in the 1950's by the almost exclusive accentuation of the symbolic register.

"The given of the [analytic] experience," writes Lacan in this text, "is first of all that of language, a language, that is, a sign" (*Ecrits*, p. 82). Let us be more precise: a sign addressed to someone. The analytic experience is that of speech, of dialogue: someone speaks to someone, to an "interlocutor" (ibid.) But to be sure, the whole question is to know *who* speaks to *whom* (ibid., p. 375). This is, for Lacan, the question of the dia-lectic.

From the start, Lacan designates he who speaks as the "subject" (ibid., p. 83). True, this "subject" is still rather poorly distinguished from the "ego," at that time described by Lacan as constituted by alienating identifications with the specular and "formative" *imagos*. It is nonetheless worth remarking that Lacan already ties this "subject" to speech: the "ego" is he who *sees* himself in the other (and who remains mute with admiration, with rage); the "subject" is he who *speaks* to the other (in place of fighting with him in the mode of imaginary rivalry). This definition of the subject will remain essentially constant for Lacan (even when he will choose to speak of a "subject of the signifier"): there is no subject except speaking, and inversely, speech always presupposes a subject.

What does this mean? For the Lacan of 1936, it means that it *means*. To speak presupposes an "intention" to signify, a "meaning" (*vouloir-dire*; ibid., p. 83). Indeed, let us imagine a speech with absolutely no relation to reality, a lying, fantastic speech or even a simply insignificant one (and, as we all know, this is the one encountered in psychoanalysis); nonetheless, says Lacan, it still signifies a subject expressing himself for the benefit of another (in the terms of the "Rome Discourse," it still represents "the existence of communication"). As Lacan will later repeat, heavily relying on citations from Augustine, Hegel, and Ferdinand de Saussure, language does not represent reality but a subject. In our text of 1936, "language, before signifying something, signifies for someone," as is seen in analysis, where the subject carries on a properly insane conversation with his analyst: "Indeed, what he says may 'have no sense whatever'; what he says *to him* receives one" (ibid., pp. 82–83). And this sense, thus constituted in the interlocutory speech and nowhere else, this signified = X, is the subject.

Let us pause briefly to contemplate the theory of language here instigated in relation to the analytic cure. It presupposes the placing in parentheses of every realist reference in favor of an entirely auto-enunciating and sui-referential model of language. The latter does not represent the real; it represents a subject for the benefit of an other subject (which Lacan, after the detour by way of Saussure, will later reformulate by saying, "the signifier represents the subject for an other signifier"). Language, which signifies this or designates that (and thus becomes rather a "wall" [or "barrier"], according to the "Rome Discourse"; cf. *Ecrits: A Selection*, pp. 71, 94, 101), is first of all speech in which a subject ex-presses himself for the benefit of an other, manifests himself in exteriority through the mediation of the other—in short, in which he speaks *himself* in his truth, by autorepresenting himself to himself.

Speech, and especially analytic speech, is, in effect, an affair of truth, in the precise sense of a subject seizing himself therein in the mode of *certainty*, removed from all objective reality (*Seminar of Lacan: Book I*, p. 21). It is true that Lacan will later affirm that the subject disappears in his appearing, is absented in the statement (*énoncé*) in which he represents himself. The truth of the subject, he will then say, is rather the *splitting* of the subject of the statement and the subject of the enunciation (and so, truth has a "structure of fiction" [*Ecrits*, pp. 17, 451, 742; *Ecrits: A Selection*, p. 306], since self-inadequation is the rule). However, it is also true that the "structure" that articulates the subject, speech and truth, will remain the same, and this structure is none other than that of the Cartesian *cogito* (of which, indeed, Lacan makes no mystery; cf. *Four Fundamental Concepts*, p. 35: "Freud's method is Cartesian—in the sense that he sets out from the basis of the subject of certainty"). The subject of speech, like that of the *cogito*, grasps himself in his truth by autorepresenting himself to himself, by posing himself in front of himself in the mode of *Vor-stellung* (a Freudian term that Lacan identified, as is well known, with the "signifier"). All this suggests the direction in which Lacan will henceforth search for the mechanism of the analytic cure: in the progressive unveiling of the truth as (auto)representation. To be cured is to know oneself by speaking oneself.

It might be objected that the *cogito* is a monologue, whereas Lacan is describing a dialogue (even if it be a dialogue with a rather mute interlocutor). But this is solely the result of Lacan's reformulating the *cogito* in Hegelian terms: it is by speaking to the other, by alienating-exteriorizing myself in a common language, that I represent myself "in front of" myself and thus become conscious of myself. The truth of the subject, for the Lacan of the 1930's, is dialectic, intersubjective, or it is nothing: the subject cannot manifest himself in his truth (he cannot make of his certainty a truth) except by passing through the mediation of the other, by making the other *recognize* him in the interlocution. Hence the correlative exclusion of affect from the field of the cure—an exclusion that is sketched out in the text of 1936 and that will, as is well known, only become more rigid (*Ecrits*, p. 225; *Ecrits: A Selection*, pp. 41, 57, etc.): what matters is not the affect as it is "experienced" in the obscurity of immanence but the affect as it is "transmitted by language" (*Ecrits*, p. 83), that is, as it makes itself recognized in the transcendent exteriority of representation.[7] Inner feeling, as Hegel had already said, remains ineffable (it cannot know itself) as long as it refuses to exteriorize itself "in the light of day" in the form of discourse:

> [He who] makes his appeal to feeling, to an oracle within his breast [note this reference to oracular speech] . . . tramples underfoot the roots of humanity. For it is the nature of humanity to press onward to agreement with others; human nature only really exists in an achieved community of minds. The anti-human, the merely animal, consists in staying within the sphere of feeling, and being able to communicate only at that level.[8]

Consequently, there is no question of making the outcome of the cure depend on some *catharsis* of affects, nor even on that "working through" of transferential affects which Freud saw as the equivalent of abreaction.[9] Affect will be accepted in the analytic cure only insofar as it is formulated in a communal discourse where it makes itself recognized.

This now allows us to specify the direction of Lacan's search for the effective mechanism of the analytic cure: in the unveiling of the truth, certainly, but more precisely in the recognition by another, in the absence of which the subject truly cannot *exhibit* himself in his truth. Transferential speech is a "community of minds," the analyst's consulting room is a public place, an *agora*, a *forum*. Or again: the *cogito* is communal, social, intersubjective, it speaks itself in first person plural (the "we" of the *Phenomenology of Spirit*; cf. *Ecrits: A Selection*, p. 86). Claude Lévi-Strauss formulates it very well in his *Introduction to the Work of Marcel Mauss*, in regard to "Dr. Lacan's profound study, 'L'Agressivité en psychanalyse' [Aggressivity in Psychoanalysis, in ibid., pp. 8–29]": "strictly speaking, the person whom we call sane is the one who is capable of alienating himself, since he consents to an existence in a world definable only by the self–other relationship."[10]

(From this, let it be said in passing, we can see to what point the nascent Structuralism was a Hegelianism.)

We were asking ourselves earlier *who* speaks to *whom* in the analytic dialogue. Our little detour through dialectic now furnishes us with the response. The "subject" who speaks is in reality the "ego," as constituting himself through the mediation of the other. As for the one spoken to, it is once again the same "ego," incarnated in an "imaginary" alter ego. The subject speaking *himself* means, for the Lacan of 1936, that he speaks *with* his ego: *to* his ego and *by means of* his ego. His speech therefore is imaginary speech, in the strict sense given that term by Lacan: in the transference, the subject starts to speak (in a mode that is aggressive, ashamed, imploring, etc.) to an image of himself, the very one he identified with to constitute his ego and was already expressing, in the mode of *méconnaissance*, through his conduct and symptoms. In the discourse of the patient, writes Lacan, the analyst finds again

the very *image* he provoked in the subject by his attitude and whose imprinted trace he recognized in his [the patient's] person . . . but which, as he himself makes it for the subject, concealed its features from his [the subject's] gaze . . . : image of the father or mother . . . image of the brother, rival infant, reflection of self or companion. (*Ecrits*, p. 84)

It can be seen that the transference, which is admittedly nothing other than a transfer of speech, is simultaneously described by Lacan as a transfer of images or "imaginary transference" (this is the term that Lacan still uses in 1948, in "Aggressivity in Psychoanalysis"; *Ecrits: A Selection*, p. 14). The transference is a projection, in that the subject ex-presses or exteriorizes through speech the identifying *imago*, until then "imprinted in his person." As for the analyst, who, Lacan says in 1948, "offers the subject the pure mirror of an unruffled surface" (ibid., p. 15), he limits himself to returning to the subject his own image, his own egoic reflection. And thus it is that he cures: by permitting the subject to see himself, to recognize himself in the image held up to him, and thus to know himself in his truth by becoming self-conscious:

[The] analyst acts in such a way that the subject becomes conscious of the unity of the *image* refracted by him into different effects, according to whether he acts it, incarnates it, or understands it. We will not describe here how the analyst proceeds in his intervention. . . . Let us simply say that as the subject pursues the experience and the living process in which the image is reconstituted, his conduct ceases to mime its suggestion, his memories resume their real density, and the analyst sees the end of his power, now rendered useless by the ending of the symptoms and the completion of the personality. (*Ecrits*, p. 85)

You will have noted the expressions "to act," "to incarnate," "to mime the suggestion" of the image. The patient, in the beginning of the analysis, *mimes* the image that possesses him instead of representing it to himself "in front" of himself (he identifies himself with the Oedipal *imagos*, says Lacan a little further on, "in order to act, as the only actor, the drama of their conflicts" [ibid., p. 90]). In other words, he suffers from *mimesis*. Mimesis is the evil (the madness) because it consists of a nonreflexive (hypnotic, "suggestive") identification with another. Here the ego *is*, quite literally, the other, without that elementary distance from self which would permit him to reflect on himself, to see himself as other. Now, for that Hegelian who is Lacan, there is no salvation except by reflection: certainly the ego is the other, but he still needs to know this, so he must expel the image that possesses him (operate the catharsis of mimesis), and transferential speech serves this end. The subject (alias the ego) puts himself outside of himself, in the specular-speculative mirror held up to him by the analyst, until the moment when he can finally recognize himself in the analyst / mirror while at the same time being recognized by him in terms of "Thou art that" (*Ecrits: A Selection*, p. 7) rather than in the mimetic crazy statement, "I am the other, I am the Father, I am God." Curative speech is that in which *I* grasp myself by the mediation of the *thou*, for salvation passes through kenosis, *Entausserung*, alienation. The "God Logos" is the one who separates himself from himself in the *dialegesthai*, dialectically: it is in the other, and only in the other, that I can see myself, speak myself, and re-cognize myself as I am.

With this brief review of Lacan's early developments, I do not in any way mean to suggest that this would be his final word on the power of speech and the magic of the verb. That same dialectical speech which in 1936 Lacan made the source of the lifting of the symptoms and "completion of the personality" is exactly the one he denounced in 1953 under the name of "empty speech" (*parole vide*), firmly opposing it, from then on, to what he calls "full speech" (*parole pleine*) (or, again, "true speech"). "To speak oneself" on the couch, to speak with one's ego, to alienate oneself in an alter ego in order to better dealienate oneself—all this is, in reality, to waste one's breath, to chatter in ignorance of self. Correlatively, the task of the analyst is not to bring the subject to recognize himself in the image projected on him. Lacan says it quite clearly in his seminar on "The Psychoses":

To authenticate . . . in the subject everything which is of the order of the imaginary is, properly speaking, to make of analysis the antechamber of madness, and we can only stand in admiration of the fact that this has not led to an even more profound alienation. (*Séminaire III*, p. 251)

To return the subject to his own image in the mode of the "Thou art that" is thus no longer, in Lacan's eyes, to dealienate him, but completely the opposite. It serves only to frustrate him further and, as he also says in the "Rome Discourse," encloses him in "an objectification—no less imaginary than before—of his static state or of his 'statue,' in a renewed status of his alienation" (*Ecrits: A Selection*, p. 43), for this "ego" in which he will recognize himself mirrorwise, "even if it were his spitting image, can never become one with the assumption of his desire" (ibid., p. 45). On the contrary, it will properly constitute its *méconnaissance*. The ego, Lacan now hammers away, is the very locus of resistance (*Ecrits*, p. 374). The subject resists "with" his ego, which also means there is never any resistance other than that of the analyst (ibid., p. 377), who incarnates that ego. The bad analyst is the one who takes the place of the ego, takes it for an ally, and finally suggests to the subject, like any hypnotist, that he abandon his resistances (ibid.). To say "Thou art that" is then just the same as saying "Thou art me, the ego"; to fortify that ego is the same as reinforcing the resistance.

Resistance to what? We have just heard it: to the "assumption of desire"—that is, once again, to the manifestation of the truth of the subject in speech addressed to the other, for it is still from this recognition of self by the intermediary of recognition by the other that Lacan continues to expect the lifting of the symptoms. From this point of view, nothing has changed. What does change is the definition of the subject who is supposed to be recognized by the other. This subject, now distinguished from that "object" which is the ego (*Seminar of Lacan: Book II*, pp. 44, 49), is characterized as *desire*, now supposed to be recognized by speech: "That the subject come to recognize and name his desire, that is the efficacious action of analysis" (ibid., pp. 228–29). The stake in analysis is "full speech" in which, says Lacan, the "desire of recognition" is united with the "recognition of desire."

As this last formulation makes clear, the "desire" now in question has nothing to do (whatever Lacan himself might say) with the Freudian *Wunsch*. In reality, it has to do with the Hegelian desire for recognition reinterpreted by Alexandre Kojève in his 1947 *Introduction to the Reading of Hegel*. If we need to clarify "the desire for recognition reinterpreted by Kojève," it is because this desire has little to do with Hegelian desire, *Begierde*. The latter, says Hegel in chapter 4 of the *Phenomenology of Spirit*, desires *itself* in the other, which is why it invariably transforms itself into a desire for recognition, having first to negate and alienate itself in the desire of the other in order then to manifest itself "outside," in the concreteness "in-and-for-itself" of the "we" of mutual recognition. Now Kojève, in his anthropologizing reading of Hegel, proposed to describe this desire of self in the other in terms of "desire of the *desire* of the other," which implicitly effects a "denarcissization" of desire. "Desire is human," we read in the first pages of *Introduction to the Reading of Hegel*, only if it desires "the Desire of the other."[11] Why? Because desire can be human only by negating itself as animal desire (as "need," Lacan will later say), and thus must

be directed toward a non-natural object, toward something that goes beyond the given reality. Now, the only thing that goes beyond the given reality is Desire itself. For Desire taken as Desire—i.e., before its satisfaction—is but a revealed nothingness, an unreal emptiness. Desire, being the revelation of an emptiness, the presence of the absence of a reality, is something essentially different from the desired thing, something other than a thing, than a static and given real being that stays eternally identical to itself.[12]

In short, the desire of recognition is a desire directed toward nothing (and that is why, added Kojève, it can only be satisfied in a "fight to the death for pure prestige").

All these traits, it goes without saying, are to be found in Lacan. "The desire of man," he repeats, "is the desire of the Other," that is, the desire of no object, the desire of nothing, and, finally, the desire of death. By the same token, we can better understand why no specular alter ego of the subject can ever "become one with the assumption of his desire." This desire-subject which is to be recognized is precisely no longer an "ego" or a "self," as it still was for Hegel and for the early Lacan. Desiring the desire of the other, he desires "himself," certainly, but only as pure desire, that is, only insofar as he is precisely not "himself," not "identical to himself," always "beyond" himself. Thus, if he "recognizes himself" in an other desire, it is only insofar as the latter "reveals" to him his own nonidentity with self or, if you prefer, insofar as it "reveals" to him his own nothingness by "revealing" *nothing*. This mirror doesn't reflect anything: the analyst, says Lacan, should be an "empty mirror" (*Seminar of Lacan: Book II*, p. 246), that is, pure desire. And this mirror is no longer a mirror but a gaping hole, a vertiginous (and vertiginously anxiety-producing) breakaway from all "self-consciousness": "desire of the Other" with a capital "O"—so writes Lacan—or, again, "unconscious desire," never presentable to consciousness understood as self-consciousness. The subject (or the desire) that must be recognized in analysis is now the subject (or desire) of the unconscious—and thus the watchword: "Return to Freud!"

But how, exactly, can such a subject (such a desire) make itself recognized? Indeed, Lacan persists in thinking that the salvation (in other words, the cure) of the subject must pass through recognition by another. And if this is so, it is because he persists in thinking of the truth of the subject in terms of automanifestation: "to make one's desire recognized" (*Ecrits*, p. 343) is to manifest it "outside," in the public square, in full daylight. Now, how can desire be manifested if it is pure unpresentable negativity, pure "nothing"? By speech, once again, but no longer by that speech with which an ego speaks *himself* by recognizing *himself* in an alter ego, a speech all the more empty in that it has only the ego on its lips; rather, by the speech with which the subject speaks "himself" in his absence, a speech all the more "full" in that it manifests him as nothing, and all the more "true" in that it attests his self-inadequation. Speech, Lacan now says in para-Heideggerian (*Hegeliano*-Heideggerian) terms, is the presence of an absence, the appearance of a disappearance, in short, the *a-lētheia*, the veiling-unveiling of the subject as desire.

We have already seen that language, for Lacan, does not represent reality, but rather the subject. Now we need to clarify why: because the subject is negativity and does not manifest himself in language except by negating reality, by reducing it to nothing. Augustine, as remarked by Lacan, already said it to Adeodatus in the *De Magistro*: the word *"nihil"* obviously has a signification, but where, in reality, do you find what it represents? (*Seminar of Lacan: Book I*, p. 252). Such is, repeats Hegel, the *"göttliche Natur des Sprechens"*[13]: speech causes to be that which is not, by negating that which is. Or again, in the formulation of Kojève and Lacan, it performs the "murder of the thing" (*Ecrits: A Selection*, p. 104; *Seminar of Lacan: Book I*, p. 174). Say the word "lion," wrote Hegel, and you create the lion ex nihilo in abolishing it as a tangible thing;[14] say the word "dog," comments Kojève, and you kill the real dog;[15] say the word "elephants," concludes Lacan, and here is a herd of elephants completely filling the room, present in its absence (*Seminar of Lacan: Book I*, pp. 178, 218, 243). Discourse, the manifestation of the negativity of the subject who poses himself by negating the "Real" (this was Kojève's word before becoming Lacan's), thus works the wonder of manifesting what is not. And in this way, adds Lacan for his part, it manifests the subject, alias desire.

Indeed, it is not enough to affirm that language is an autoenunciation and that the subject speaks himself in it by negating every real referent. We must go so far as to propose that he speaks himself in it while abolishing himself in it (exactly as he abolishes the dog or the elephants): to say "I" is, at bottom, always to say "I am dead," or "I am nothing." In this sense, autoenunciation becomes an enunciation *of nothing* (that is, in Lacan's terms, an enunciation of desire; cf. *Four Fundamental Concepts*, p. 141), since the subject of the enunciation disappears by appearing in the subject of the statement. Thus there is no longer, as there would be in good dialectic, identity of the subject of the enunciation and the subject of the statement. The subject, as he is redefined by Lacan following Kojève, is no longer the subject who manifests himself in and by *means* of, or by the *mediation* of, speech addressed to the other (he is, if you prefer, no longer the signified of that signifier, and hence Lacan's later affirmation of the "autonomy" of the latter in relation to the former). Rather, the subject *is* the speech addressed to the other (or the "discourse of the Other," as Lacan would soon say), in the precise sense of that speech manifesting him as nothing, of his appearing / disappearing in it as pure desire. The *cogito*, while remaining a *cogito*, is henceforth an empty *cogito* because the subject is definitively exorbitated in the representation which represents him, irreducibly alienated in language, in that Other where he appears by disappearing.

Therefore, speech is the presentation of that unpresentable which is the subject understood as desire, and it will thus be all the more true, will all the better express the truth of the subject of desire, in that it manifests him *as* absent. Desire, said Kojève, is a "revealed nothingness." Now, how can such a nothingness "reveal" itself, if not by negating everything which might present or incarnate it, realize or satisfy it? Thus, for Lacan, it "reveals" itself always and only in the mode of *Verneinung*, the denegation that poses in absenting: "It's not my mother," says Freud's patient about the content of one of his dreams—by which he presents the emptiness of his desire in the *absence* of the mother. "*Fort!*" (Go away!) cries little Ernst to the bobbin that he throws away—and there it is, his desire is "there" (*da!*) in the disappearance of its object. In other words, the repression (which denies, negates, reneges, etc.) is the very presentation of desire, insofar as the latter is nothing (no thing, no object, no being). Repression, Lacan will thus say in complacently paradoxical formulas, is the same thing as the return of the repressed (*Seminar of Lacan: Book I*, p. 191); the slips of the tongue, the memory lapses, the bungled actions are "successful" actions; and truth surges forth in the "mistake" (ibid., p. 265), especially in that "mistake of the subject supposed to know": the transference (*Four Fundamental Concepts*, p. 230 ff.). Far from hiding anything, as Freud believed, repression tells the truth; it manifests desire in its retreat. Lying speech, which negates reality, is paradoxically the most true with regard to the subject, insofar as it reveals the nothingness that he "is." To paraphrase (just slightly) the famous prosopopoeia of "The Freudian Thing": "I, truth, lie."

Must we then conclude that curative speech is lying speech, and that analytic action consists not in the lifting but in the *maintenance* of repression (in an "eternalization of desire," as Lacan often says [*Ecrits: A Selection*, p. 104], and thus in an "eternalization" of the neurosis)? In a certain manner, yes. But that is because in Lacan's desperate "logic" there is no possible un-veiling of desire, unless it be in its veiling (in its repression and, more generally, in the symbolic order understood, in the wake of Lévi-Strauss, as the Law of language, signifying system, and "discourse of the Other"). Analytic speech is not a *means* to arrive at the truth of the subject; it *is*

that very truth, as manifestation—the only possible manifestation—
of the subject as "nothing," as pure desire of nothing. From this
point of view, what Lacan calls "full speech" is no more "true" than
"empty," "false," "lying," "resistant" speech. On the contrary, it is
a matter of that *same* lying speech, insofar as it progressively puri-
fies itself during the course of the analysis, finally arriving—such,
at least, is Lacan's hope—at its pure and simple essence of speech
addressed to the other.

Indeed, full speech is not "full" of something (of a message, information, a content of sense). On the contrary, it is speech that
communicates nothing, nothing other than the "existence of communication" (ibid., p. 43). Analysis is a long speech, a very long-
winded speech, because the subject must be led to pierce the "wall"
of objectifying-representative language in order to learn simply to
speak, that is, to say nothing ("Words, words, words"). Then speech,
instead of saying something, says itself and so tells the truth, which
is precisely that speech says *nothing*—nothing other than that *nothing* which is the subject as soon as he speaks. And where can such
a speech be found, a perfectly sui-referential, autorepresentative,
and autoenunciating speech? Everywhere (since "full speech" is the
essence of all speech), but more particularly in the *given* word. "Full
speech," the authentically speechlike speech which manifests itself
(or should manifest itself) *as such* at the interminable term of the
analysis, is speech in which one gives nothing other than one's
word—in short, in which one engages oneself. When you sign a
contract, when you say "Yes" in front of the Justice of the Peace,
or again, when you tell someone that you recognize him as your
master (or disciple), you do not communicate (you do not give) anything other than your word. And in fact, all the examples of "full
speech" given by Lacan are of that type: "you are my wife," "you
are my master" (ibid., p. 85; *Ecrits*, p. 351; *Séminaire III*, pp. 47–48),
"you are the one who will follow me" (*Séminaire III*, p. 315 ff.). These
are words that not only have no referent, but moreover have no
"signified" other than themselves. In Lacan's terms, they "are first
and foremost signifiers of the pact that they constitute as signified"
(*Ecrits: A Selection*, p. 61). Indeed, the given word "*constitutes*," "*effects*"
the pact which it itself is—a pact that Lacan calls "symbolic" both
because it is without ties with reality ("symbol" here taken in the
Lévi-Straussian sense) and because it operates like a sign of recogni-

tion (*sumbolon*). By saying "you are my wife," I recognize you and institute you as such, while at the same time recognizing and instituting myself as "your husband." In short, I receive, as Lacan says, my own message in an inverted form. I institute myself (I manifest myself, publicly) as subject in and by speech addressed to the other, by becoming *other* than I was before: Look! Now "I am your husband," submitted from now on, for better or for worse, to a differential / symbolic order where I am no longer *nothing*—nothing *other* than the signifier that represents me for an other signifier.

From this we can see that "full speech" finally has much more to do with what Austin called, at about the same time, "performative utterances"[16] than it does with "speech" in the Saussurian sense. "Full speech," like the Austinian "performative," does not "constate" or represent anything prior to its enunciation. On the contrary, it instigates (one could even say *creates*) a reality, which is, moreover, purely linguistic since it resides uniquely in the act of its enunciation (I am not "your husband" unless I *say* "you are my wife," etc.). Performative speech, as Austin had already said, is thus neither "true" nor "false" in the traditional sense (that is, in the banal representative-constative sense). Lacan adds, for his part, that it is thus all the more "true" with regard to the subject, since the latter is nothing before the speech in which he autoenunciates himself by and while abolishing himself. Psychoanalytic speech, as such, insofar as it returns speech to its performative essence, thus implements the paradoxical "realization of the subject" (ibid., p. 40) by creating him ex nihilo. In the beginning is the word—that is, the *act* of speech, the "speech act." In it, the subject constitutes and accomplishes himself in his *being*, which is *nothing* outside of the speech that causes him to appear / disappear. And thus it is that speech cures, since the subject finally makes himself recognized in his truth, "beyond the reality principle."

This is what Lacan explains quite clearly in relation to the first hysterics cured by Freud, in a passage of the "Rome Discourse" at which I would now like to pause. Indeed, why were the hysterics treated by Freud and Josef Breuer cured of their symptoms, and in such a spectacular manner? Freud and Breuer, as is well known, attributed the fact to the *prise de conscience* of a pathogenic and "traumatic event," or more precisely to its rememoration through speech.

However, these traumatic events, as Freud was quickly forced to admit, were most often fantasies without any relation to reality. Thus the cures were real, but they were provoked by perfectly fictitious "reminiscences." Hence Freud's hesitation, here ruthlessly resolved by Lacan:

> The ambiguity of the hysterical revelation of the past is due not so much to the vacillation of its content between the imaginary and the real, for it is situated in both. Nor is it because it is made up of lies. The reason is that it presents us with the birth of truth in speech, and thereby brings us up against the reality of what is neither true nor false. . . . For it is present speech that bears witness to the truth of this revelation in present reality, and which grounds it in the name of that reality. . . . I might as well be categorical: in psychoanalytic anamnesis, it is not a question of reality, but of truth, because the effect of full speech is to reorder past contingencies by conferring on them the sense of necessities to come. (*Ecrits: A Selection*, pp. 47–48)

In other words, it does not matter whether or not hysterical speech adequately represents a past reality; what matters is that it "founds," performatively, the truth of the subject in the here and now of its enunciation, with all the consequences that this implies for the future (and for the past which is thus "reconstituted"). To say, "I am a woman of the last century," as did Emmy von N. in her states of somnambulism, or to claim no longer to speak German, as did Anna O., is undoubtedly to lie with regard to reality (to "simulate," as used to be said of hysterics), but only to better institute oneself in one's truth as subject (as "English" or as "a woman of the last century"). In short, the more one lies, and the more one tells the truth, the more one "affirms that speech constitutes truth" (ibid., p. 43). As for the analyst, he need not search for truth beyond the speech addressed to him, but must simply confer upon it "its dialectical punctuation" by "sanctioning" it with his response (ibid., p. 95); indeed, Lacan goes so far as to suggest that Freud's cures were all the more effective because his interpretations were erroneous, that is, simply "endoctrinating" (ibid., pp. 77–79). As the poet Bruno Goetz remarked in relation to his analysis with Freud, the latter could have simply contented himself with saying "abracadabra"—the beneficent effects of his speech would have manifested themselves nonetheless.

This brings us back to the question of "*truquage*" evoked by Lacan toward the end of his life, for if speech cures as *pure* speech, what distinguishes it, finally, from the "*truc*," the "*machin*," [17] and more generally, from all those "zero symbolic values" which, in his *Introduction to the Work of Marcel Mauss*, Lévi-Strauss said have the function of furnishing signifiers for what escapes from the symbolic system? [18] By the same token, what distinguishes pure analytic speech from *any "machin" whatsoever*, from this or that magical formula or *mana* object, for example? Is psychoanalysis then to be a deception, like that of the shaman who pretends to expel a malady by spitting a bloody object out of his mouth? Yes, certainly—with the exception, Lacan would add, that it exhibits the truth of deception, which is precisely that the truth of the subject, being purely symbolic, has a "structure of fiction."

In two articles that obviously influenced Lacan, [19] Lévi-Strauss explains that the deception of the shaman is more and other than a deception. Fanciful as they may be, shamanic cures undoubtedly have "the effectiveness of symbols," in that they furnish the sick person (and the social group) with "a *language* by means of which unexpressed, and otherwise inexpressible, psychic states can be immediately expressed." [20] In other words, they are sociotherapies founded on the phenomenon of "group consensus" [21]: the shaman, the sorcerer, the magician procure for the sick person and the social group a *myth* [22] in which both can integrate ineffable psychical or physical pain in a common language. And, adds Lévi-Strauss, exactly the same principle applies to "the modern version of shamanistic technique called psychoanalysis." [23] To this argument Lacan has clearly subscribed, making as he does of the "individual myth of the neurotic" [24] the very truth—the completely social, symbolic, and linguistic truth—of the subject. Curative analytic speech falls within the province of *mana*, of the "*truc*," but this "*truc*," precisely because it is completely empty, implements the symbolization (socialization, recognition) of the subject—"what Lévi-Strauss calls a 'zero-symbol' (*symbole zéro*), thus reducing the power of Speech to the form of an algebraic sign" (ibid., p. 68). [25] End of the timeworn mythemes, beginning of the glorious mathemes: capital "A," small "a," "abracadabra!"

Now here, I feel, it becomes quite impossible to follow Lacan and Lévi-Strauss, for in reality it is not just any speech that will cure, whether in analysis or elsewhere. If that were so, it is hard to see why a medical diagnosis (which may well be considered a form of symbolization of the illness) would not have, ipso facto, the same "effectiveness of symbols" as analytic or shamanic speech. But this is simply not the case, as Lévi-Strauss himself remarks.[26] For speech to have its effect (the famous "placebo" effect, for example), something else is necessary. Not all symbols are valuable, as the algebra of Lévi-Strauss and Lacan would have it: there are "myths" which are effective and others which are not.[27] How, then, can this difference be accounted for?

We might be tempted to look for the answer in the content of the therapeutic myths—exactly what Lévi-Strauss declares is unimportant.[28] Indeed, it is remarkable that "illness" is always symbolized in traditional societies either as a possession of the sick person by a "spirit" or a "demon" (which the shaman must then exorcize), or as a dispossession of the soul (which the shaman must then bring back after his "journey," in the mode of what Luc de Heusch has called an "adorcism").[29] The "illness" (whether physical or psychical) is thus constantly interpreted as a depropriation, which is itself deciphered in social terms as a violence perpetrated against the subject. Such a "structuralist" constancy cannot be purely indifferent, and it would undoubtedly be easy to find multiple equivalents in the "individual myths" of our modern neurotics and psychotics (the paranoiacs, to begin with).

But let us resist this temptation, and, as Lévi-Strauss and Lacan suggest, stick with the form of the therapeutic myths, that is, with their mode of enunciation rather than with what they state as content. Now, from this point of view, it is difficult not to notice that the form of the myth always reflects, in one way or another, its content (to such an extent that the difference simply disappears): curative speech reproduces (mimes) the (mimetic) illness that it is supposed to cure. Indeed, it must be emphasized that the supposedly "possessed" sick person is most often urged to abreact-expel the haunting spirit during the course of a possession trance induced and directed by the shaman. In the same way, it is at the end of a trance, carried out in place of the sick person, so to speak, that the shaman (often formerly mentally ill himself)[30] returns the soul, of which the patient is reputed to have been "dispossessed," to the body of the patient. (I will ignore the multiple intermediary variants that interpose themselves between these two structural poles.) In short, it seems that traditional therapies unanimously treated illness with illness: possession with a trance of possession, and depropriation with an increased depropriation. Now it appears, if one follows the indications furnished by de Heusch, that it is precisely the "ecstasy" or "transition to another psychic state" that Lévi-Strauss himself admittedly neglected[31] which assures the passage between "a situation originally existing on the emotional level"[32] and its symbolic assumption by the group. By way of the trance (the *provoked* trance), the group indeed *recognizes* the illness of the patient instead of excluding it. It does not take much speculative imagination to extend this observation to all the other curative techniques that integrate an element of trance, whether slight or profound, from Christian exorcism to contemporary neocathartic therapies, by way of the magnetic cures of Mesmer, the "artificial somnambulism" of A. M. J. de Chastenet de Puységur, the medical hypnosis of Jean-Martin Charcot and Hippolyte Bernheim, and even (let's be scandalous) the analytic "transference" of Freud.

According to this hypothesis, which I believe to be the correct one, curative speech is always, in one way or another, *mimetic* speech—that is, according to the definition given by Plato in the *Republic*,[33] speech in which I speak "under the name of an other." Thus it is not speech addressed or given to the other but speech (be it vehement or calm) in which I *am* the other, without the slightest distance or mediation. Nor is it intersubjective speech, but rather speech of no subject (even an empty one), speech of trance in which the "I" is quite literally spoken by the "other" which it incarnates— while this "I," the complete actor, simultaneously experiences all the affects of his role. In short, curative speech would be exactly that which Lacan, it will be remembered, had excluded from the start in "Beyond the Reality Principle," under the double heading of (ineffable) affect and (nonreflexive) *mimesis*: that is, in a word, the mimetic and cathartic speech of hypnosis.

Yet this kind of hypothesis was not entirely foreign to Lacan himself, as that passage in the "Rome Discourse" from which we started attests. Significantly, Lacan has no difficulty here admitting that the cure of Breuer and Freud's first hysterics took place under hypnosis. Moreover, he invokes this fact in order to deny that these cures were the result of a *"prise de conscience"* of the traumatic event, as Freud believed at the time. Lacan explains it quite clearly in regard to the "talking cure" of Anna O.:

If this event was recognized as being the cause of the symptom, it was because the putting into words of the event (in the patient's "stories") determined the lifting of the symptom. Here the term *"prise de conscience,"* . . . retains a prestige that merits a healthy distrust. . . . The psychological prejudices of Freud's day were opposed to acknowledging in verbalization as such any reality other than its own *flatus vocis.* The fact remains that in the hypnotic state verbalization is dissociated from the *prise de conscience,* and this fact alone is enough to require a revision of that conception of its effects. (ibid., p. 46)

Up to this point everything goes well: Lacan admits, and even emphasizes, that curative speech is a hypnotized speech. But how does it cure? Here begins a very close argumentation that concludes two pages later with a nonrepealable "disavowal" of every foothold in hypnosis, "whether to explain the symptom or to cure it" (ibid., p. 49):

But why is it that the doughty advocates of the behaviorist *Aufhebung* do not use this as their example to show that they do not have to know whether the subject has remembered anything whatever from the past? He has simply recounted the event. But I would say that he has verbalized it . . . he has made it pass into the *verbe,* or, more precisely, into the *epos* by which he brings back into present time the origins of his own person. And he does this in a language that allows his discourse to be understood by his contemporaries, and which furthermore presupposes their present discourse. Thus it happens that the recitation of the *epos* may include a discourse of earlier days in its own archaic, even foreign language [an allusion to Anna O.'s glossolalia], or may even pursue its course in the present tense with all the animation of the actor; but it is like an indirect discourse, isolated in quotation marks within the thread of the narration, and, if the discourse is played out, it is on a stage implying the presence not only of the chorus, but also of spectators. Hypnotic recollection is, no doubt, a reproduction of the past, but it is above all a spoken representation—and as such implies all sorts of presences. (ibid., pp. 46–47; translation modified)

As will undoubtedly have been understood, Lacan here is attempting to interpret hypnotic speech in terms of "full speech" addressed / given to the other, but only at the price of suspending that oracular speech in strange "quotation marks," for Lacan knows quite well that hypnotic speech is a mimetic speech, as his labored references to hysterical theatricality attest. It was indeed "with all the animation of the actor" that the hysterics, once under hypnosis, acted and mimed the roles that haunted them (let us not forget that Anna O. and Emmy von N. were both cases of "double personality," that is, modern cases of "possession").[34] And it is from this intensely experienced "repetition" (this *Agieren*, as he will later say of the transferential repetition) that Freud, for his part, expected the "cathartic" abatement to arise. As he wrote in the *Studies on Hysteria*:

> Recollection without affect almost invariably produces no result. The psychical process which originally took place must be repeated as vividly as possible [*lebhaft . . . wiederholt*]; it must be brought back to its *status nascendi* and then given verbal utterance.[35]

It is this same mimetico–affective "verbalization," the most "direct" possible, that Lacan here invites us to understand as "indirect discourse" interior to a "narrative" or, more exactly, to an "*epos.*" The allusion to Plato's theory of *mimesis* is clear (supplementary proof, if there be any need for it, that Lacan knows quite well of what he speaks). Indeed, Plato says in the *Republic* that the epic poet "mixes" narration and imitation (*diegesis* and *mimesis*); for example, Homer starts by narrating Chryses in the third person and then quotes him in the first person "as if he were himself Chryses."[36] According to Lacan, it was exactly the same for the hysterics under hypnosis: they mimed, certainly, but only so as to give more "life" to the narrative in which they narrated themselves for the benefit of the other—the important thing for Lacan being that they included that other in their speech and did not confound themselves completely with their role. In a word, the hysterics would stage themselves. They would separate themselves from themselves by adopting the point of view of the spectator, of that other *for* whom they played as actresses. Or again, they would put themselves *in representation* in order better to see themselves "in front" of themselves, from the exterior, through the gaze and speech of recognition of the other—of *all* the others assembled in a circle at the center of the "City State" (ibid., p. 47). They were actresses and simulactresses, consequently, but only to better seal the pact of truth in the "lie" of self-representation.

Now, it is quite impossible to follow Lacan on this point (which is the point of view of the complete spectacle, of the panoptic of representation), for the hypnotized person, no less than the possessed one in a trance, can in no way distance himself from the role that he plays. To narrate himself, in Lacan's sense, is completely impossible (if he did so, he would simply no longer be under hypnosis, no longer be possessed). By the same token, lying also becomes impossible, because this person can no longer separate himself from himself by adopting the point of view of the other in order to delude him into believing his tall tales. On the contrary, he *tells the truth*, nothing more. Such is the true "paradox of the actor" as attested to by the trance of the hypnotized: that is, he *is* that "other me" spoken of by Anna O., he *himself* is that spirit, that demon, that *zar* or *loa* which haunts him. And that is also why he experiences all the affects, all the emotions of the "other ego," in the mode of the most irrepressible passion: those emotions are his own—the most his, the most his own. In this sense, mimetic speech engages a completely other concept (?) of the truth-of-the-subject than that manipulated by Lacan: not at all truth in the sense of representation, where I speak myself to myself *through* an other who is "in front" of me, but truth in the sense of affective passion, where I speak (myself) *transfixed, traversed* by the other that I am. Without a doubt it was that truth— that truth which is completely unspeakable unless it be spoken in "first person"—which hypnosis allowed the hysterics to manifest, that is, to put into an act, for mimetic speech, too, is truly a "speech act," and perhaps even *the* "speech act" par excellence. But it is the "speech act" of the "other me"—of that other who I *am* in saying it (and not, as Lacan would have it, of that Other who I *am not*).

Having come this far, we must choose—and it is on this choice, I feel, that the "future prospects of psycho-analytic therapy" (to borrow Freud's title) [37] today depend, for once it is admitted that the speech which cured the hysterics does not belong to the model of "full speech" in the Lacanian sense, there remain only two possibilities. First, we can persist in thinking that it is pure speech addressed to the other which is effective in the cure, and then we definitively prohibit ourselves from understanding the effectiveness of the first hypnotic "talking cures." This was Lacan's choice—rejecting hypnotic speech, after having made a show of explaining it, in order finally to retain nothing but pure speech without hypnosis. The result of this choice is well known: a cure amputated from every affective and mimetic element, conclusively reduced—as Lacan, quoting Mallarmé, says—to that pure exchange of word and coin "that people pass from hand to hand 'in silence'" (ibid., p. 43).

Second, we can admit that it is indeed mimetic speech which cures, and then we are obliged to reconsider, from top to bottom, that model of the cure always more and more purified since Freud broke with the "impure origins" of psychoanalysis. The result of such a choice? It is certainly too early to say, even if some, here and there, are already working on exploring the possibilities. But we can certainly bet that the patients will stand to gain everything—and above all the recognition of their "illness," which is the secret of their "cure." As for the psychoanalyst, if you think about it, there is really little for him to lose, except perhaps his rather futile concern for separating himself from his "precursors, the shamans and sorcerers." [38]

Translated by Douglas Brick

# Mimetic Efficacity

To the memory of Léon Chertok,
hero and troublemaker.

Invited to speak "About Hypnosis," I asked myself what this title was supposed to mean. Did the organizers of the conference wish to invite us to put hypnosis at the *center* of our discussion? According to this first, most evident reading, it would then be proper for us to converge toward that unique and central object in order to examine it, each in his or her own way, in one or another of its many aspects: the usual program for all "interdisciplinary" colloquia. But why, then, did they not simply opt for "Hypnosis"? Why this timid "about," which seems to condemn us to an indefinitely peripheral discourse? Is it not rather because we are invited to think of hypnosis as a phenomenon whose center is everywhere and whose circumference is nowhere? With this second hypothesis, which I suspect is the correct one, it is, on the contrary, by being on the circumference that we would truly be at the center.

But the center of what? Of an enigma that simultaneously mobilizes and defies the most diverse disciplines. As we all know, this phenomenon has many aspects—spectacular cures, rituals or crowd phenomena, disturbing psychic or somatic manifestations—and thus it falls within the province of psychiatry, sociology, the history of religions, as well as medicine, biology, or even ethology, which undoubtedly means that it does not fall within any one of them, nor is there much to be hoped for in their possible agglomeration. As Léon Chertok and Isabelle Stengers write, we are in the presence of an "irreducibly bio-psycho-sociological phenomenon," which "at present has successfully escaped from interdisciplinary 'reshuffling.'"[1] Now, to call this phenomenon "hypnosis" immediately exposes us to many methodological difficulties, for "hypnosis" is only one name among many that designate the elusive "X" we are trying to grasp. You will call it "animal magnetism," "waking somnambulism," or "transference" if you happen to be a psychotherapist; "suggestion," "hysteria," or "modified state of consciousness" if you happen to be a psychiatrist or psychologist; "trance" or "ecstasy" if you are an anthropologist; "demonic possession" if a theologian. And each of these ways of naming brings with it not only a different *theory* but also a different *phenomenon*, as if the most remarkable property of our "X" was not to have any property and to vary in accordance with the discourse brought to bear on it.

I am all the more aware of this problem in that I myself have tried, within the limits of a work devoted to psychoanalysis, to emphasize the profound continuity between hypnosis and the analytical "transference." I would invariably come across the objection that there are differences between these two psychotherapeutic techniques: did I mean to say, totally improbably, that the analytic transference is the same as Jean-Martin Charcot's authoritarian and nontherapeutic hypnosis, or Hippolyte Bernheim's "suggestion"?[2] Obviously not, and so I had to clarify that I meant a light hypnosis, with neither hypnotist nor direct suggestion, characterized by an identificatory and "emotional tie" with the therapist, that is, the same one that analysts, for their part, call "transference." Hence the second, and predictable, objection: why, under these conditions, speak of "hypnosis" at all? For my part, I still think that this heuristic reversal is not without utility, if only because it helps to emphasize the theoretical and practical problems that analytical theory (or theories) of the transference tend to occult. But I must admit that, in the end, it is not much help to translate the word "transference" as "hypnosis," if this is supposed to mean that it is a new phenomenon, proper to analysis and its therapeutic setup. It would be better to find a third term, one large enough to encompass both preanalytic hypnosis and transference. But, precisely, which one?

Indeed, the same thing may be said of every other theoretical attempt at identification of the phenomenon "X" that concerns us here. Thus Franz Mesmer attributed the convulsions of those possessed by demons to the effects of "magnetic fluid"; Charcot attributed them to manifestations of hystero-hypnotism; and Freud to an Oedipal neurosis. Just as Charcot saw hypnotism as a pathological phenomenon, the magnetizers saw it as a therapeutic technique, and Freud as a mixture of the two (transference-neurosis). More recently, psychologists study, in the laboratory, what they think are objective manifestations of the hypnotic state, whereas others denounce it as a "suggestive" construction or an interactive artifact. And finally, there is a whole psychiatric, psychoanalytic, and ethnopsychiatric tradition that has conditioned us to discovering manifestations of neurosis, psychosis, or depression behind trances of possession and shamanic phenomena (Ohlmarks went so far as to speak of an "arctic hysteria" with regard to Siberian shamanism). To this anthropologists inevitably object that a shaman or possessed person cannot be equated with a mental patient, since the former's conduct is considered normal by the group and that, in any case, this conduct is a "function of a collective order which is not even neutral in relation to exceptions."[3]

Consequently, no matter how we approach the question, we find ourselves confronted with desperately contradictory answers; each identification of the phenomenon inevitably elicits a converse rival identification. Thus, before any discussion, we should ask ourselves what we are talking about, and whether we are even talking about the same thing. In other words, is there some constant that we can, if not use as a foundation, at least agree upon? Or is this quest for an improbable "essence" of the phenomenon (or, what comes to the same thing, a conciliating metadiscourse) definitely illegitimate and predestined to failure?

To begin with, it seems to me that it is not impossible to spell out a certain number of recurrent and invariable traits. In fact, no matter how we approach the phenomenon, we are always confronted by a more or less deep state of trance, which is neither the "official" waking state nor sleep pure and simple, and which is, above all, apprehended as *other*, either because it is rejected as pathological and dangerous; because, on the contrary, it is considered sacred; or, finally, because it manifests itself through extraordinary phenomena: insensibility to pain, somatic conversions and reconversions, glossolalia or the "gift of tongues," hyperawareness, and so on. Moreover, this state regularly makes itself conspicuous by a more or less marked *depersonalization*, which overturns the ordinarily accepted borders between "self" and "other": sometimes the person in the trance identifies totally with a foreign personality (as in cases of possession and double or multiple personalities), sometimes he enters into an extraordinary communication with a spirit (as the spiritualist mediums or shamans during their "journey"), sometimes he is content to entertain an exclusive rapport with the hypnotist and / or analyst who induces the light or deep trance. Finally, this de-personalization constitutes an incommunicable *lived experience*, quite logically so, since one cannot simultaneously *be* (an) other while distinguishing oneself from that alterity. This also explains why we have many narratives of mystical ecstasy but no "Memoirs of a Som-nambulist," unless in the fictional form given by Charles Brockden Brown.[4] Paradoxically, the experience of being-other, when pushed to the trance state, can be only "interior" and lived "from within," as Georges Bataille said,[5] and so it cannot be communicated to another by language (even if it can be communicated quite well by "affec-tive contagion"). Let this be a warning to us: every discourse on the trance—the one we are trying to entertain here, as much as any other—can do nothing but miss its object, precisely because it makes an object of it. Our metadiscourse is condemned to circulate "around" the trance, except on the condition of entering its mael-strom, all lines cast off, and definitively dismissing every hope of remaining above it.

In short, it seems reasonable to admit that in each case we are in the presence of a phenomenon that we can represent to ourselves only as "other," because it is the other of representation. Indeed, the latter defines itself by difference (subject / object, self / other, body / spirit, etc.), whereas the phenomenon we are trying to speak of is totally unaware of difference (hence its close connection with body and affect, as well as its disconcerting relation with memory, will, and self-consciousness, which are never suppressed and yet are pro-foundly modified or "altered"). Under these conditions, it is not sur-prising that, practically unanimously, trance is considered extraor-dinary—that is, depending on which vocabulary is used, "sacred," "pathological," "prelogical," or "regressive"—since it transgresses both the symbolic order of societies and our scientific reason. And yet, as extraordinary as it may be, it appears really to be also a very ordinary phenomenon (I was almost going to say "banal"), since it is found everywhere, both in time and space, whether in cultures that make it the center of a cult or in those, like ours, that have a tendency to reject or marginalize it. This truly is an anthropological con-stant, which obstinately defies historical and cultural differences and which, nevertheless, is not completely natural or biological, even if, in this regard, ethology poses some rather formidable questions about the continuity between human and animal hypnosis (trembling, catalepsy, exophthalmos, etc.).[6] Indeed, it is not sufficient to say that the trance has a physiological or biological substratum (in the end, what human activity does not?), for the fact is that it is always culturally molded. It is better to admit that it is a paradoxical cultural invariant that, as Claude Lévi-Strauss said differently of the incest prohibition, takes us back to the juncture of nature and culture, at least to the point where that opposition becomes confused and undecidable.

Having thus summarized the common and rapidly vanishing denominator of the phenomena we are facing, we really must recognize that all the rest is subject to infinite variation, for how are we to orient ourselves among all these trances—light or deep, spontaneous or induced, hyperaware or dazed—which, whether or not they are accompanied by memory and language, are sometimes a sign from the gods and sometimes the sign of a curse, sometimes the patient's affair and sometimes the doctor's? Hence it seems that this universal invariant corresponds to an equally universal variation: each culture, each epoch, each theoretical setup emphasizes one or another aspect of the phenomenon to the detriment of the others, in order to try to master its disconcerting ambiguity. Thus, at the end of our second effort, we appear to be obliged to agree that the invariant, in this case, *is variation*. And this is indeed what I believe happens: the trance is, by its very definition, transitory and variable, because it operates a *passage* between terms that, from the point of view of symbolic normality, can only be diametrically opposed. More exactly yet, it is this highly paradoxical operation that makes things pass from the domain of nonopposition, from the irrepresentable and nonsymbolizable, to that of opposition, representation, and the symbol. Thus is explained both its universality (since it is founded on humanity's common "*part maudite*") and its diversity (since it is always–already moving toward a separation from that "*part maudite*").

This is what I would like to try to show, assisting myself with certain data furnished by anthropology. Indeed, anthropologists are the professionals of cultural variation and thus they have not failed to attempt to put a little order in the trance phenomena that confront them. I am thinking most notably of two important articles by Luc de Heusch dedicated to possession and shamanism,[7] with which

I would now like to support my arguments rather freely, so as to draw, at my own peril, several very speculative hypotheses. These two articles by de Heusch present themselves as a general theory or, at least, a general classification of therapeutic rituals, conceived as a universal response to illness and ill[8] in general. Indeed, what causes someone to be ill in traditional societies? This or that, but, more precisely, a spiritual *aggression*, which explains why someone has broken a leg or been struck by an enemy arrow. In this regard, the etiological theories of traditional societies have a remarkable consistency: where we Westerners seek an organic or psychic cause for the illness, traditional societies almost unanimously attribute it to violence perpetrated by a sorcerer or spirit. As the Siberian Bouriates say: "All evil [*mal*] comes from the spirits."[9] More precisely yet, summing up the etiologies, which can be quite diverse on this terrain, we shall say that illness consists either in a *possession* of the soul by a malefic spirit or substance, a possession that consequently calls for an *abreactive* or *exorcist* procedure, since the malefic influence must be expelled, or in a *dispossession* of the soul, which thus requires a procedure that de Heusch calls *adreactive* or *adorcist*, by means of which the soul is returned to its rightful owner.

In psychiatric terms, we might then say that traditional societies profess a paranoid and hypochondriacal theory of illness (cf., for instance, the famous "murder of the soul" that afflicted President Schreber). But such a diagnosis would be doubly erroneous, first, because this "paranoid" theory is that of society in general (and not that of a "mental patient"), and second, because it limits itself to giving a social (and, finally, very down-to-earth) interpretation of illness: possession or dispossession of the soul arises from a violent intrusion or theft, that is, from a transgression that affects the proprieties and good order of society. To use Jean Pouillon's excellent expression, the "primitives" are *sociosomaticians* who see illness as a social disorder, and who consequently apply to it a therapy that is also resolutely social.[10] Besides, do we do anything different when, under cover of a "psychosomatic" interpretation, we attribute our pains (*maux*) to some family or professional difficulty, that is, in the final analysis, to some person who "gives us a pain (*mal*)"?

However, this should not distract us from our interrogation concerning the relation between social "ill" and what we call "mental illness" or "madness," for in each case it is a matter of a possession or dispossession of the soul: the intrusion or abduction affects an *iden-tity* that we might call "subjective" but that it would undoubtedly be more prudent to call "social." Whatever the case, the patient is con-sidered no longer master of himself but alienated or possessed by a malefic entity from which he no longer distinguishes himself. From this point of view, "possession" and "dispossession" are nothing but two converse ways of designating the same malady of identity, that is, what we would describe as a personality disturbance, or at least as a brutal collapse of the boundaries between "self" and "other." This, of course, does not mean that the patient himself is "mad," and even less that the society that applies this diagnosis is deliri-ous. Nonetheless, illness in general is usually interpreted in terms of "madness," as if the latter represented the social ill par excellence ("mimetic violence," as René Girard would say).[11]

Now, this will be verified if we pass from possession in the larger sense to the strict sense, and from there to the possession trance. Indeed, we must distinguish the possession / dispossession to which illness in general is attributed from possession properly so-called, which belongs rather to madness in our sense of the word, and which primitive etiologies often differentiate quite clearly from other illness by imputing it to specific aggressors. As to the posses-sion trance, which is a ritually induced state, it regularly intervenes in the medico–religious response directed as much against illness in general as against the specific illness of spontaneous and mad "pos-session." From this we may already draw two conclusions. The first, as de Heusch writes, is that

in the archaic perspective, mental illness is nothing but the strongest ex-pression of the general idea of illness, conceived as the intrusion of a patho-genic agent.[12]

The second conclusion, which arises quite naturally from de Heusch's second article (although I take the responsibility for for-mulating it so clearly), states that the first conclusion results from the fact that "mental illness" (i.e., possession in the strict sense) is the illness that traditional societies cure the most efficaciously. How so? By way of the trance.

Having come this far, we in fact fall into a double paradox that will very quickly bring us to the center of our problem. The first paradox is that the possession trance is considered by traditional societies sometimes as a maleficent state, which ritual functions to exorcize, sometimes as a freely chosen state called up in the course of adorcist possession cults, which apparently have nothing to do with a therapeutic aim and which (from the structural, if not the historical, point of view) soon lead to the phenomenon of prophetism, on the one hand, and that of theater, on the other.[13] The second paradox (but, in reality, the same) is that the trance which intervenes in exorcist rites is sometimes the patient's affair and sometimes the doctor's.

This leads de Heusch to sketch out a sort of typology of several African societies, according to whether they adopt a more exorcist or adorcist attitude toward possession and the trance. At one extremity of this spectrum we have, according to de Heusch, the frankly exorcist attitude of the Thongas of Mozambique. At the other extreme are, on the one hand, the cults of adorcist possession of the Ethiopian and Dahomian type (the latter having given rise, on the other side of the ocean, to Haitian voodoo) and, on the other hand, shamanism (traditionally confined to Eastern Asia and the Amerindian territory, although de Heusch unearths an example in the Vandaus of Mozambique and hence suggests that shamanism lies "dormant" in African sorcery). Between these two poles, we find all sorts of intermediate variants, according to whether the trance is induced in the patient for diagnostic ends, whether it is combined with the treatment, or whether the doctor puts himself into a trance to diagnose the ill, in the fashion of a true medium.

Having outlined this diagram, it behooves us to find out what we are supposed to do with it. De Heusch's avowed intention is to view it as a group or "field of transformation . . . founded on differential intervals of weak or strong amplitude."[14] We can immediately see that the idea of a "transformation" of exorcism into adorcism is strongly tempered by that of "differential intervals." In fact, shackled by a sort of conventional structuralism, de Heusch contents himself with giving us a synchronic classification of the diverse attitudes toward the trance, without ever directly confronting the problem of the mechanism by which one goes from exorcism to adorcism. This is all the more astonishing in that he gives us all the elements necessary to see that this passage, in reality, operates *internally* in each of the medico-ritual situations he examines, and that, in each situation, the operator is the trance itself.

To demonstrate this, I shall use the example of the Thongas in relation to the possession trance, which de Heusch classifies with pure and simple exorcism. Here we are concerned with possession in the strict sense, which the Thongas impute to the ancestral spirits of the neighboring populace (the Vandaus mentioned above), and which they themselves describe as a "madness," the "madness of the Gods":

> The patient, "possessed" in the strict sense of the word, lives in chaos, deprived of all language. He comports himself in an eccentric manner, trembles, has crises of aggressiveness.[15]

Here, then, is a case of explicitly malefic or, as Gilbert Rouget says,[16] "reproved" possession, which thus must be exorcised. And in fact, the gobela or Thongan "doctor" proceeds exactly like Christian exorcists, to whom I shall return shortly. In the course of a gathering in which chants and drums intervene, and whose officiants are, significantly, formerly possessed persons,[17] he deliberately induces a possession, which, from a confused agitation, suddenly becomes a true possession trance, and, at the same time that an animal is being sacrificed, he questions the spirit that speaks through the mouth of the possessed person in order to identify it. This being done, the possessed person throws himself on the animal, sucks its blood, and spits it out on an altar to which the spirit attaches itself, being transformed from the malefic spirit that it was just a moment before into a sort of tutelary spirit of the patient. As the latter, henceforth invested with the powers of a seer, which may lead him to become a gobela in his turn, he is reputed to be cured. But is he, really? Henri Junod, the author of a celebrated monograph on the Thongas that I have consulted, is categorical on this point: the patient is not cured, at least not in our sense of the word, and the proof is that he will continue to have crises.[18] Thenceforth, however, these are considered normal, for they can be attributed to his tutelary spirit and a few offerings on the altar suffice to calm them. Hence everything has returned to order, after a passage through the greatest disorder.

Now, how can we explain this undeniable efficacity of the ritual, this astonishing transmutation of malefic possession into beneficial possession? The theory that immediately comes to mind is the one called "symbolic efficacity," which Lévi-Strauss proposed, in his *Structural Anthropology* (hereafter *SA*), with regard to the shamanic ritual of the Cunas,[19] and whose effects on Lacan's theory of the analytical cure are well known. According to this generally accepted theory, the ritual furnishes the patient and the group with a myth, that is, with "a *language*, by means of which unexpressed, and otherwise inexpressible, psychic states can be immediately expressed" (*SA*, p. 198), thus "making explicit a situation originally existing on the emotional level" (*SA*, p. 197). More exactly yet, the ritual furnishes a "zero symbol," a "floating signifier," "meaningless" in itself and destined, like all *mana* categories, to symbolically integrate a state or situation that escapes from the symbolic system.[20] In short, as Lacan will later say about the cures of the first hysterics treated under hypnosis by Josef Breuer and Freud,[21] what is important in this case is that the ill be symbolically *recognized* by the group, through the intervention of speech. And this really is the sort of thing we see in the Thongan ritual: as soon as it is named and symbolically identified, the possessive spirit loses his malefic powers. Thus we could say that the whole operation of this ritual consists in symbolically separating the possessed person from his possessive spirit, such that the fearsome loss of identity that characterizes the "madness of the Gods" is replaced by a new order in which each— the self and the other—finds once again his differential place. As de Heusch writes on this point: "It is a matter of substituting the relative distance of dialogue for the pure and simple confusion of man and spirit."[22]

But this explanation, although it admittedly touches one of the aspects of the process, is not sufficient, first of all because, structuralism *oblige*, it deliberately parenthesizes the persecutive content of the myth in favor of its pure symbolic form. As Lévi-Strauss writes regarding shamanism and psychoanalysis, "the myth *form* takes precedence over the *content* of the narrative" (*SA*, p. 204)—another way of saying that the content is totally unimportant and that any "zero symbol" would do the trick. Besides, this is why Lévi-Strauss, in his analysis of the Cuna myth, takes such little interest in the narrative of the "journey," during which the shaman battles with the supernatural power that steals the "soul" of the patient, retaining only the aspect of symbolic "manipulation" (*SA*, pp. 197–201). Now, as we have seen, this theme of possession / dispossession of the soul by a malefic power is nonetheless an important recurring trait of therapeutic myths, and hence cannot be unimportant. In reality, it is not just any symbol that is efficacious: the only ones that work are those that stage and, by the same token, recognize the dangerous and paradoxical indistinction of "self" and "other." Thus it is not the symbol per se that does the curing, but only a very particular symbol, which indicates a confused experience that actually escapes from the symbolic system.

In addition, the theory of "symbolic efficacity" does not say a word about the nonetheless important and massive role of the trance, which attests precisely to that "inexpressible" experience. Besides, Lévi-Strauss specifically recognizes this in his article (*SA*, pp. 187–88), and we can easily understand why: the trance preeminently upsets the "differential intervals" so dear to the structuralist, and thus it is not "good to think" (*bonne à penser*), according to the famous formula of *The Savage Mind*. Structuralist thinking can do nothing but violently expel it, classifying it on the side of the unclassifiable, the unthinkable, and, more generally, the guilty nostalgia for the immediacy proper to the ritual (see *The Naked Man*). This is tantamount to saying that the theory of symbolic efficacy prohibits itself from explaining its object, since the trance, whether "good to think" or not, always intervenes in one way or another in therapeutic rituals.

Now, if trance intervenes in such a necessary fashion, it is because it *dramatizes*—as much or more than it *symbolizes*—the lived experience of the indistinction between possessed person and possessing or dispossessing spirit. We have just seen this in the Thongan example, but it is obviously valid for all the therapeutic rituals that de Heusch so pertinently places in series with it: the trance *induced* by the doctor is continuous with the possession *suffered* by the patient, since the latter is asked to mime his possession by letting the spirit speak through his mouth. We could say, in a more precise fashion, that the patient is urged to stage, to make publicly visible, and thus to communicate a mimetic indifferentiation that, by rights, can only be lived "in the first person," were it not precisely the experience of a "nonperson." Perhaps we should add, to be totally rigorous, that this indifferentiation is "mimetic" only from our point of view, since the "possession" is already a first symbolization of the ill. But how can we say it otherwise? We are at a point where words necessarily fail us. At any rate, we can see that the "remedy," which is the trance, begins by faithfully modeling itself to the "ill," such that the "cathartic" exorcism is rigorously contiguous with "mimetic" adorcism. In this case, it is a matter of a *catharsis of mimesis by mimesis* (which, in passing, may throw some light on the tie established by Aristotle between these two venerable notions). De Heusch, for his part, expresses this, in relation to the Thongan trance, by speaking of a "dialectic stage" and a "resolution of the contradiction,"[23] undoubtedly a way of introducing a little movement into the rigid "differential intervals" of structural analysis. But this reference to dialectic is deceptive, for dialectic starts by separating the terms that it unites, whereas, in this case, the trance separates the possessed person from his spirit only on the condition of having previously united them, and doing so in the most spectacular manner. In reality, de Heusch continues to interpret the indifferentiation of the trance from the symbolic point of view, that is, from language and its differential "normality," whereas the Thongas, as more generally all traditional societies, recognize it "as such" by deliberately provoking it. And, it seems to me, this is what constitutes the whole efficacity of the trance, its properly mimetic efficacity: the trance (or, if you like, the "possession" that it dramatizes) is *attested to* by the group, by the simple fact of being ritually induced. At bottom, this all happens as if the society communicated to the "madman" (or whatever he is to be called) the following message: "Truly you are no longer yourself, *but that's normal*, so be yourself, that is, another." This is an extraordinarily simple process that brings to mind the "paradoxical prescription" of the symptom recommended by the Palo Alto school, following Milton Erickson. We can understand why this procedure must remain definitively closed to any description made from the symbolic point of view, since, in short, it consists of admitting that language and the symbolic are, quite simply, not the whole of human experience. By not admitting this, in its turn, anthropology condemns itself to seeing the trance and symbolic rituals as nothing but symbols "empty of sense," as in Lévi-Strauss, or as "stupid actions," as Frazer was already accused of doing in Wittgenstein's admirable *Remarks on Frazer's Golden Bough*.[24]

Thus we do not wish to deny that recognition by the group plays a decisive role in the process of the cure, nor that this process finally arrives at a symbolic naming (or renaming). In fact, it is always such a symbolic reintegration that we have in mind when we speak of the "cure" with regard to illnesses that are not exclusively organic. But this observation remains abstract and without any scope as long as we do not admit that this recognition aims first and foremost at the nonsymbolizable and that it happens by way of the trance. In fact, everything else does belong to the symbolic (including the sacrifice and the search for a scapegoat that a Girardian interpretation would probably emphasize). But the trance itself is never anything but the very ill that it exorcizes through repetition and ritualization, so we might say that it is both "madness" itself and its first "symbolization," since it is really both at once, an astonishing sort of "go-between" that vaporizes the instant we try to grasp it.

As for the role of speech and language, which an ethnologist under the influence of the Lacanian theses would undoubtedly emphasize, here again, we do not wish to deny them. The possessed person, *who no longer speaks*, really is asked, in the course of the trance, to name the spirit and the malefic power that haunts him. But in what form? In the form of mimetic speech in which the possessed person vaticinates, as Plato said of the poet-mimetician, "under the name of another." Hence, this speech is not a speech of dia-logue (with the spirit, with others in general); rather, it is a matter of "inspired" speech in which the "self" is indistinguishable from the "other" (even if, from the doctor's point of view and from that of the assembled spectators, it serves to put an end to that pathetic identification). By privileging the role of speech in the trance, we consequently risk forgetting its very particular character, which is to indicate an experience that is lived outside of representation, and which, by this very fact, can be communicated, *in language*, only in the form of the mimetic indistinction between "self" and "other." Speech is efficacious only if it is, first and foremost, speech of the trance, a speech enacted, heart and soul.

However it may be with this last question, which could take us far toward a revision of the role of speech in the analytic cure, we can undoubtedly now better understand why the trance is everywhere present in therapeutic rituals and equally well why it takes such diverse forms. It is everywhere present (even if "dormant," as de Heusch writes) because it is the remedy par excellence, through which the illness par excellence—the "madness of the Gods," mimetic madness—and hence, by extension, all illnesses are cured. And it takes diverse forms because, being both illness and remedy, that is, the pure paradox of a *homeopathy* that cures the "same" by the "same," it inevitably elicits contradictory symbolizations, each society differently accentuating the extremes that it links together. Thus the Thongas, as we have just seen, accentuate its malefic character, not without seeking in it the very principle of the operation of exorcism. In contrast, the cults of possession accentuate its beneficial side to the point of almost forgetting its noxious side, if certain indications, such as the initially malevolent character of the Ethiopian *zar* or the Dangalean *margai*, did not regularly call to mind the therapeutic origin of these cults.[25] As to shamanism, it might be objected that here the trance is the affair of the doctor and not of the patient. But it would undoubtedly be easy, as de Heusch suggests in regard to Vandau shamanism,[26] to discover in the shamanistic technique of exorcism by suction an attenuated form of adorcism, by which the medicine man takes the patient's possession, and hence his trance, upon himself. In any case, the fact remains that the shaman himself is a formerly possessed person who has victoriously traversed the experience of the trance,[27] or who at least has simulated it by the ingestion of toxic substances such as tobacco juice.[28] The shaman cures *all* illnesses only because he has cured *the* illness par excellence, and thus, as "technician of ecstasy" (Mircéa Eliade), he can master the paradoxical operation of the trance.

What will happen now if, armed with these already temerarious hypotheses, we pass, via a no less temerarious leap, to our Western societies and to the diverse responses (or ripostes) that it has opposed to the trance? Can we mechanically apply our schema to them? It is doubtful, if only because our societies are exemplified by a general allergy toward the trance. This fact is perhaps related to the fundamental dualism of Christian thought, which prohibits, as de Heusch notes in passing, all alliances with the spirit of evil and thus every "transformation of Evil into Good."[29] Whatever the case with regard to this last consideration, which we shall have to modify somewhat, it is quite true that the trance and, more generally, all the forms of possession / dispossession are universally excluded from our Christian or scientific societies. By simplifying to the extreme, and taking inspiration from a distinction proposed by Lévi-Strauss in *Tristes tropiques*, we might perhaps say that our societies adopt a resolutely "anthropoemic" attitude toward madness, whereas traditional societies generally adopt an "anthropophagic" one: whereas the latter societies exclude the ill, but only by diversely "absorbing" and "digesting" the patient, we tend rather to "vomit" both the patient and the ill out of the social body. In this regard, read or reread the chapter "*Stultifera navis*" that opens Michel Foucault's *Madness and Civilization*. In the Middle Ages, the madman was ritually expelled from the city, with all the effects of reverse sacralization that this might entail.[30] Now, as Foucault once again shows, this structure of exclusion has been integrally maintained into our own time, since psychiatric incarceration is merely its historical transformation. Incarcerated during the seventeenth century, along with drunks, syphilitics, and blasphemers, in establishments constructed on the site of former leprosariums, the madmen remained, as is well known, long after the general practice of incarceration had ended. Hence, liberated from their chains by Philippe Pinel, they remained nonetheless excluded from society, just as they had always been. This means that the therapeutic objective of the asylum, when it exists, is secondary in relationship to the gesture of exclusion, and by this very fact it is rendered impossible in advance. In any case, the phenomena of "possession" or "dispossession" of self that interest us no longer have the slightest chance of being recognized for what they are, that is, a call for the ritual of the trance to take charge. Even less can they be deciphered as the very instrument of the cure. When Pinel, for example, speaks of "religious madness" or of "melancholia by devotion," when Jean-Etienne Esquirol includes "demonomania" in his nosography,[31] the case is closed: the "madness of the Gods," in all its forms, is definitively *alienated*. It becomes, under diverse names ("paranoia," "hysteria," "melancholia"), an *object*, which the psychiatrist and his colleague the psychologist attentively scrutinize but with which they hardly ever have more of a relation than that of the astronomer with a distant galaxy. By an extraordinary sort of autoexorcism, psychiatry, itself the heir of the ancient rituals of expulsion, has come to expel, under the name of "mental illness," the sacred and all its distressing ambivalence.

Thus it is that, once placed in the framework of the asylum or the laboratory, the phenomena of possession or the trance have become perfectly unrecognizable, since they have been separated from all recognition and all therapeutic response. In this regard, one should read Pierre Janet's exemplary book *De l'angoisse à l'extase*: while Madeleine, the "ecstatic" patient in his service, fell into trance states of pure possession,[32] Janet was imperturbably measuring physiological modifications with dynamometers, ergographs, and oesthesiometers. In a more general fashion, it is undoubtedly no exaggeration to say that the whole of the nineteenth-century experimental psychology, from Janet to Théodule Ribot by way of Alfred Binet and Charles Richet, has been nothing but a fantastic objectivization of trance phenomena, the hysteric functioning like a "psychological automaton"[33] or "man-machine,"[34] and hypnosis like a "marvelous machine of psychological vivisection."[35] This last formula of Richet makes the point quite well: the trance (since this is really what is in question under the name of hypnosis), in the eyes of the psychologist, cannot be a means to a cure. Even when it is feverishly cultivated (as was the case, for example, at the Salpêtrière, which Charcot had transformed into a veritable voodoo for psychiatrists), it is never seen as anything other than an instrument of experimentation, as neutral as a scalpel—when it is not considered purely and simply a pathological phenomenon arising merely from hysteria. As is well known, this was Charcot's claim, in his polemic with Bernheim, and, by the same token, we can better understand why he forbade himself the use of the therapeutic possibilities of hypnosis, which he knew quite well. These cures "which . . . cause people to cry out 'miracle,' but of which charlatans alone make their glory,"[36] were attributed by him to the clinical picture of hysteria, *that is to say, to the illness itself.* Hence it is quite evident that this disquieting indistinction between the ill and its remedy had to be severely rejected; otherwise the psychiatrist would have become a banal miracle worker, if not quite simply a hysteric.

Certainly, it might be objected that this was not the attitude of other psychiatrists, like Bernheim or Breuer, and that from Nancy to Vienna, by way of Paris, the royal road that leads to psychoanalysis was being opened. And, in fact, we have become accustomed to thinking that it is with Freud that the adventure of modern psychotherapy began, finally taking care to put itself at the diapason of the patient and to heal by way of hypnosis, affective rapport, or transference analysis. But things are undoubtedly more complex than that, first of all because the spectacular "cathartic" cures of Anna O. or Emmy von N. were not the first of their genre: ever since A. M. J. de Chastenet de Puységur, and throughout the nineteenth century, there is no lack of examples of somnambulists who were cured after having dictated to their therapist, from the depths of their trance, the treatment proper to them,[37] such that psychoanalysis does not in the least hold the historical monopoly on the discovery (or rediscovery) of the therapeutic virtues of speech under hypnosis. Next, it can be claimed with validity that Freud, for his part, never completely broke with the attitude of his master Charcot with regard to the trance, as witness his rapid rejection of hypnosis, his reiterated critiques in regard to the *Zauberwort* "suggestion,"[38] and his polemic with Sándor Ferenczi on the subject of "neocatharsis." In reality, Freud integrated the trance only in the slight and, most importantly, "doseable"[39] form of transference, attributing the process of the cure to its *analysis*, that is to say, as Lacan later insisted, on symbolic interpretation by way of speech and dialogue.

Be that as it may, if there is a rupture between psychoanalysis and the psychiatry represented by Charcot, it operates in continuity with another tradition: that of the magnetizers and hypnotists. Indeed, it has become impossible, after the work of Henri-Frederic Ellenberger, Chertok, and Franklin Rausky,[40] to remain ignorant of the fact that psychoanalysis is the heir of a long series of "treatments of the soul" that begin with Mesmer's "animal magnetism." As Chertok cheerfully repeats: psychoanalysis is nothing more than a chapter in the history of hypnosis, which I, for my part, would rather reformulate more generally, calling it a chapter in the history of the trance.

Indeed, it should be known that the universally "anthropoemic" attitude of Western Christianity has always had for its counterpart, even if in a more marginal form, an "anthropophagic" attitude, centered on the curative power of the trance. The Church, in particular, has never denied (and, in fact, continues to admit) the possibility of possession: the spirit (or, according to a more ancient tradition of the Church Fathers, the flesh) can truly be "possessed" by a demon. Now, this possession may well be diabolic (with the exception of the mystical union with God, which represents the adorcist pole of the Christian religion), but the possessed person is not held responsible (with the exception, this time, of the contractual "sorcerer"), so he can therefore be redeemed by an exorcism that reintegrates him into the community of believers. Must we then conclude, as does Foucault, that accepted possession and expelled insanity have nothing to do with each other, the latter pertaining to a "history of madness" and the former to a "history of religious ideas"?[41] It seems to me that this historical rigor is excessive, for, from the beginning, it is really a matter of the same indistinct ensemble of phenomena of depersonalization and desymbolization, the only difference being that in the one case they are captured by a symbolic setup that recognizes them and integrates them as such, whereas in the other they are purely and simply rejected. In this sense we could say that Foucault's *Madness and Civilization* is written from the point of view of what it denounces: it is the history of banished madness, reduced to silence and the "absence of work"; it is not that of the madness that Western Christianity, and later the magnetizers, made to speak abundantly, integrating it by way of the trance.

In this regard, let us note that, simultaneous with the "great confinement" described by Foucault, the famous episode of the possession of Loudun was taking place. Now, it is sufficient to read the works that Aldous Huxley and Michel de Certeau dedicated to this remarkable affair to realize that it modeled itself quite faithfully on the exorcism of the Thongan "madness of the Gods": there was the same persecutive interpretation of the ill that struck the Ursulines, since this ill was attributed sometimes to "obsession" (that is, to possession in the larger sense), sometimes to "possession" in the strict sense; the same theater of the trance,[42] in the course of which Astharoth, Zebulon, and Behemoth spoke "live" and in a foreign tongue (Turkish); and the same final resolution, since everything returned to order once the guilty principal was identified. Someone might perhaps object that in this case there was a man who died, and that the "sorcerer," Urbain Grandier, really was burned at the stake. But this violent sacrifice, which arose from Christian dualism (and, accessorily, from the political aims of Richelieu), is quite evidently symbolic with regard to the possessed persons themselves, for, contrary to what happened, for example, in the nineteenth century, during the "demonopathic" epidemic at Morzine,[43] the Loudun nuns were reputed to be cured and were reinserted into the community. Sister Jeanne of the Angels even made a brilliant career as an ecstatic, with the apparition of stigmata, thus passing without transition from the status of failed mystic to successful possessed person. As for Father Surin, he experienced the same fate as many a Siberian shaman,[44] since, after having victoriously exorcised the Ursulines, he himself became possessed, thus testifying, against his will, to the upsetting indistinction between the "ill" and the "remedy."

Obviously, then, there is no reason to go to Africa or Siberia to observe the curative effects of the trance. We can observe them in our own recent history, as is testified to, even today, by the presence, in each bishopric, of an exorcist who is regularly summoned in instances of countryside sorcery.[45] It might be said that these are nothing but archaic remains that are condemned to disappear with the religious institutions that supported them. Perhaps. But it would then be necessary to remark, at the very least, that Mesmerian magnetism, which inaugurated the "therapeutic revolution" that ends in our modern psychoanalysis, very explicitly took over the ancient rituals of exorcism. Indeed, it is well known that Mesmer attributed the convulsions induced by his colleague and rival, the exorcist Gassner, to the misunderstood effects of "magnetic fluid"—an "enlightened" translation with scientific pretensions, but one that truly manifests the identity of the phenomenon in question: the vehement "magnetic crises" induced by Mesmer were, quite obviously, nothing but secular possession trances. And one need not have a great deal of speculative imagination to apply this diagnosis to Puységur's "waking somnambulism" and its diverse historical avatars: the waking trance of spiritualist mediums, Ambroise Liébeault and Bernheim's "suggestive" hypnosis, Breuer and Freud's cathartic hypnosis, the "light hypnosis" of free association in psychoanalysis,[46] autogenous training, sophrology, Ericksonian hypnosis, primal scream, and so on. That this usually involves a calm trance obviously does not change its nature as a trance. As Octave Mannoni says quite well (although unduly privileging the psychoanalytic end of the story):

When the devil is eliminated, the convulsives remain. When the relics are eliminated, Mesmer's "magnetized" remain. When the tub is eliminated, hypnosis and the "rapport" remain. When hypnosis is eliminated, the transference remains.[47]

Now, from our point of view, this is very interesting, for here we are witnessing the emergence of a possession trance *without possession*. By this I mean that the "possession" is now relieved of any persecutive or demoniacal interpretation in favor of a resolutely "adorcist" valorization of the trance. Admittedly this can lead to new forms of persecutive interpretation on the part of the patient; he might impute the origin of his illness to some imaginary "trauma," or the therapist might become, in the patient's eyes, an "obsessive" figure (significantly, this last phenomenon occurs when the doctor himself remains ambivalent about the trance that he induces: Janet's "somnambulic passion," Freud's "negative transference"). But in the eyes of the magnetizers themselves, it is clear that the trance is not an illness that must be exorcized, but rather the cure itself. Either the "magnetic crisis" is considered to be good in and of itself, or else, as in the case of African medical mediumism, it is what allows for a diagnosis of the ill and a prescription of the remedy, or even, in its spiritualist and quasi-shamanistic development, for a communication with the "spirits." Most of the magnetizers took this therapeutic optimism so far that they were blinded to the obvious tie between the treated illnesses and the treatment itself, putting as much energy into denying the pathological character of the trance as Charcot, conversely, put into affirming it. From this point of view, it would be rather easy to demonstrate that all the great hypnotico-magnetic therapies were initially modeled on the phenomenon of the illness itself, proposing to artificially induce one or another spontaneous trance whose beneficial effects had been observed by Mesmer, Puységur, Breuer, and Freud (the crisis of Fräulein Oesterlin, the "sleep" of Victor Race, the self-hypnosis of Anna O.). Conversely, there is no doubt that the spontaneous crises or trances of the patients were modeled, in turn, on the hypnotic therapies that they called forth; hence the flowering in the nineteenth century of cases of hysterical somnambulism, double and multiple personalities, or glossolalia.

But all of this, which allows us to understand the profoundly interactive character of the process, is still not the most important. What is decisive and new is that the trance is deliberately valorized and cultivated, outside of any persecutive interpretation. Now, it is the trance itself that does the curing, excluding any naming or expulsion of a "guilty" party. In truth, this does not exclude the possibility that the trance continues to be interpreted, and even superinterpreted, symbolically. And we must go so far as to say that these interpretations or theorizations, as "scientific" as they might be, invariably take us back to variations on the theme of possession and / or dispossession of self. It is not difficult, for example, to read in the "fluid" that circulates from magnetizer to magnetized a penetration and hence a "possession" of the latter by the former: "Your fluid and mine," said one of Tardy de Montravel's patients, "are now one; I must be affected by all the things that affect you."[48] The same could be said of Bernheim's "suggestion," Janet's "somnambulic passion," and Breuer and Freud's "dissociation of consciousness"; and, in any case, the phenomena of personality alternation and glossolalia induced under hypnosis suffice to prove it: in the trance, it is always a matter of a state in which one's own proper identity (or, at any rate, the social identity) is abolished, in favor of a "possession" by a foreign identity (or language).

But, once again, this possession by the other, or this dispossession of self, does not call up any exorcism or symbolic separation from the menacing indifferentiation. On the contrary, the latter is considered perfectly "normal" (which it is, in a sense) and it is repeated as many times as necessary. We are as close as possible to the "adorcist" solution of the possession cults, with the one exception that here it is set in motion for exclusively therapeutic ends. By an extraordinary short circuit, the trance is unburdened (almost) of the entire symbolic paraphernalia that dissimulated its paradoxical efficacity, to finally be confronted as such—in its absence of "as such."

Having come this far, I really must draw the conclusion that is to be derived from this trajectory. It seems to me rather evident: far from being an aberrant and pathological phenomenon that must be rejected or mastered, the trance is what universally allows the cure of a certain type of illness that affects, let us say, the identity. And it does "cure" it (I put this term, and the majority of those that follow, in quotes) in proportion as it makes of it, not a "morbid illness" but a perfectly "normal" state that we must always recognize and elicit "as such," without excluding it or superimposing on it mythic or persecutive symbolizations.

This conclusion, evidently, takes us to the polar opposite of Freudian or Lacanian analysis, in the eyes of which the trance is either what, under the name of "transference," must be interpreted and resolved at the end of the analysis, or what must be resolutely evacuated from the curative setup in favor of a pure symbolization through speech. Now, it seems more and more evident to me that, especially in Lacan, this is a fundamental error that goes against the incontestable evidence of magnetic and hypnotic therapies. Indeed, it is difficult to see how a purely linguistic interpretation could accomplish the reinsertion into "the symbolic" of patients who are manifestly *sick (malades) of the symbolic*, that is, both sick from the point of view of the symbolic and sick because they cannot make themselves recognized in it. As we have seen, even the societies that adopt the most rigidly "exorcist" attitude toward it begin by recognizing the ill and attempting to speak its own "language," which is that of the trance. From this point of view, Lacan's categorical exclusion of every form of the trance[49] is, in reality, equivalent to a foreclosure on the illness of the symbolic (which, as everyone knows, is the Lacanian definition of psychosis) and, by the same token, a foregone prohibition against curing it. Where Freud, in spite of everything, recognized in the transference a manifestation of a "demonic" unconscious resistant to reason, its linguistic interpretation by Lacan definitively bumped it in the direction of an unconscious that is conceived, with Lévi-Strauss, in purely symbolic terms. How then, under these conditions, could it ever authorize any passage, any *transition* between the symbolic and an unsymbolizable realm thence expelled into the external shadows of the ineffable or an impossible "real"?

But what is to be done, then? Return to the practices of the magnetizers and their touching confidence in the powers of the trance? The objection to that is predictable: if Freud and, even more so, Lacan gave up the slightest hope in the therapeutic virtues of the trance in order to center the cure on the power of symbolic interpretation, it was because we live in a society that can no longer believe in "possession," no matter what form it might take; the proof, one might add, is that the magnetizers, like their much removed Reichian, "scientologist," or "humanistic psychologist" heirs, were forced to dress up the trance with a whole mytho-science of rubbish in order to make it acceptable in our desacralized symbolic system. Why not admit it, then, in all consciousness, and bank on the manipulation of symbols *that we know are symbols*, pure "zero myths"?

This objection, which, to all appearances, is reason itself, seems to me, in reality, to participate in a sort of obscurantism of reason that our time has mostly transcended, for if it is true that we no longer believe in possession, it is equally true that we cannot believe in a subject who, to take up Freud's formula, is "master in his house." That myth, too, has exploded in fragments, and not merely because of psychoanalysis. In reality, when "the Symbolic"—that linguistic and differential order to which "the subject" must be brought— is pompously invoked, this unduly applies to our modern societies a model utilized by anthropology to envision traditional societies.

Now this rigid model, even if it is applicable to traditional societies, certainly is not appropriate for our perfectly demythologized, desymbolized, and desubjectivized mass societies, for who still believes in the subject, defined by *his* place in *the* society?

Hence it seems to me that it is rather the confidence accorded the power of the symbol which is largely archaic. As for the trance, which upset traditional societies just as much as it does our modern anthropology, perhaps we are in a better position today to approach it without guilt or mythology, as the magnetizers had begun to do: no longer as our *part maudite* but as a sleep of reason that no longer engenders any monsters—in short, as just as banal and beneficent as our nightly sleep—no longer, therefore, as a terrifying and mysterious Other but as our true mirror.

Translated by Douglas Brick

The Unconscious and Philosophy

⌒ The Unconscious,
Nonetheless

Michel Henry's thesis in *The Genealogy of Psychoanalysis* (henceforth *GP*)[1] is truly upsetting. For a long time now, we had become accustomed to thinking that psychoanalysis "leads us," as Jacques Lacan wrote, "to oppose any philosophy directly issuing from the *Cogito*,"[2] whether it be Cartesianism, Hegelianism (even Marxist Hegelianism), or phenomenology. With the help of a certain Heideggerianism, we had become convinced that Freud started where Descartes stopped—in the infinitely elusive zone of dream, phantasm, or transference where the certitude of the subject assuring itself of itself in representation must, in the end, give up its place to that completely other "certitude" of an unconscious thought. Lacan said it well: "Freud, when he doubts . . . is assured that a thought is there, which is unconscious, which means that it reveals itself as absent."[3] And that "It [*Ça*] thinks" without me, without the *ego*, was a certitude whose non-Cartesianism we had not doubted for a second. Even when the profound identity of the Freudian subject and the Cartesian subject was rigorously recognized,[4] the question was settled: undoubtedly the subject had no other being aside from thinking; yet the fact remained that it was exactly *that*—the representation, the "signifier," as we also used to say—that initially disconnected it from itself, that prevented it from ever being consciously present to itself. As close as possible to the Cartesian *cogito*, the Freudian *cogito* thus seemed to depart from it all the more decisively, deepening the infinite *desire*, the infinite *want*-to-be of the subject: "I think where I am not," announced Lacan, "therefore I am where I do not think."[5] The philosophical genealogy of psychoanalysis was, in that sense, self-evident, since, at bottom, it was really an anti-genealogy. It all started with a parricide—like all parricides, undoubtedly a difficult one, and yet irreversible, since it was

radical enough to call back into question the radicalness of the Cartesian foundation (or *subjectum*) and, at the same time, the root of our
common genealogical-philosophical tree.

It is this parricidal "genealogy" that Henry reverses and overturns right from the start, affirming, against all our prejudices, that
it truly is a *genealogy*, a continuous filiation. Far from being that
philosophical orphan whom we imagined, Freud was, according to
Henry, only a "belated heir" of Descartes. Worse yet, he was only
the illegitimate son of a philosophical lineage that was unfaithful
to the Cartesian Beginning, the final and slightly monstrous off-
spring of a disastrous misinterpretation of the *cogito*—one that, since
Descartes himself, and even with Heidegger, was an "I think" in
the sense of an "I *represent* myself." However, "I think, I am," as
we learn from Henry, "means anything but thought. I think means
life" (*GP*, p. 7)—that is, as we also learn, an "I feel myself" that
is unrepresentable because it exceeds all objectivity, all transcendence, including the light that would open its possibility. Once again
opposing the philosophical tradition issuing from Descartes with
a beyond-consciousness, with unconscious "*thoughts*" and "*representations*," Freud had, according to Henry, done nothing other than
rashly renew that tradition at the price of manifesting, in the fashion
of an enormous symptom, its phenomenological absurdity. Hence
what we took to be a new beginning—psychoanalysis—was really
nothing other than an end, the somnambular and lethal accomplish-
ment "of the long history of Western thought, of its incapacity to
grasp the only important thing" (*GP*, p. 6).

And what is that? Life—life that is always started and starting
anew, "the tireless and invincible coming-into-itself of life," burning "through us in the invisibility of our night" (*GP*, p. 15). We
had thought to found a new filiation, to take root in a new soil (an
abyss, we used to say, to distinguish it from that "terra firma" of
which Hegel spoke in relation to Descartes). We had simply forgotten, fascinated as we were by the still too luminous images of the
"tree" planted in its "clearing," that life never starts or finishes, being
the very Beginning itself, and that it is always the same blood, the
same sap running in our veins. We had *imagined* our life "over there,"
"elsewhere," instead of feeling it well up in us. Our "ontology of
the unconscious" (*GP*, p. 346 ff.) was nothing but sap transformed
into light.

Thus we must relearn life, begin again to live, that is, (re)begin at the Beginning by Being or, to say it even better, by simply *being*, for here, right from the start, Henry separates himself from Heidegger: Being does not begin by dis-appearing, it begins by appearing, before any distance from itself. Here, Being is living-being, and this signifies that Being, right from its first "illumination," appears to itself *in itself* by "expelling nothingness" (*GP*, p. 18). Therefore, this Beginning is absolute in the strict sense, since it is "not the first day, but the very first" (ibid.), the unpreceded "coming" of the living present "into itself," the radical initialness of life before which there is quite simply nothing (this nothing—and here is undoubtedly the most profound root of the disagreement with Heidegger—this no-thing *is* not). Always-already beginning by "coming into itself" (always-already enclosed in that absoluteness of the Beginning that it itself is), the living-being neither arrives nor commences anyplace in the world, and so, as Edmund Husserl also said of the transcendental ego,[6] it is innate and immortal.

And that is also why the Beginning is not Greek but Cartesian. It all begins, for Henry as well as for Hegel and Husserl, with the *cogito*, without this privilege being in any way historic, for if Descartes is the Beginner par excellence, it is because he is the first *in* history to have returned to what is properly *without history*, "to the most initial moment of the Beginning, by which history begins and never ceases to begin" (ibid.). And that "moment"—that "flash," as Henry also says, underlining the instantaneous character of the *cogito*—is the one when, having doubted everything, having suspended all natural or naive belief in the existence of the world (my own intraworldly existence included), I finally know, with absolute certainty, that this world *is* insofar as I think it (insofar as it "appears," adds Henry) and that I *am* "as much as" I think it, for "as long" (*autant de temps*) as I think it (as long as it appears).

Being, such would thus be the original evidence, begins at the present, as living presentation to oneself in thought (let us not yet say consciousness): "I think, I am," or, once again, according to Husserl's formulation, which Henry would undoubtedly not deny, "I *am*, this life is, I live: *cogito*."[7] "Original presence," "living presence" (*GP*, p. 189), "initial appearing to itself of appearing" (*GP*, p. 123), the Beginning attained at the zenith of the hyperbolic and metaphysical doubt consequently exceeds all historicity. There is no "history of Being," no "history of metaphysics" as forgetfulness or destiny of Being, since Being, for Henry, never withdraws or dissimulates itself from itself. The Beginning, according to Henry, does not *begin* by losing itself. On the contrary, never beginning in time or history, it is profoundly un-losable, since it is untemporal or a-temporal in the strict sense. However un-appearing it may be, it can consequently always be re-found, (re)begun outside of history. History, in this sense, is not that of an original "errancy," it is only the history, at bottom unessential, of a "long error" and a periodic return to truth—that is, to the Beginning; that is, to the *cogito*.

Up to this point, you will have recognized, with just a few differences, the classical path of phenomenological reduction, in its at least provisional recourse to Descartes. Indeed, for Henry it is a matter of returning, beyond all the historical deviations of the phenomenological motif, to that very returning of transcendental Life upon itself for which the *cogito* had furnished the initial model. And, in fact, Henry's project is overtly given as phenomenological. "Being," it is clearly stated, "means: to appear, to be manifested" (*GP*, p. 26), that is, to be phenomenalized. The thing that is "ignited and catches fire" (*GP*, p. 18) in the *cogito* is, once again, nothing other than pure phenomenological light, the pure illumination of the *phainestai*:

A thing that thinks is nothing other than the flash of lightning, the light which is lighted . . . the materiality of phenomenality as such. (*GP*, p. 20)

Henry nonetheless separates himself from Husserl, in a properly imperceptible separation, when he returns the luminous evidence of the *cogito* to the obscurity that inhabits it. Indeed, it is no accident that Henry speaks of the "illumination" of the *cogito* through the metaphors of "flash" and "lightning" (*GP*, p. 18). Illumination is blinding, just as blinding as the bolt of lightning that flashes forth from the night only to return immediately to it: recall, for example, the long mystical tradition of the "black sun," which was also that of Georges Bataille attempting to express, in the language of "thingish transcendence," the irreducibly immanent and living "intimacy" of "interior experience."[8] Illumination of the visible, the phenomenological light of the *cogito*, would itself be invisible, according to a hyperbolic "invisibility" necessarily betrayed by the classical oppositions of the visible and the invisible, veiling and unveiling, the clear and the obscure, and, finally, consciousness and the unconscious.

Ultimately, what is the "certitude" obtained at the end of the "Cartesian *epochê*"? Does it suffice to say that it is that of pure phenomena, of the *Seinsphänomen*? Is it only the certitude, every worldly position suspended, of the transcendental egoic life, as Husserl thought? Or, in still other words, is it that of the immanent experience of intentional consciousness, of that "consciousness-*of*" that has as a fundamental quality, "as a *cogito*, to bear within itself its *cogitatum*"?[9] It would undoubtedly be so if Descartes had been content to *suspend* every thesis concerning the existence of the world, ready to recover immediately this last in its full phenomenological positivity, as *noema* "irreally" included in *noesis*. But Descartes *doubts* the existence of the world, and that negating doubt, which in Husserl's eyes still appeared too much in solidarity with the natural attitude, would, according to Henry, go much further than phenomenological "reduction," in that it would suspend even the *transcendence* (even if it were an immanent transcendence) of intentional consciousness itself.

Doubting everything—even doubting, at the "extravagant" extremity of hyperbolic doubt, that he had a body, eyes, ears—the Descartes of the *Second Meditation* not only doubts *what* he sees but also *vision* itself, the "phenomenological gaze" as such. And, as Henry writes in some very powerful pages (powerful with all the *violence* of interpretation), if Descartes doubts seeing what he sees, "it is, it can only be because vision itself is fallacious, it is because the gaze is, in itself, of such a nature that what it sees is not as it sees it" (*GP*, p. 25). Cartesian doubt, in other words, would reject what Husserl explored as a sort of New World: that is, the evidence which is given to intuition (since *intueri* is to see); that is, also and especially (and here the accusation encompasses Heidegger), the "element of visibility," the "pure horizon" of ob-jection of the ob-ject, the "opening of openness as the ontological difference on which all ontic presence is founded" (*GP*, p. 26). In contesting vision, Descartes would not only contest the eido-logy to which philosophy has confided itself since Plato, he would also contest the *opening* of the possibility of the transcendental gesture, what Henry calls, with a term that he diverts from Heidegger and returns against him, *ekstasis*, the being-beyond-itself of transcendence.[10]

It is in this point, this perfectly unseizable point by which the *cogito* withdraws in a single motion from the "natural light" and from the "vision of essences," that "everything," it seems, "vanishes" (*GP*, p. 25), for if doubt goes as far as to exceed the pure element of phenomena's appearing, what remains for us as evidence, as certitude? Once again, vision, but this time a "vision" that is perfectly blind, a "seeing" without any(thing) seen. Supposing that what I see is not as I see it, says Descartes in the *Second Meditation*, "at least, it is very certain that it seems to me that I see light, hear a noise and feel heat." [11] *At certe videre videor*. The certitude, here, has nothing to do with the *videre*, the "seeing-of-something." It deals with the *videor*, that is, with a "semblance" or an "appearance" (*GP*, p. 27) that must not be interpreted in terms of visibility, [12] since it itself is *invisible*, anterior to what presents itself to be seen in the doubtful exteriority presented to me by the Evil Demon. "It seems to me that I see" and not "I see myself seeing (myself)": the certitude of the *cogito* is not the reflexive or specular certitude of the self-observing "disinterested onlooker" spoken of by Husserl; [13] rather, it is that immediate and, in this sense, more naive, absolutely native and absolutely beginning certitude of an eye that only sees what it sees on the condition of not seeing itself. In short—and here we are getting close to Henry's fundamental thesis, the one that, among others, allows him to disassociate himself from the Heideggerian reading of the *cogito* [14]—that strange "certitude," which could almost be called exophthalmic, is not that of a con-sciousness assuring itself of itself in representation, is not the subjectal co-positioning of the ego "with" all the *Vor-stellungen* that it poses before itself. The *ego*, according to Henry, does not pose itself by ob-posing itself in and as representation. On the contrary, it de-poses itself in them. It is in withdrawing itself from everything that it poses *before* itself—according to a "retreat from the world" (*GP*, p. 52) that is all the more irrepresentable in that it makes way and space for representation—that the ego knows that it is, with a "knowledge" that is precisely no longer the *self*-knowledge of a *self*-consciousness.

A "non-knowledge," then? Or an "unconscious"?

Having come to this point, which is a vanishing point, Henry could, in effect, have attempted to burrow into that abyssal retreat of the ego into its ownmost *cogito* and to find again "in" the Cartesian subject itself that non-subjectal essence or Being which Heidegger, for his part, had searched for "outside," in the ek-static character of the *Dasein*. He could thus, in his own manner, have prolonged all the non-Heideggerian (which is not to say anti-Heideggerian) readings of the *cogito* begun here and there in France over the last twenty years: that of Derrida, for example, insisting (in terms sometimes strangely similar to Henry's) on the *cogito*'s uncontrollable excess to itself;[15] or again, those of Lacan and Jean-Luc Nancy, emphasizing, each in his own way, the initial "abortion" of the subject in the utterance, "*cogito*,"[16] or its "retrenchment" in the enunciating (*énoncer*) "*ego sum*."[17] He could, finally—and this is basically what Lacan proposed—identify that disappearance or that "fading" of the subject into its own representation with what Freud called the "unconscious."[18]

However, this is exactly what Henry refuses to do, refuses with an obstinacy that makes his remarks profoundly untimely, very profoundly unsettling. To speak of the "un-conscious," of the "disappearance" of the subject in its very appearance, of the "retrenchment" of the ego in its own autoenunciation, and so forth would in effect be to continue, under the appearance of a reversal, to speak the very language of representation—that language of ekstatic phenomenality for which "each new content of experience offers itself to the light of seeing only if that which precedes it makes to it the sacrifice of its own presence" (*GP*, p. 50), every veiling thus being equivalent to an unveiling, every "showing" to a "hiding," every presence to a retreat or to a re-presentation. In short, it would be to continue to speak that oppositive language of the *videre* that the "mute" certitude (*GP*, p. 51) of the Cartesian *videor* had already outmoded. The fact that the certitude obtained at the end of the hyperbolic doubt can no longer *speak itself* (reflect itself, speculate [on] itself) in no way diminishes, for Henry, its character of certainty. Far from constituting a sort of negative "certitude," it is all the more positive for having definitively escaped from that exteriority where representational consciousness must necessarily be demeaned and lost in order to (re)seize itself. This, of course, supposes that this absolutely positive certitude, at the very least, *appears* to itself. But in what mode of appearing, then, if that of phenomenality is refused?

In the mode of affect. "Being" means to appear, and to appear anteriorly to every exteriority and every alterity (*GP*, p. 100; *Essence of Manifestation*, p. 392 ff.); it means feeling (oneself) in feeling. Immediately after having affirmed that "it seems to me that I see," Descartes adds, "and this is properly what in me is called feeling and this, taken in this precise sense, is nothing other than thinking." Such would be, not the intuition, but the dazzling "revelation" of the Cartesian Beginning: that of a thought that, before thinking of anything, feels itself think (that is to say, live), and only thus *is* what it is, that "thing that thinks. That is to say, a thing that doubts, perceives, affirms, denies, wills, does not will, that imagines also, and which feels."[19] Anterior to every empirical affection and to every a priori receptivity of horizon as its condition of possibility, there would be that pure affection of itself by itself, that "autoaffection" so immanent to itself that it can no longer even reflect upon itself, conceive itself, or seize itself, *but that nonetheless feels (itself), experiences (itself)*. Henry's whole thesis is summed up and exhausted in that affirmation, basically inaudible to classical philosophical discourse, of a manifestation (to itself) *in immanence*. Indeed, where the transcendence and appearance outside itself of consciousness ends (and thus where the thought of a Friedrich Schelling, half asphyxiated, no longer knew anything but an "unconscious" Identity, and that of a Hegel, more crudely yet, nothing but a "night in which all the cows are black")—there, in reality, begins the *other* phenomenality, the *other* "mode according to which phenomenality is phenomenalized" (*GP*, p. 36). This was the thesis of Henry's great book *The Essence of Manifestation* (henceforth *EM*), in its combat against what Henry at that time called "ontological monism":

There exist *two* specific and fundamental modes in conformity with which the manifestation of what is takes place and is manifested. In the first of these modes, Being manifests itself to the outside. . . . This is why . . . its very manifestation refers to that which does not manifest itself. In the second of these modes, in feeling, Being arises and reveals itself in itself, integrates itself with self, and experiences itself, in suffering and in enjoyment of self, in the profusion of its interior and living Being. (p. 684)

Thus Being arises immediately, without any distance, in an interiority and an immanence all the more transparent to itself insofar as it is all the more opaque to the "seeing" that it "makes possible" (*GP*, p. 36).

This is the moment, it appears to me, to pose several questions to Michel Henry. Is it true, in effect, that we can so easily subtract the sphere of affective life from the duality characteristic of the *ek-stasis*? To feel *oneself*, to *auto*affect oneself, does that not already imply, however narrow it might be, the pleat of a reflection? And thus of a departure from oneself? And thus also of a receptivity, as is testified to by the important theme (already present in *The Essence of Manifestation*) of the "passivity" of affectivity in regard to itself? And if immanence "makes possible" the transcendence where nevertheless it loses itself, does this not presuppose that it *opens itself*, of itself, onto and as that possibility? Finally, is it purely by accident (historical accident) that we have so much difficulty in thinking of a phenomenon that does not present itself *to* us, "*in front of*" us—so much difficulty, in other words, in thinking life and living thought? These first questions bring us to the presentiment that it is difficult, that it is perhaps simply impossible to follow Henry in his project of a *phenomenology* of the essence of phenomena or, what amounts to the same thing, of a phenomenology of Being. This is not, to be sure, because we would forbid ourselves from following Henry in his passionate quest for a "beyond" of ek-static phenomenality (and even less because we would refuse to go searching for that "beyond" in affect), but rather because it is hard to see how that "beyond" of phenomenon (that "completely other than representation," *GP*, p. 361) could continue to be formulated in the very terms of what it is supposed to exceed.

Indeed, it is one thing to say, according to a typically Heideggerian form of reasoning, that "what is seen is always foreign [to] the seeing itself" (*GP*, p. 36) and that the essence of manifestation (or of transcendence) does not manifest itself (being the "*transcendens* pure and simple" spoken of in *Sein und Zeit*).[20] It is another thing to conclude, as Henry already had (*EM*, p. 39 ff.), that this essence phenomenalizes itself differently—*especially if that other and more original "phenomenon" integrally recuperates, under the name of "affectivity," all the properties refused to the phenomenality and representation called "ekstatic"*: living self-presence and proximity, positive infinity, absoluteness, Parousia, and so on, for in reality Henry does not contest phenomenology in its Husserlian literality except in order to return it even more profoundly to its intention, according to a gesture that was already Husserl's with regard to Descartes. At bottom, he does not criticize the "ek-static" representation of the Moderns for an alleged intrinsic failure of its assurance of the autopresentation of the subject. On the contrary, he criticizes it precisely for *failing* as soon as it requires a "phenomenological distance" (*EM*, p. 59 ff.) that removes (*é-loigne*) the proximity to self as such. That is also why the return to the Cartesian Beginning proposed by Henry is presented without mystery as an nth re-foundation of the Subject, this time on the basis of a more ultimate and more fundamental autopresentation: thus it is *always the same* autopresentation, with the difference that here it is a question of Sameness itself, of an Identity or Unity (*GP*, p. 33) so "close" to itself that it takes the breath away from every thought and always seems to be on the point of fainting away into that nothingness to which Hegel condemned it at the beginning of his *Science of Logic*.

Thus, like Nietzsche according to Heidegger, Henry only criticizes the metaphysics of subject(iv)ity inaugurated by Descartes in order to fully carry it out—the whole difficulty and equivocality of his gesture being that he must then oppose Descartes to Descartes, Schopenhauer to Schopenhauer, Freud to Freud, and, finally, perpetually criticize what he accomplishes and accomplish unendingly what he criticizes. Indeed, in the end, how can one reconcile, in all the rigor of the concept, the masterly demonstration of the unseizable character of the *cogito* with the pure and simple reinstallation of an "absolute," "radical subjectivity" (*GP*, pp. 52, 392)? How can one contest, at the depth which is Henry's, the very notion of phenomenality while at the same time continuing to speak the very language of phenomenology? And, still more radically, how can one *say* what, exceeding all ex-position and all representation, can only be un-sayable, inexpressible, irrepresentable? Does it suffice to *say* that "feeling-oneself" (*se-sentir*) escapes from the fate of the reflexive "oneself," to *say* of immanence that it is "mute" (*GP*, pp. 44, 51), of the intuition of the *cogito* that it is "blinding" (*GP*, p. 56), of the original transparence that it is "invisible" (ibid.), of the interiority of the ego that it is "hardly thinkable" (*GP*, p. 32)? Finally, can Henry avoid the Modernist gesture that he never ceases to denounce so spiritedly: that is, the confirming of the empire of the language of representation at the very moment of attempting to hint at its "completely other," at the radical "non-sense" of life (*GP*, p. 358)?

Let us be clear. There is no question here of simply confining Henry to the "closure of representation" that he so brilliantly challenges. It is obvious that remaining comfortably (or even tragically) "within" that closure will never get one "out," and in this regard Henry's critique is extremely pertinent: no matter what is *said* about it, Being is not only said *in the sense* of representation, *from the point of view* of ek-static phenomenality, it is also said in the mode of that more than passive passivity of the feeling that I experience before any "receptivity," of that more than active activity of the hand that I move before any "spontaneous decision." Nevertheless, the whole question is whether it is possible simply to install oneself *outside* of representation, or rather, whether it is (to speak the language of Emmanuel Lévinas) only in a perpetual "unsaying" (*dédire*) of the ekstatic-representational "said" (*dit*) itself that, paradoxically, one can escape from it. At the very least, its extraordinary power of envelopment should first be recognized: the language of representation literally has no outside, since it is precisely the language of Outside. That is undoubtedly why we cannot content ourselves with making of it the sort of more or less superficial and illusory "veil of Maia" that Henry attempts so constantly to open before our eyes—before our eyes of living blindmen—for such is perhaps the major illusion secreted by the *ekstasis* of representation, its properly transcendental illusion: re-moving (*é-loignant*) everything that it draws closer, veiling everything that it unveils, it unavoidably creates the mirage of a "beyond the mirror," of a "before" representation as such, as if the veil of the veiling / unveiling structure itself could, in the end, be lifted, removed, *aufgehoben*.

In this regard—and as Henry himself shows, without seeming to notice that it is eminently applicable to his own enterprise—the critique of representation is as old as the thought of representation. Always, the ex-position of the subject in representation has deepened the desire for an even closer proximity; always, the mediation of transcendence has called up the nostalgia for an immediacy even more "naive," more primordial, whether it be that of feeling or of the expressive voice, that of the body or of power, that of life or of genius. But that is exactly the dream *of representation*—the dream of an Outside of the Outside, of a "Before" the spatio-temporal Removal. Therefore it does not suffice to say, as did Bataille, contrary to Henry, that once the transcendence of "self-consciousness" appears, it definitively prohibits us from returning to that burning immanence of life other than by a "poetic leap."[21] It must be thought that immanence was never lost *elsewhere* than in transcendence. True life has never been elsewhere than in the representation that makes it shimmer outside of itself, as its inaccessible beyond, and thus it is not elsewhere than in representation. According to a paradoxical but perfectly rigorous structure, the "beyond" of ek-static transcendence can only be its "beyond" on the condition of somehow being internal and immanent to it, anterior to the ob-position of immanence and transcendence, and thus also anterior to the opposition of representation and its "completely other": what we need if we want to do justice to the irrepresentable is an *other* thought of representation rather than an *anti*-representational thought. Whether we like it or not, the irrepresentable is not to be sought outside of representation.

Now, this is exactly what Henry does, as soon as he claims to give us access to the immanence of affective life beyond the transcendence of representation, to the living eye of the *videor* beyond the ecstatic vision of the *videre*. And thus we must ask ourselves whether, in reality, he does not succumb to the mirage of language and of representation in thinking that he can see himself without a mirror and speak himself beyond language. After all, can the eye feel itself without seeing (even, and especially, in the dark of the most profound night)? Is it not precisely this that makes vision blind, that prevents it from seeing itself see, as it *feels itself* see? In other words, wouldn't it have been better to insist on the irrepresentability of representation itself (not the provisional but the radical invisibility of vision as such), rather than to repeat the gesture of all post-Cartesian modernity that always burrows more profoundly through representation toward its improbable and unseizable subject? Wouldn't this have been preferable to producing, at the exhausted extremity of a discourse which is perpetually destroying itself, that sort of monster which is so astonishingly close to what it never ceases to denounce: an *irrepresentable* subject, an *unconscious* consciousness? Indeed, if (and how not subscribe to it?) "the last word of the philosophy of consciousness, its limit, its paradox, the extreme point where it returns against itself and self-destructs, is truly *the unconsciousness of pure consciousness itself as such*, the unconsciousness of 'transcendental consciousness'" (GP, p. 352), doesn't this statement return eminently against Henry himself as soon as he in his turn tries to *escape* from the paradox, from the very moment when he, too, searches to regrasp the life of consciousness before its deadly disassociation into "consciousness" and "unconsciousness"?

It is from this unassailable position (unassailable because it is, by right, situated prior to any opposition and thus prior to all communicability) that *The Genealogy of Psychoanalysis* can claim to dismiss, back to back, both the "philosophy of consciousness" and the "ontology of the unconscious." This is the central affirmation of the book: "Consciousness and the unconscious are the Same" (*GP*, p. 78), or again, "The concept of the unconscious [makes its appearance] *at the same time as that of consciousness and as its exact consequence*" (*GP*, p. 6). "At the same time" means ever since Descartes, ever since the dazzling certitude of the feeling of self was understood and reflected as representational consciousness, self-presence in the light of the "clear and distinct" idea. Why this disastrous misinterpretation of the *cogito* must necessarily have given rise to the idea of an "unconscious" is at present much easier to understand: because ek-static representation only presents the subject to itself on the condition of simultaneously absenting it, because its luminous "in-face" always and in principle carries with it the hidden, veiled, obscure face. Consequently, "the more radically is operated the eidetic determination of the soul as consciousness, the more stingingly surges forth its refutation, the contrary affirmation that only a part of our being, and naturally the most superficial part, is offered to the light" (*GP*, p. 75).

Now, once consciousness is reduced to the finitude of "seeing" (of intuition, perception, evidence), we must indeed affirm, as does Nietzsche, that "the principal great activity is unconscious," consisting of the "obscurity" and "confusion" of the soul's passions for Descartes (*GP*, p. 56 ff.); "unconscious perceptions" for Leibniz (*GP*, p. 79 ff.); "apperception" escaping from every experience for Kant (*GP*, chap. 4); the "unconsciousness" and "irrepresentability" of Schopenhauer's Will; Hartmann's "instinct" (*GP*, pp. 213–14); "latency" of memories according to Freud (*GP*, p. 75); and, we might add, the incompleteness and non-self-presence of intentional consciousness for Husserl. Right from the beginning, in other words, the unconscious accompanies consciousness as its shadow, as the shadow carried by *its* light. The more ekstatic-representational consciousness searches to see itself, and the more it flees from itself, the more it drops the prey, if I may be allowed to express it thus, and picks up the shadow by always searching elsewhere for the absolute, in an "other place," whereas it is really already there, in the nocturnal illumination of affective life. According to Henry, this results in the insatiable desire for clarity and unveiling that animates the "philosophy of consciousness" as a whole, which is constantly in pursuit of a transparence that its very seeking expels to infinity, and thus, finally, leads to the implacable paradox that always turns it more and more into a "philosophy of the unconscious," since it always seeks to *represent* that impossible transparence under the name of "the unconscious" or of "desire."

According to Henry, Freud (let us speak of him at last) was the ultimate and most flagrant representative of this "paradox of modern thought" (*GP*, p. 194). Like Schopenhauer, he had the presentiment that the essence of the psyche cannot be reduced to the light of representational consciousness. Like Schopenhauer, and more especially like Nietzsche, he searched for that invisible essence of the *Seele* where it effectively is: in affective life, in the dynamism of "drives," "tendencies," and "motions," acting im-mediately, because being effected without the transcendent mediation of representation. But also like Schopenhauer, he allegedly failed to seize that "other of representation" (*GP*, pp. 193, 349, 361) in its own phenomenality, apprehending it rather *through* representation and its language, whether as an "X" that is always inaccessible because it is always-already represented to consciousness or, worse yet, as a collection of "unconscious representations." "Thus," writes Henry with regard to Schopenhauer's doctrine of representation as impassable appearance and phenomenon of the Will,

an astonishing reversal is produced . . . that finds its conclusion in Freudianism: the calling into question of representation ends in the establishment of its undivided reign and, properly speaking, in its own diktat. (*GP*, p. 194)

However, it is just this modern dictatorship of representation that we must relinquish so as finally to reach the true unconscious, that is to say, *consciousness*, the "affect," says Henry, "*that is never unconscious*" (*GP*, p. 10).

Here, it is true, Henry's angle of attack is limited, but it is decisive: it is on the Freudian doctrine of the *Repräsentanz des Triebes*, the "representative" (or "representance") of drives. Indeed, it is well known that Freud, ever since the *Project* of 1895, had conceived of the psyche as an apparatus confronted with two types of excitations, the first qualified as "external" because the subject can flee from them or protect itself from them (in the best of cases), the others as "internal" because they are constant and impossible to avoid (hunger, thirst, sexuality). It is this second group of excitations that he subsumed under the name of "drive" (or "instinct," as it is usually, and poorly, translated into English), meaning thereby a "pressure" "originating from within the organism" and imposing itself on the psychism as an imperious "demand for work"[22]—that is, as Henry immediately emphasizes (*GP*, p. 366), as a demand for *exteriorization*, for *objectivation*. Whether this demand be fulfilled or rejected by the psyche (and that is its normal or morbid "vicissitude"), the Freudian drive, like the Will of the Moderns, effectuates and realizes itself—manifests itself—only by representing itself, by going outside of itself by pro-ducing itself in front of itself, and it is only from this *point of view*, that of ek-static light and representational consciousness, that it can be said to become "conscious" or "*unconscious*." This would be proved, if there were any need for proof, by this passage from "The Unconscious," which Henry qualifies quite justly as a "key-text" (*GP*, p. 364):

I am in fact of the opinion that the antithesis of conscious and unconscious is not applicable to instincts. An instinct can never become an object of consciousness [*Objekt des Bewusstseins*]—only the idea that represents the instinct [*die Vorstellung, die ihn repräsentiert*] can.

But, continues Freud very significantly,

Even in the unconscious, moreover, an instinct cannot be represented [*repräsentiert sein*] otherwise than by an idea [*Vorstellung*]. If the instinct did not attach itself to an idea or manifest itself as an affective state, we could know nothing about it.[23]

The important thing in such a text is not so much that the drive is here conceived of as *represented* by the psychism, whereas in other places it designates rather the "psychic *representative*" of the excitation coming from the body or, in an even more deliberately ambiguous fashion, a "concept on the frontier [*Grenzbegriff*] between the mental and the somatic."[24] What is more important is that Freud, here as elsewhere, conceives of this "pressure" of energy *only* as represented, that is, as "translated" in the "psychic." Indeed, if we can "know nothing" of the force of the drive as such, it is precisely because its psychic *Repräsentanz* is supposed to constitute the very condition of its accession to being-conscious-and / or-unconscious—that is, to being, pure and simple. Here, to be is to-be-psychical, and to-be-psychical is to-be-represented, to-be-object(iv)ized, so that everything that escapes from the representational gaze and consciousness is condemned either to sink into pure and simple nonmanifestation (the "X" of the force of the drive) or, once again, to "exist" only as representation (the unconscious, the *Unbewusst*). Indeed, the unconscious is the "other" of representational consciousness only because it is fundamentally the "same," which is sufficiently attested to by the little *"auch"* via which Freud slides from the domain of consciousness, where only the *Vorstellung* can become *Objekt des Bewusstseins*, to the domain that is still and always representational, the domain of the unconscious: "Even [*auch*] in the unconscious, moreover, an instinct cannot be represented otherwise than by a *Vorstellung*." It is not surprising, then, that Freud can nourish the project of "translating" the unconscious into consciousness,[25] since representation's "completely other" has always-already been "translated" into representation: into "bound" or "psychically worked over" energy, the drive seized in its representations, libido invested in its "objects," affect "attached" to its representations, and so on. Similarly, everything that initially came to upset and overflow representational consciousness—affect taking over the hysterical body, the constraining "efficiency" of obsessional thoughts, the uncontrollable "acting-out" of the transference and of repetition, the involuntary flash of the *Witz* or of slips of the tongue, somnambular execution of suggestions, undelayed "fulfilment" of the "primary processes"—all this is completely integrated into representation, interpreted as unconscious "thoughts," decoded as repressed "phantasies," in a word, *psycho*analyzed.

Certainly, it will be said that such a reading is only possible at the price of a play on the word "representation," and that it illegitimately confounds the German *Repräsentanz* with *Vorstellung* by forgetting that, according to Freud, the drive "represents" itself equally in the form of *Affekt*, of qualitative "tonality." But this would merely be grasping at words by making light of the problem that they designate in Freud, for it is no accident that Freud writes, in the passage from "The Unconscious" already quoted, "Even in the unconscious, moreover, an instinct cannot be represented [*repräsentiert sein*] otherwise than by a *Vorstellung*," despite immediately adding, as though with remorse, that the drive would remain unknowable if it "did not attach itself to an idea or *manifest itself as an affective state*." In reality, it is only the *Vorstellung* that *repräsentiert* the drive, for the good reason that the affect, for its part, *presents*[26] it immediately, without the slightest mediation. This is attested to by the fact—many times emphasized by the commentators, but of which Henry is undoubtedly the first to extract the consequences so rigorously—that affect, by Freud's own admission, cannot possibly be unconscious, as if it would short-circuit every distance and every exteriority between the drive and the psyche (between "body" and "soul"). Affect either is or is not. Contrary to the *Vorstellung*, which can be and yet not appear, the affect *is* only in appearing, exists only as manifest:

> It is surely of the essence [*Wesen*] of an emotion that we should be aware of it, i.e., that it should become known to consciousness.[27]

This is why, according to Freud, there cannot be, in all rigor, any "unconscious affects." And so, in speaking of "unconscious anxiety" or, still more paradoxically, of an "unconscious consciousness of guilt" (*unbewusstes Schuldbewusstsein*), the psychoanalyst would only mean that the representation to which the affect was initially attached has succumbed to repression. But the affect itself would never cease to impose itself on consciousness. In other words, the affect may well be "suppressed" ("inhibited," "blocked," reduced to the state of a "rudiment"), but it can by no means be *repressed*.

We will then conclude with Henry that the affect, far from being a second psychic *Repräsentanz* of the drive in addition to the *Vorstellungs-Repräsentanz*, is, rather, its very manifestation. That affect always be "conscious" means, in effect, that the psyche can never "distance" it, never flee it (repress it) like an exterior reality, never ob-pose itself to it in the light of the *Vor-stellung*, and thus neither can it ever dissimulate it from itself. In short, this signifies that the opposition of consciousness and the unconscious is not applicable to affect. But is this not precisely what Freud says *of the drive*? And is it not also the *drive* that he most often describes as that constant excitation from which the psyche can never escape? From then on, it is easy for Henry to challenge as artificial and "speculative" the distinction between the drive (or the quantity of excitation) and the affect supposed to represent it. This distinction is only valid for the *Vorstellung*, which is, in effect, incapable of representing to itself the originally upsurging interiority of life except by ex-posing and pro-jecting it (as Freud said of the "endopsychic knowledge" of the unconscious) outside of itself, here in the form of a fantastic "topography" of the psyche. But if Freud stubbornly qualifies the drives as internal, this is because, phenomenologically speaking, they really never affect the psyche from the exterior[28]—because they are, translates Henry, a name for the pure and spontaneous *auto*affection of the "interior life":

> Drive, in the end, never designates for Freud a particular psychic motion, but rather the auto-impressing of itself without ever being able to escape from . . . the weight and the burden of itself. (*GP*, p. 374)

The "weight," the "burden": we see that Henry insists as much on the passive side of this "receptive spontaneity" as on its active side. We can easily understand why, for what would a perfectly controllable love, hate, or anxiety be, one whose initiative rested solely on the subject? It would no longer be a *passion*, it would no longer be a *"drive."* Nevertheless, Henry, according to a decision that is in no way innocent and that *orients* his whole argumentation, implants and finally reabsorbs the passion of affect in an activity (just as he reabsorbs, as we will see in a moment, its unconsciousness in a pure and simple consciousness). And it is precisely in that irreducible passivity of the affect that Henry, at the extremity of words, sees the "effect" of its very spontaneity, which is also to say, its fundamental immediacy. Far from affect being the effect of an exterior cause ("body," "drive," "traumatic event," etc.), it is on the contrary precisely because life, in its free "coming into itself," deals only with itself that it *experiences itself*, that it makes the ordeal of being— which is each time pathetic, enjoying *and* suffering (*GP*, p. 283; *EM*, p. 658 ff.)—incapable of fleeing before itself. Life is a passion but, according to Henry, only because it suffers *itself*, suffering being nothing other than the pleat of enjoyment *of* self. Thus, in regard to the "eternal suffering and contradiction" of "the originary One" in the early Nietzsche, he states:

> In the essence of life, the enjoying of self . . . consists of a self-experiencing of self, which is originally a self-suffering of self, that is, the proper possibility of suffering. (*GP*, p. 292)

More passive than any passivity would thus be the *free*, very *spontaneous* affection of self by self, in the very measure of its absoluteness without exterior: hyperpassivity of the "hyper-power" (*GP*, p. 394 ff.), and radical un-power of what is power without limits. Indeed, how can the ipseity escape from itself if it is no longer free even to oppose itself to itself, if it is "alone in the world" (*GP*, pp.

39, 97), literally walled up in its "solitude" (*EM*, p. 284)? At the extreme, how *can* it do anything at all, if every possibility is closed to it, if its power, as Freud said of "wish" and of "primary processes," knows no delay in its realization—*knows no "exterior reality," no "temporality," no "negation, no doubt, no degrees of certainty"*?[29]

This last and very famous quotation will have made us understand: it is that singular powerlessness of the living consciousness with regard to itself that Freud never ceased to *represent* under the name of "the unconscious," wanting at any price to see it as an alterity ob-posable to consciousness. This is the last attempt of representational thought to control what escapes it, and what can indeed do nothing but escape it: itself, its own irrepresentable life. That there is an "unconscious" can thus be said only from the point of view of consciousness "in the sense of representation" (*GP*, p. 365). But, as Henry ends by saying bluntly, "the unconscious does not exist" (*GP*, p. 384). Freud's unconscious was only a "name" (*GP*, p. 348) for what cannot be named, for what I can only feel without ever saying it: the life, absolutely mine, that I never cease to experience, the "affect . . . *which is never unconscious*." The unconscious, in the end, was nothing *other* than my consciousness *itself*.

Before such an enormous, demented affirmation, psychoanalysts could easily diagnose a particularly flagrant form of resistance to psychoanalysis. And, in fact, could we possibly imagine a more massive "defense" than that complete dissolution of the unconscious in consciousness, a more narcissistic "*méconnaissance*" than that determination to preserve the ego from any wound, any alterity?

Nevertheless, psychoanalysts would be wrong to hold to this position,[30] first of all because they would then have to incriminate Freud himself, for it is not Henry but Freud who returned the unconscious to consciousness. That the "unconscious" is finally nothing other than "consciousness" itself is indeed what Freud affirms very clearly in the beginning of *The Ego and the Id*, in a very troubling proximity to the theses of Michel Henry. The opposition of the conscious ego and the repressed unconscious, Freud recognized, cannot furnish the last word on neurosis (nor on the *psuchê* in general), since the "resistance" that the first opposes to the second is itself unconscious: the neurotic has no knowledge, no con-science of his own repression. Thus it is necessary to admit, Freud continued (preparing the turning point of the "second topography," that the ego) that "this ego [to which] consciousness is attached"[31] is itself unconscious, unconscious of itself: "A part of the ego, too—and Heaven knows how important a part—may be *Ucs.*, undoubtedly is *Ucs.*"[32] This, it is true, in no way signifies that the unconscious must from then on be reabsorbed in consciousness, as Henry would certainly be tempted to think, but rather that the unconscious invades consciousness itself; indeed, here everything depends on that infinitesimal and yet decisive difference of accent between a *conscious* unconscious and an *unconsciousness* of consciousness. Nonetheless, by bringing his attention to the unconsciousness of repression itself (this is the whole sense of the famous "analysis of the ego"), Freud made the opposition between the unconscious and consciousness (between the repressor and the repressed) very problematic. This at the same time prevents us from taking too lightly the affirmation of their identity by Henry, for how can we continue to speak of a resistance *to* the unconscious if it is, rather, the resistance of the ego (in this case, the superego) that resists its own becoming conscious?

This is not the end of it, however, for it would all risk remaining at the state of irritating paradox were we not to become aware that this unconscious consciousness or unconsciousness of resistance is that of affect. It is affect *as affect* that "resists" analysis, understood as insight or coming-to-consciousness (*prise de conscience*) of repressed representations, as remembering of forgotten "memories," and so forth. Indeed, it must be recalled that when Freud spoke, in the 1920's, of "resistance," he was thinking primarily of that eminently affective manifestation, "transferential resistance." It is that resistance, recognized since 1912 as the "strongest of the resistances" opposed to the treatment,[33] which he refers to when he evokes, in chapter 3 of *Beyond the Pleasure Principle*, the transformation of the "art of interpretation" that analysis was initially into the strange confrontation of force and affect that is the "working through" of the transference. Nor is it sufficient, in order to "make the unconscious conscious," to "discover the unconscious material that was concealed from the patient . . . and, at the right moment, [to] communicate it to him," nor even to encourage the lifting of resistances by "inducing him by human influence—this was where suggestion operating as 'transference' played its part." This more or less persuasive maieutics remains without effect, for the patient not only does not want to, but most especially cannot remember the whole of what is repressed in him, and what he cannot remember may be precisely the essential part of it. . . . He is obliged to *repeat* the repressed material as a contemporary experience instead of, as the physician would prefer to see, *remembering* it as something belonging to the past. These reproductions, which emerge with such unwished-for exactitude . . . are invariably acted out in the sphere of the transference, of the patient's relation to the physician.[34]

Indeed, it is all too often forgotten that "repetition," before losing itself in the labyrinth of metapsycho-biological speculation of *Beyond the Pleasure Principle*, first and above all names, for Freud, the transferential repetition in its remarkable resistance to analytical treatment. The patient, in his relation to the analyst, relives the never-ending scenario of his loves and hates, clinging obstinately to his illness and suffering. But he does this *without hiding anything*, and this is the "unforeseen situation" that motivated the "turning point" of the 1920's: the patient "resists" the treatment all the more tenaciously insofar as he literally opposes no resistance to the "repressed unconscious." The latter, far from being dissimulated, is exhibited without the shadow of a reservation, (re)produced *in statu nascendi*,[35] and repeated with "fidelity," so that Freud ends by admitting, always according to the same paradox, that it is the unconscious that resists its own unveiling, and that it resists as *"consciousness," as "ego."*

Now, all of this, rather mysterious in Freud's texts, is cleared up if we remember that the "resistance" of transferential repetition rests uniquely *in affects*. Freud says it well (and it must be recalled with force, since the reduction of the phenomenon to nothing but words has become so current in French psychoanalysis). The transference is an "intense emotional relationship" (*eine intensive Gefühlsbeziehung*)[36]: the patient "loves" the analyst with an excessive and devouring love that regularly reverses itself into hate; he feels obscurely guilty with regard to the analyst; he suffers anxiety about him; he suffers and enjoys the suffering. And so he "resists," Freud then says, since he refuses to remember the real cause of these affects and does not want to know anything of the representation— "traumatic memory," "phantasm," Oedipal "*imago*"—to which the affects belong. Here we clearly see that it is from the point of view of representation, *and only from that point of view*, that the transferential affect can be said to "resist." It is because Freud stubbornly continues to think that affect hides *representations*, because he thinks of it only as "tied" or "attached" to representations, that he wants to see it as an obstacle to the becoming conscious of the "repressed," that is, as a "not-wanting-to-*know*" the unconscious. But in reality affect does not resist anything, especially not itself, which is why Freud feels the need to emphasize that it is always conscious, always perceived by the patient as "something real and contemporary."[37] Indeed, its profound passivity (its "compulsion to repeat") is such that it can never differ or take the slightest distance from itself. Thus it is forced to perceive itself "as a contemporary experience." And so we must ask ourselves, in the end, if that "resistance" of the affect is not much more passive than active.

After all, can it still be said that the patient, in feeling this or that affect, does not *want* to know anything about the representations that haunt him? Rather, should it not be admitted that he *cannot* know anything, at least in the sense of representation? And isn't this the key to that singular "resistance" to analysis? In *Being and Nothingness*, Sartre had already emphasized this difficulty, and Henry recalls it in relation to Schopenhauer's theory of repression (*GP*, p. 230): *wanting* not to know, the subject must at least know what he does not want, think of those representations that he does not want to think—so how can we understand his not knowing anything of his own action? Thus it is undoubtedly elsewhere, in the involuntary and irrepresentable "acting"[38] of the affect, that we must go to find the solution.

Indeed, it turns out that affect, as Freud says elsewhere of the "dream work," does not think. It is *acted*, according to an efficiency that has absolutely nothing to do with a will deliberating before moving and thus knowing what it wants. Freud insists very much on this; the affect of transference is an *Agieren* of the drive, an "acting" of the repressed, and this means, before anything else, that it short circuits representation. The patient "acts" his passion (or experiences his action) before thinking about it, without thinking about it:

The patient does not *remember* anything of what he has forgotten and repressed, but *acts* it out [*Agieren*]. . . . The greater the resistance, the more extensively will acting out (repetition) replace remembering.[39]

However, if things proceed in this way, it is because the drives, in the transferential affect, are immediately effected, without the mediation of representation. It is this contemporaneity, this immediacy exclusive of any delay, that Freud had primarily in mind when he spoke of *Agieren*, much more than the putting into action as "acting-out," which is, everything considered, nothing other than its conse-quence, itself immediate. If, here, the gesture so often accompanies words, it is primarily because the affect, as such, exists only as ac-complished, according to a "wish fulfilment" that knows no delay (no difference, no separation) between the so-called "wish" and its execution.

That the affect is "acted" in the transference is thus to be under-stood in the sense of being felt and experienced in the present, with-out detours, that is to say, without the mediation of any representa-tion. "I love you, I hate you," says the patient, not "I love you, I hate you because you make me *think* of so and so." The affect does not think before acting. It is, indissociably, thinking *and* acting, acted thought, thought *in actu*, a thought that is all the more active as it is more passive: pure passion-of-the-present that never has the time to think, to which is never accorded the time for *reflection*.

This is but another way of saying, one more time, that the affect (i.e., the acting, the repeating, the transference) knows no delay, no time, "no negation, no doubt, no degrees of certainty." All the "peculiar properties of the unconscious" described by Freud are emi-nently suitable to affect, which is thus like the very experience of the unconscious—and its completely conscious experience. Affect is the peculiar *cogito* of the unconsciousness; affect is the peculiar uncon-scious of the *cogito*. Thus we must conclude that it is the unconscious itself, in the hyperconscious passion of the transference, that resists the analysis. This is what Freud ended by saying in the astonishing final paragraph of "The Dynamics of Transference":

> In the process of seeking out the libido which has escaped from the patient's conscious, we have penetrated into the realm of the unconscious. . . . *The un-conscious impulses do not want to be remembered in the way the treatment desires them to be* [emphasis added], but endeavour to reproduce themselves in accordance with the timelessness [*Zeitlosigkeit*] of the unconscious and its capacity for hallucinations. Just as happens in dreams, the patient regards the products of the awakening of his unconscious impulses as contemporaneous [*Gegen-wärtigkeit*] and real; he seeks to put his passions into action [*seine Leidenschaften agieren*] without taking any account of the real situation.[40]

All this, needless to say, confirms Henry's analyses, and now we can better see the extent to which they are in accordance with certain of psychoanalysis's most fundamental aporias. After all, if "the unconscious impulses do not want to be remembered in the way the treatment desires them to be," it is really because the unconscious, in the profound passivity of its acting, does not *want* to enter into the Freudian *concept* of "the unconscious"—because, finally, the unconscious itself has nothing to do with memories or fantasies susceptible of being recalled *to* consciousness or represented *before* it. That the famous "unconscious resistance" is here nothing other than the extremely open and very conscious resistance of the unconscious itself proves this enough: it is the very opposition of consciousness and the unconscious (of the visible and the hidden, the manifest and the latent) that no longer functions. Simply that. Thus, if we want to understand anything of what Freud called "the unconscious," we should agree to abandon that opposition. The unconscious does not oppose itself to consciousness, any more than consciousness opposes itself to the unconscious. They are, the one like the other, prior to that opposition, which is representational ob-position as such, and they resist it tenaciously, obstinately. What Freud, under the name of the transference and repetition, desperately struggled to think of as a resistance of consciousness to the unconscious was nothing other than their common resistance to that very ob-position, to the becoming-conscious in the sense of being-represented: it was, as Henry aptly puts it, the profound oblivion of affect, in its insurmountable opposition to opposition, to representation, to remembering, to "ek-static temporality" in general.

Hence psychoanalysts would be wrong to reproach Henry for limiting himself to an analysis of consciousness. The quasi-somnambular sureness with which he rejoins certain of the most problematic propositions of the late Freud attests to this sufficiently: this blind consciousness of affect is none other than the unconscious in its enigma thus *revived*, and it is really here that, to be truly fruitful, the dialogue with Henry should begin. Fundamentally, just as psychoanalysts would be out of place in neglecting the enormous problem he raises (it is *their* problem, the properly vital problem of a psychoanalysis become bloodless for having confined itself to the powers of representation, of language and the signifier), so they would be correct in questioning him when he claims to have solved it—when he dissolves and, so to speak, "sublates" the enigmatic alterity of the unconscious into pure and simple self-consciousness.

Indeed, it is one thing to say that the unconscious is the irrepresentability of consciousness as such, the irrepressible passivity of its
affect; it is quite another to affirm that this passion is simply the consequence of the *auto*affection of life by itself, in short, the "effect"
of an activity or spontaneity more buried (and thus more subjectal)
than those of will or desire "in the sense of representation." Why
not admit it? That conclusion is a great deception, for how can we
not be struck here by the ambiguity of Henry's gesture, which is
constantly occupied with transgressing the *subject*-of-representation
toward its irrepresentable and more fundamental subject? And is it
not, the psychoanalysts might legitimately retort, precisely this so-
called subject of affect (this "self," this "ipseity") that disappears in
the privileged experience of the transference?

In fact, can it still be said that the patient, in the context of his
relation to the analyst, experiences *himself*, feels *himself*, is passive in
regard to his *own* actions? That he experiences his passion (at least
more often than not) is quite certain. That he experiences himself
in it is already much less certain, as indicated by the profoundly
constraining (*zwanghaftig*) character of the transferential passion. The
patient is *subjected* to these contradictory feelings without at any moment being able to control them, and to the point of very literally
fainting away in the somnambulant execution of the "acting-out":
"Was it me that did that? I was not myself. . . ." Isn't it most remarkable, consequently, that the patient forgets himself in the transference, that he experiences his passion beyond "himself"?

Besides, it is not just a matter of the patient, experiencing this or
that affect, not *knowing* why he experiences it with that ravaging intensity that pushes him into the analyst's arms or, contrarily, inhibits
him to the point of being mute. At the extreme, he does not even
feel the passion. Indeed, it must be remarked that Freud's insistence
on affirming the always conscious character of the affect is equaled
only by his very significant obstinacy in speaking, nonetheless, of
"unconscious feelings." Here I will only quote a single passage from
The Ego and the Id about the feeling of unconscious guilt that drives
the patient to become ill:

But as far as the patient is concerned this sense of guilt is dumb; it does not
tell him he is guilty; he does not feel guilty, he feels ill. This sense of guilt
expresses itself only as a resistance to recovery which it is extremely difficult
to overcome.[41]

This example shows it sufficiently: there is here, in the subject (in the affect), something that goes beyond the subject (that goes beyond his autoaffection). The affect is not experienced by the subject—it is not experienced by anyone—and yet it acts, it exercises its cruel effects. Whether we like it or not, there is, in the passion of the transference, truly something more and other than "self-suffering" in Henry's sense. The patient suffers his passion, and he suffers it "beyond the pleasure principle," beyond all enjoyment of self, to the point of no longer being able to bear himself (*se souffrir*). "Atrocious face of the death drive," writes Henry in this regard (*GP*, p. 384), in which he thinks Freud misunderstood the "feeling of Self" (*GP*, p. 379) where "the unsupportable is not separable from extreme joy" (*GP*, p. 384). To this Freud responded in advance, speaking of the "demonic" character of the compulsion to repeat:

> The subject appears to have a passive experience, over which he has no influence, but in which he meets with a repetition of the same fatality.[42]

Indeed, would Freud have said anything at all had he not cited precisely that—the radical non-self-presence of the subject, the "demonic" alteration of his consciousness, his visitation by the all-other—had he not said the unconscious, consequently, the unconscious, nonetheless?

For those who are decidedly loath to hold this "nonetheless" to be nothing, the task is clear: we must now ask ourselves what the singular alterity is that haunts the affect, who the demon is that possesses the transference. That it is not a question of any "other" in the world (of any personage in the empirical history of the subject, of any representation deposited in some unconscious memory) should, from the very first, be accorded to Michel Henry. And we can grant him this all the more willingly in that it is, in the end, the psychoanalyst's most quotidian experience. Inevitable in the cure and perceived by the patient as reality itself, the affect of the transference has about it, nonetheless, nothing "real" in the usual sense of the word, since it does not address itself to the analyst's empirical person. Such is, as is well known, the paradox of the transference: the more the analyst hides himself as a real other, the more intense becomes the affect dedicated to him by the patient. Provoked by no one in the world, this affect can thus be called "spontaneous" in its very passivity—which, to remain within a pure phenomenological description of what is experienced in the "parenthesis" of the cure, admittedly moves in the direction of the thesis of a transcendental autoaffection.

Nonetheless—and this changes everything—this parenthesis of the transference does not close itself upon a self, since this time it includes the stranger (the "demon," the "evil Genius"). The transference takes place *only* in a certain rapport with the other, in which it undoubtedly only reawakens a trait that is essential to affect in general. Null, perhaps, the very absent presence of the analyst is indispensable to the birth of the affect, as if there were never affection except by the other, and by an other all the more other in that he is no one. Such is thus the redoubled paradox of the transference: the affect, provoked by no one, is nonetheless *affected* by no one, and so all the more intimately and essentially passionate in that it is more spontaneous, more "transcendental."

This rapport without rapport with another, this nontranscendent transcendence of the other in affect—what can we name it, then? Perhaps "rapport" (*Rapport*), as Freud did in speaking of the transference, reviving a word used by the old magnetizers to designate the enchanted relation of hypnosis:

We can easily recognize it [the "intense emotional relationship" of the transference] as the same dynamic factor that the hypnotists have named "suggestibility," which is the agent of hypnotic *rapport* [*des hypnotischen Rapports*].[43]

Indeed, how not recognize, in the paradox of transference, the very paradox of hypnotism: that of a receptivity (a suggestibility, an affectability) all the more total with regard to another in that it is perfectly spontaneous; that of a rapport with the other all the more massive in that it is perfectly somnambulant, forgetting of the other as other? The patient "under transference," it is well known, starts by submitting to (even if it be in order to reject with rage) the "influence" of the analyst; he gives credence to (or withholds it from) the analyst's interpretations and constructions, submits himself to (or rejects) his injunctions—but all this absolutely freely and, at the hypnotic limit of the transference, without even knowing it. And, to finish, it is when the other, in the extreme manifestations of the transference, is no longer there (when the analyst is no longer anyone) that it exerts its most obsessional, most "demonic" influence: uncontrollable anxiety, guilt to the point of suicide, hate to the point of murder, suffering that incarnates itself in the symptom. Just as the person under hypnosis executes his posthypnotic "mission" without remembering that it has been suggested to him by the physician, so the patient under transference acts and repeats all the more blindly his affection for the other *when he no longer represents that other to himself.* Now, isn't it this nonrepresentational rapport with another, this spontaneity that is all the more receptive when it does not represent what it receives, that, in 1889, Freud called "suggestion," defining the latter as "a conscious idea, which has been introduced into the brain of the hypnotized person by an external influence and has been accepted by him as though it had arisen spontaneously"?[44]

It is at this point, the "point of otherness"[45] between auto- and heteroaffection, that everything is decided—above all, the status of what is called "the unconscious." Now admittedly, since the transferential rapport is spontaneous, we can insist on the first-person experience of the patient, what Henry would call the irreducible "ipseity" of his affect. But in this case we would definitively prohibit ourselves from taking into account the transferential *rapport* as such (as well as its undeniably transformative character: whether we like it or not, the patient does not remain the *same* from the beginning to the "end" of the analytic process). We could also, as Freud did, think that the transference onto the analyst repeats an affective rapport with a "third person" (*dritte Person*),[46] that is, to this or that "other" from the individual history of the subject. But then we would remain prisoners of "ekstatic" thought, in Henry's sense of the word: first, because we would understand affect in general as the effect of an exterior cause (this or that "object" or "personage" from the Oedipal scenario having provoked this or that libidinal "cathexis" or aggressive "impulse"); and second, because we would be making the transferential affect into a (secondary, deplaced, false) re-presentation of a previously experienced affect, instead of considering it in the uncontrollable immanence of its "here and now."

Does this mean that we would be condemned to choosing between the thesis of autoaffection and that of heteroaffection—between the "same" and the "other," "ipseity" and "rapport"? That is not at all sure, and undoubtedly it is Freud, once again, who can help us understand why, although not because he ever questioned his official theory of the transference as repetition of "emotional relations which had their origins in [the] earliest object-attachments during the repressed period of . . . childhood." [47] But this in no way prevented him from speculating elsewhere on the "prehistory" of the Oedipus complex, whether under the title of "primal narcissism," of the archi-incorporation of the primal Father, or again of the "original emotional tie" of identification. All these so difficult themes of the "doctrine of drives" correspond, as we know, to the necessity of legitimizing "affective relations" that are irreducible to the "object cathexis" of the anaclitic-Oedipal type (and thus also to the official theory of the transference): the libidinal "egoism" of falling in love (*Verliebtheit*), homosexual or paranoiac "narcissism," the "affective ambivalence" of the oral incorporation and / or primal identification.

Now, these themes, which so radically upset Freud's earlier hypotheses, not only confronted him with rapports with another that are more "archaic" than object-love; narcissism, incorporation, identification also confronted him with the properly immemorial "prehistory" of the ego because they escape from representational ob-position and ob-jectality as such. Whence also the considerable difficulty Freud encountered in integrating these "emotional ties" in his first theory of the drives: along with the "object" of desire or of the drive, it was the very possibility of a *representation* of the affect that disappeared, for how can one represent (to oneself) if not in a completely *exterior* fashion, a state such as primal narcissism where "the ego had not yet marked itself off sharply from the external world and from other people," [48] and thus where only the unlimited indifference of the "oceanic feeling" exists? In the same way, how can one represent (to oneself) this "ego" of the oral relation which *is* the "object" that he incorporates, or again, this "ego" of the primal identification which *is* the "model" that he incarnates? Try to imagine this, which forms the ultimate and bizarre Freudian *cogito*: "I am the breast." [49] You would simply see nothing: no *Objekt*, no *Vorbild*, no *imago*—not even a mirror or a Double. In reality, such an "I" cannot grasp itself or conceive of itself because of the lack of that elementary distance from self and / or world that would permit it to pose itself in front of itself, to reflect itself, to take itself as theme or object, in short, to become self-conscious. And thus this "I" is also not the *ego* of a *cogito*, at least not if this is understood as an "I think myself" or an "I represent myself," but rather (try to imagine this, which is unimaginable) a Narcissus without a mirror, who would instantly drown himself in the water of his reflection and who would thus never manage to think himself, to want or desire himself.

Can we then say that this irrepresentable ego of narcissism, this consciousness without an object (who has no rapport with anything and who is thus, in all rigorousness, neither a consciousness nor the unconscious) is the "self" of the affect, in its blind and yet living immanence, as Henry would probably have it? In a certain manner, yes, but in an other manner, not at all—and, in the end, everything turns on that *other* manner of thinking the *same* thing, which is here the sameness or identity of the ego itself, for what is the "ego" or the "self" of narcissism? Or, to put it even better, *who* is the Narcissus who feels and experiences himself as soon as he is himself, without ever being able to separate himself from himself? Is he the same as himself, or is he not, in his very identity, an "other"—for example, the "father of personal prehistory" (spoken of in *The Ego and the Id*) with whom he identified himself before representing him to himself, before being an ego, "in order" to be an ego, or again, that breast, which is certainly no object, but which nonetheless makes up all its irrepresentable substance of subject?

Whatever may have been his fascination with regard to narcissistic self-sufficiency (and it is blatant in a text like "On Narcissism: An Introduction"), Freud never believed that the ego can be by itself, can be absolutely and thoroughly it*self,* for he knew, with a perfectly *naive* knowledge (in all senses of the word, and first of all the Husserlian sense), that the ego *is born*: here or there, by chance and by destiny, without being at its own foundation. He knew, in other words, that life is not absolute and that the coming to being is not the "coming to itself" of a *subject,* however invisible and irrepresentable it might be. To live (to be a "self") always presupposes a coming into oneself from something other than self, a begetting and a genealogy. And it is thus always a beginning to live, starting from an immemorial beginning that is not the Beginning spoken of by Henry, that is not the orphan innateness of an *ego* that always starts from itself. Such a Beginning, Freud said quite abruptly, with regard to the self-sufficiency of the young infant, is a "fiction":

It will rightly be objected that an organization which was a slave to the pleasure-principle and neglected the reality of the external world could not maintain itself alive for the shortest time, so that it could not have come into existence at all. The employment of a fiction like this is, however, justified when one considers that the infant—provided one includes with it the care it receives from its mother—does almost realize a psychical system of this kind.[50]

The *autos* is a fiction—admittedly ineradicable, inevitable, but a fiction just the same. Undoubtedly the ego must, in principle, remain ignorant of its birth (ignorant of the other who gave it birth, of the past that always-already preceded it, and also of the impossible future that is its own death). Nor can it avoid feeling itself as soon as it is itself, from its absolute Beginning of absolute Ego and Narcissus. But it is nevertheless *starting from* an other beginning, and all the more other in that it is its ownmost beginning—its own *being*, the maternal "womb" or "breast" that it itself *is*, without in any way being able to represent them. The ego has no rapport with itself other than starting from the rapport (the ombilic) that is a rapport with no one—no one other than itself.

Such would then be Freud's strange *cogito*, and this explains why he finally attempted to think of ipseity *as* rapport and of the ego *as* other: as the "original emotional tie" of identification, for example. Indeed, it is remarkable that Freud, without in any way abandoning the theory of narcissism, always more obstinately formulated it in terms of affective "relations" and "ties," as if to make understood (obscurely, with difficulty) the inherent *rapport* of narcissistic *auto*affection. Rapport with what, we might ask? With nothing, with no one, with no object, and yet rapport *nonetheless*, despite the absoluteness, without limits or exterior, of the narcissistic ego. Hence if the narcissistic ego has no rapport with anything, it is not because it has a rapport only with itself, because it only affects itself with itself. Freud says it well (even if he says it obscurely and with difficulty): it is because its only rapport with "objects" and with "others" is narcissistic, *because it itself is (that with which it has) the rapport*. And such a rapport can, from this very fact, be nothing other than a non-rapport or a rapport with nothing, which Freud then calls "affective ambivalence" in relation to the identification tie:

Identification . . . is ambivalent from the very first; it can turn into an expression of tenderness as easily as into a wish for someone's removal. It behaves like a derivative of the first, *oral* phase of the organization of the libido, in which the object that we long for and prize is assimilated by eating and is in that way annihilated as such.[51]

"As such"—that is, as object. Such an ambivalence of the affect, as we can see, is not a double rapport with an "object," any more than it is the indissolubly enjoying and suffering passion of the rapport with self, as Henry would undoubtedly prefer. It is, rather, a rapport with a non-object (with an "annihilated" object), non-rapport with self, and, to say it all, affection by nothing.

But it is an affection nonetheless, and that is what "I" am, in the most irreducible and singular feeling of "myself": in the initial beginning, Michel Henry would say, that "expels nothingness and takes its place" (*GP*, p. 18); in what Freud, for his part, called my "character" (i.e., the sum of my identifications)[52]; in the "demonic" repetition of my amorous adventures and my "transferences"; in the triumphant and murderous affect of my maniacal joys or in my inexpiable "super-egoic" guilt; in that unexplainable hate for myself; and, finally, in anxiety. Anxiety of what? Of my birth—that is, of nothing, of the nothing that is nonetheless not nothing, since it is my very being, the "emotional tie" that relates me to all those "others" with whom I identify myself unknowingly, whose place I take without ever representing them to myself, and whom I banish into nothingness without ever posing them before myself, without ever knowing or recognizing myself in them. "I am the breast," "I am my mother," "I am the father himself."[53] Where? Nowhere in the world, obviously, nowhere in that world of mirrors where I never cease to bang about in rage. But neither *in me*, in *my* rage, *my* pain, *my* joy.

In an other place then? A place that is no place, no other, and no me? Yes, perhaps. In what is always unknown—in the unconscious, nonetheless.

Translated by Douglas Brick

☞ *The Alibis*
of the Subject

Does psychoanalysis have anything to do with philosophy? As is well known, Freud answered this question with a serene "no!" In *The Ego and the Id*, he says that philosophers are simply incapable of understanding the idea of a psychical unconscious; and he continues:

Here we have the first shibboleth of psycho-analysis. To most people who have been educated in philosophy the idea of anything psychical which is not also conscious is so inconceivable that it seems to them absurd and refutable simply by logic. I believe this is only because they have never studied the relevant phenomena of hypnosis and dreams, which . . . necessitate this view. Their psychology of consciousness is incapable of solving the problems of dreams and hypnosis."[1]

It would be easy to demonstrate the naïveté and even ignorance of this declaration of independence, and there has been no lack of professional philosophers to do so. If, however, the philosopher wants to consider the uncanny character of psychoanalysis, and not simply reduce it to the history of philosophy's "well-known facts," he must constantly keep Freud's declaration in mind. What, in fact, does Freud tell us? First of all, he says that the unconscious will always remain foreign and allergic to every philosophy that makes the psyche identical to being conscious. It may be said that this incriminates merely the philosophy of consciousness, which is not all of philosophy. But we would have to admit that, in fact, this is the dominant trait of Modern philosophy, from Descartes to Husserl (and beyond): the total assimilation of being into being-represented, by and for a subject, by and for a *con-scientia*, which assures itself of itself by posing itself "before" itself, in the fashion of *Vor-stellung*. For such a philosophy, psychoanalysis represents a real scandal or, at best, a terrible embarrassment: in dreams, in symptoms, in the transference, something "happens," something manifests itself, but without my representing it. "I" do not accompany all my representations, not because I cannot grasp myself in them (this is Lacan's interpretation, which we will examine in a minute), but because what happens to me does not happen in the mode of representation, does not take place in its space. In what space, then? In an "other scene," one that has precisely nothing to do with representation, one whose uncanny characteristics Freud spells out for us—absence of delay and reflection, ignorance of negation and time, carelessness about contradiction and communication, lack of doubt, absolute "egoism" (that is, pre-egoism), and, finally, lack of knowledge of spatiality: "Psyche is extended; knows nothing about it."[2]

Here Freud produces two "witnesses" for the unlocalizable "place" of the unconscious, neither of which is acceptable in the high courts of consciousness and philosophy. The first witness is the dream, and the second, hypnosis. This second witness, however, is uncanny not only for philosophers but for Freud's readers as well, for we can understand why Freud calls on hypnosis in this context: where could he find a better illustration or "proof" of what he calls the unconscious than in the hypnotic trance, that unquestionably psychical behavior which is nevertheless completely removed from the reflexivity proper to representative consciousness? (Just try to imagine, for example, a somnambulist's *cogito*.) But we also know that, in 1921, Freud himself totally rejected the practice of hypnosis, preferring the method of free association and conscious recall of repressed-unconscious representations, just as we know that, two years earlier, in *Group Psychology and the Analysis of the Ego*, he had been forced to admit that hypnosis defied all "rational explanation," even psychoanalytic ones.[3] In reality, by invoking hypnosis against the philosophy of consciousness, Freud calls up a phenomenon that escapes from his own theory of the unconscious. And it could be argued that the inability of psychoanalysis to establish a theory of hypnosis comes from its clandestine roots in the philosophical problematic of the subject, especially from its propensity for describing the unconscious in terms of "unconscious *thoughts*," "repressed *representations*," or "*Vorstellungsrepräsentanten des Triebes*." How, then, can it hope to account for so-called unconscious phenomena—those of hypnosis, in this case—if it retains the major concept of the philosophy of consciousness? The concept of "unconscious representation" is inconsistent not only from a philosophical point of view but also from that of psychoanalysis, at least if psychoanalysis wants to understand why this so-called representation acts without being represented.

Perhaps these few remarks have managed to convey the uncanniness of Freud's statement, and by the same token the uncanniness of psychoanalysis for philosophy, for it remains true that Freud *does* oppose psychoanalysis to philosophy, and that he found no better way to do so than by calling on a phenomenon that remains estranged not only from philosophy but from psychoanalysis itself. Could Freud have been trying to tell us that psychoanalysis is not really "itself" or "at home" except when estranged from itself? Such, then, would be its *Unheimlichkeit* for the philosopher, even for that (perhaps perennial) "philosopher" who is the psychoanalyst himself: namely, that discourse on the unconscious speaks only in knowing that it can know nothing of what it speaks—and this, this *Unbewusst*, is what makes it speak.

If we now turn to that self-proclaimed Freudian heir Jacques Lacan, we are confronted by a totally different discursive stance. Obviously, Lacan does not have the same reservations about philosophy as his predecessor, even though he regularly insists on the different status of psychoanalytic and philosophic discourse. Even the most cursory reading of the *Ecrits* suffices: it would be extremely difficult to avoid terms like "dialectic," "truth," "being," "intersubjectivity," "desire," or "subject"—all obviously philosophical. This immediately raises the question of the status of these "philosophemes" in Lacan's text. Are they simply "didactic" or "propaedeutic" references, as Lacan himself said in relation to Hegel and Heidegger (*Ecrits: A Selection*, p. 293; *Four Fundamental Concepts*, p. 18)?[4] Or are they really reformulations of the "fundamental concepts" of psychoanalysis in terms of a particular philosophy—and, in that case, which philosophy? Hegel's? Heidegger's? Or, as has been recently suggested, Kojève's or Sartre's?[5]

Lacan, however, generally refuses these filiations, preferring Descartes's patronage: "Freud's method is Cartesian—in the sense that he sets out from the basis of the subject of certainty" (*Four Fundamental Concepts*, p. 36). This statement is obviously a far cry from Freud's, in *The Ego and the Id*, concerning the difference between philosophy and psychoanalysis. Indeed, doesn't this statement simply equate the Freudian unconscious and the subject of the *cogito*, which Freud implicitly incriminated in speaking of "philosophy" and "psychology of consciousness"? Lacan, of course, would object that his "subject" is split, barred, and divided by the signifier, and therefore not the subject of the *cogito*—the subject that consciously assures itself of itself in its representations—but this same subject separating itself from itself in the very act of self-representation and disappearing into the gap between the *cogito*'s enunciation and its statement, "I think where I am not, therefore I am where I do not think" (*Ecrits: A Selection*, p. 166). Elsewhere he writes:

Of course, every representation requires a subject, but this subject is never a pure subject. . . . There is no subject without, somewhere, *aphanisis* of the subject. (*Four Fundamental Concepts*, p. 221)

This divided subject, nonetheless, divides itself only because it represents itself; therefore it is nothing but the Cartesian subject. In other words, the "subject of the unconscious" *is nothing but the subject of consciousness* severed from the moment of self-presence. Indeed, Lacan constantly denounces every conception of the unconscious that tries to make it "other" than representative. As early as his 1946 "Remarks on Psychical Causality," he bluntly proposes replacing the word "unconscious" with "imaginary mode":

For I hope that people will soon stop using the word "unconscious" for what takes place in consciousness. (*Ecrits*, p. 183)

He then restates this theme most explicitly and dogmatically in "Position of the Unconscious":

The unconscious *is not* a species that defines a circle in psychical reality of what does not have the attribute of consciousness. (ibid., p. 830)

In reality, the Lacanian unconscious is never anything but the unconscious of representative consciousness itself, and it obviously does not take long to discover this as a sort of radicalization of that old aporia confronted differently by Leibniz, Kant, Fichte, Husserl, and the Sartre of *The Transcendence of the Ego*: If transcendental consciousness is what it is (i.e., self-consciousness) only in being conscious of an object ("consciousness of . . ."), then that consciousness cannot be conscious of itself, since it can grasp itself only reflexively, by representing itself "before" itself as an object, a phenomenon, a transcendent ego, and so forth;[6] or, indeed, as a signifier, a *Vorstellungsrepräsentant*.

On this account, it could be said that the Lacanian unconscious is *the unconscious of philosophy*—the unconscious that the philosophy of consciousness presupposes while remaining ignorant of it—but also the unconscious *of* that same philosophy, *its* unconscious, for, once again, that "unconscious" cares very little about the affirmation made by psychoanalysis of a scene other than intentional, representative, cogitating consciousness. This is another case, Freud would say, of the philosopher's eternal inability to admit that the psychical cannot be reduced to consciousness. Another sign (or symptom) of this could be seen in Lacan's obstinate refusal to have anything to do with hypnosis, on either the theoretical or the practical level. At this point, the difference between Freud's and Lacan's discursive stance becomes glaringly obvious: whereas Freud, despite all his ambivalence toward hypnosis, never stopped referring to it as the very enigma of the unconscious, Lacan simply did not want to hear about it, going so far as to make it the diametric opposite of psychoanalysis, a sort of shibboleth in reverse, which then signs Lacan's membership in the tribe of philosophers.

This is the suspicion, at least, that I would like to back up with the support of three passages from three different periods of Lacan's thought. Not that I want to prove that I know more about hypnosis than Lacan; I willingly confess that I do not know any more about it than Lacan, Freud, or anybody else; and, as far as that goes, I do not even have much to say about it. But the respect for its *Unheimlichkeit* strikes me as an excellent test of our capacity to respect the more general *Unheimlichkeit* of what Freud, for want of a better word, called "the unconscious." Either we will acknowledge its irrepresentability, the fact that our consciousness cannot be contemporary or commensurable with it, or, under the pretext of vigilance, we will lock ourselves up in the fortress of the representable and speakable—and then we will be on the side of those whom Freud called "philosophers," in their fundamental inability to do justice to the unknown.

The first text that I intend to examine, "Beyond the Reality Principle" (1936), is a text from Lacan's youth, belonging to the period of theorization of "the mirror stage" and the imaginary-paranoiac constitution of the ego. There is, however, under the title "Phenomenological Description of the Psychoanalytic Experience," a brief passage on the function of language in the cure that to a large extent anticipates Lacan's future developments. "The given of that [psychoanalytic] experience," Lacan says, "is, first, language, that is, a sign" (*Ecrits*, p. 82), or, more precisely, a sign *addressed to someone* (i.e., what he will later call "speech"). At first, removed from the demands of everyday communication, the patient's discourse signifies nothing, refers to no reality:

But the psychoanalyst, in order not to detach the experience of language from the situation it implies, that of the interlocutor, touches on the simple fact that language, before signifying something, signifies for someone. By the sole fact that [the analyst] is present and listening, the man who speaks addresses himself to him; and because he imposes the condition of meaninglessness on his discourse, what that man *wants to say to him* [*veut lui dire*] remains. In fact, what he says may "make no sense," but what he says *to him* harbours a meaning. (ibid., pp. 82–83)

In other words, the psychoanalyst knows that meaning is not to be found in *what* language says (its statement) but in *the fact of saying it* (its utterance). And this meaning, which is constituted in interlocutive speech and nowhere else, this "signified = X," is the subject (as Lacan already calls it), insofar as the subject "wants to say" (*veut dire*) and *ex*-presses itself to another. Note that this trait remains constant in Lacan, beyond all the ulterior changes: the essence of language is not to represent reality or communicate a preexisting meaning but solely to represent a subject, a subject reduced to the pure fact of speaking and communicating with another (of making itself common). Language, in its essence of speech (or, in Lacan's later terminology, of the signifier), *is* the subject, and conversely, the subject *is* that speech (or signifier), which publicly manifests him and is his sole "place" or being-there. This explains why, for Lacan, analytic speech is not a matter of reality (of memory, for example, or of social adaptation) but solely of truth, in the sense of *certitude*. As he formulates in the overture to his *Seminar*,

What is at stake is the realization of the truth of the subject, like a dimension peculiar to it which must be detached in its distinctiveness in relation to the very notion of reality. (*Seminar of Lacan: Book I*, p. 21)

Need I elaborate? This "dimension" is merely that of the *cogito* reformulated in terms of speech: the same *epochê* of any realistic reference, leaving only a pure subjective representation; the same certitude, inherent in the fact of thinking or speaking. Indeed, it is impossible for me to say something, no matter how meaningless, unless "I am" at the very moment of my saying it (even if I am nothing but that utterance or *pronuntiatum*):

This proposition [*hoc pronuntiatum*], *I am, I exist*, is necessarily true whenever it is put forward by me or conceived in my mind.[7]

It might be said that Lacan makes much of the utterance of the *cogito* —something that Descartes "forgets" (*Four Fundamental Concepts*, p. 36). It might also be said that the analysis described in "Beyond the Reality Principle" is a dialogue that takes time, not a solitary and instantaneous monologue. But this difference is merely the result of Lacan's then current formulation of the *cogito* in Hegelian terms. If the subject must *speak* himself, and speak himself to another, it is because he can come to full self-consciousness only at the price of reflecting himself, of separating himself from himself in order to better (re)present himself "before" himself. The privilege accorded to speech and dialogue corresponds to the typically Hegelian demand for mediation: the subject manifests himself in his truth only by exteriorizing himself, alienating himself in a common language, and having himself recognized by someone else in the full light of a public space, an " 'I' that is 'We' and [a] 'We' that is 'I.' "[8] The *sum* presupposes an *existo*, an ek-sistence outside of oneself, which is the very condition of self-representation—in this case, of analytical autoenunciation. In turn, that ek-sistence, in order to take place, presupposes the opening of a space (the same space-time that, according to Freud, the unconscious is ignorant of).

This is confirmed in the rest of Lacan's text: the subject's auto-exteriorization in speech is made equivalent to the exteriorization of a specular *image*. At that time, as is well known, Lacan takes "image" to mean the principle of formation and identification of the "ego" (which he still does not clearly distinguish from the "subject"): the ego constitutes itself by identification with an image, whether its own or that of a specular alter ego. Because that image is seen spatially, the *ego*, from the very beginning, is an object for itself. This is the principle of its originary "alienation" (or "transcendence," as Sartre said at about the same time): the ego exists only as an image; it can represent itself (i.e., see itself) only at a distance from itself. It therefore misunderstands itself (*se méconnaît*) at the very moment it knows itself (*se connaît*). Self-representation, *precisely because it is a representation* (a *Vor-stellung*), is an absentation from self, an *alibi* of the subject. The subject is always elsewhere than where it is, because it can see and know itself only in an image of itself.

Lacan says that this alienating image is developed transferentially (but also like a photograph is developed), by projecting it onto that "pure mirror," the analyst (*Ecrits: A Selection*, p. 15). The patient speaks to the analyst, but he also speaks to him as an alter ego, as an ego-alibi. Speaking *of* his ego *to* his ego, he then progressively gains consciousness of the fact that the subject of the statement and the subject of the utterance (the locutee and the locutor) are identical. Please allow me to quote at some length here, for Lacan's extremely ambiguous formulation is very instructive. He writes that, in the patient's discourse,

> The analyst discovers the very *image* which, by means of his game, he has aroused from the subject, whose trace he recognized imprinted in his person [The analyst's person or the subject's? It is impossible to tell], that image . . . which, as he himself does for the patient, hid its features from his gaze [His or the subject's? Once again, a mystery]. . . . But the very image that the subject presents through his behavior, and which continually reproduces itself therein, *is unknown to him*, . . . while the analyst finally recognizes that image, the subject, by the debate he is pursuing, finally imposes the role of that image upon him. It is from this position that the analyst takes his power to act on the subject. Henceforth, the analyst acts in such a way that the subject becomes conscious of the unity of the *image* that refracts through him into different effects, depending on whether he enacts, incarnates, or acknowledges them. At this point, I will not describe how the analyst proceeds in his intervention. . . . I will simply say that as the subject pursues the experience and lived process through which the image is reconstituted, his behavior ceases to mime its suggestion; his memories take back their real density, and the analyst sees the end of his power, now rendered useless by the end of the symptoms and the accomplishment of the personality. (*Ecrits*, pp. 84–85)

The notable expression "to mime the suggestion of the image" obviously brings us back to hypnosis. Analytic speech consists of a "de-suggestion," a "de-hypnotization," or again, a "de-mimetization." As Lacan says, the patient "incarnates," "enacts," or "presents" the image with which he has identified himself, while remaining ignorant of it until the moment when, projecting it on that specular mirror, the analyst, he learns to recognize himself in it, to become conscious of himself in it by seeing himself at a distance from himself. The course of the analysis, which is conflated with that of dialogic speech, proceeds from a mimetic *Darstellung* to a specular *Vor-stellung*, from an unreflective identification to a reflective identification, from a miscognition (*méconnaissance*) of the other "in" oneself to a recognition of oneself in the other. This comes as somewhat of a surprise, since we thought we had understood that the *méconnaissance* inherent in the image came from its specular-alienating character. But now Lacan not only asks us to see the specularization of the image as the mainspring (the dialectical mainspring) of the subject's final dealienation, but seems to be imputing the initially "suggestive" or hypnotizing character of the image to a nonspecular identification as well. This also allows us to clear up the ambiguity in the last citation: the "trace" of the image "hides its features from [*the subject's*] gaze" because it is "imprinted in *his* person," and thus he is condemned to repeat it in ignorance and "mime its suggestion." How could he possibly be conscious of it, since he could not see it in front of himself—since he "himself" *was* it, prior to any self-representation?

The stakes in this passage are considerable; what is in question is the very nature of the unconscious, the unconscious as it presents (rather than represents) itself in the repetition and affect of the transference. Also at stake is the way in which we understand the constitution of what Lacan calls the "subject" (or the "ego"): Are we to understand it as constitution by image and self-representation, as Lacan usually affirms, or, as he suggests here, as an unrepresentational, hypnotic, and prespecular constitution, and thus as a-subjective, profoundly blind and dispossessing, since anterior to every possession of a *self*? This last suspicion seems to be confirmed if we turn to the article "Family Complexes," written two years later than "Beyond the Reality Principle," in 1938. Here again, we find the theme of suggestion, this time explicitly linked to the imaginary formation of the ego, as part of what Lacan at that time calls the "intrusion complex" (instead of the "mirror stage"):

As long as the image of the counterpart plays only its primary role, limited to the expressive function, it triggers similar emotions and postures in the subject. . . . But when he submits to that emotional or motive suggestion, the subject is not distinguished from the image itself. . . . The image only adds the temporary intrusion of a foreign tendency. Call it narcissistic intrusion: nonetheless, the unity that it introduces into the tendencies contributes to the formation of the ego. But before the ego affirms its identity, it becomes one with the formative, yet primordially alienating, image. (*Les Complexes familiaux*, p. 45)

We understand why Lacan speaks here of "suggestion," qualifying it as "emotional": The image is truly irresistible because the subject cannot distinguish himself from it by posing it before himself, and it is "affective" or affecting (as Freud also said of the identificatory *Gefühlsbindung*) [9] because it no longer pertains to representation. The image being an "intrusive" one (and, strictly speaking, this term is inadequate, since there is no ego before the intrusion), the image is not elsewhere (*alibi*) but here (*hic, da*), without the ego being able to separate itself from the image in order to be conscious of it. Therefore, it is no longer an *image* but a "role," an obsession. One might object that Lacan does continue to speak of "image," "form," and "alienation," and this appears to retain us in the realm of visual representation; but Lacan averted us to this problem earlier in the same article: The formative power of the image is itself pre-imaginary, in-formal. Behind the *imago* of the counterpart, which we have just been dealing with, lurks the maternal *imago*, whose character, as Lacan takes some pains to emphasize, is "affective," "proprioceptive," and nonimaginary: "At this point, I am not speaking, with Freud, of autoeroticism, since the ego is not yet constituted, nor of narcissism, since there is no ego-image" (ibid., pp. 29–30). But it is from this irrepresentable (because nonobjective) content of the maternal *imago* that the later *imagoes*, as Lacan emphasizes, take their "modeling" and "formative" power:

That imago is given, in its content, by the sensations proper to first infancy, but it *has no form* until they begin to mentally organize themselves. Since this stage is prior to the emergence of the form of the object, it appears that these contents cannot represent themselves in consciousness. But, as I already said, they reproduce themselves in the mental structures that *model* later psychical experiences. They are associatively re-evoked when these later experiences occur, but *they are inseparable from the objective contents that they in-form.* (ibid., p. 28; emphasis added)

There is not enough time to comment properly on this subtle blurring of the opposition between form and content (that is, of opposition, period). Suffice it to say that Lacan, from 1936 to 1939, is very close to founding the identificatory power of the image in a pre-specular and affective identification or "suggestion," which, as he explicitly states, escapes from representation and consciousness, and to which he implicitly refers the phenomena of suggestion and transference. Later, however, he simply abandons this hypothesis, leaving no explanation of the ego's constitution other than the imaginary-specular one. This abandonment, it seems to me, is in conformity with the dialectical model of the cure that we have seen sketched out in "Beyond the Reality Principle." If the objective of the cure is a *prise de conscience* of the subject's alienating image, it goes without saying that the cure cannot deal with anything but an *image* that can be explicated by dialogical speech. By definition, everything that escapes from representative ob-position escapes from the *prise de conscience*. The result is that there is no reason to be concerned with it in the cure, and, in fact, there is every reason to avoid it. Better still, one must say nothing of it, not even of its possibility, since it goes against the proclaimed objective. Exit the "emotional suggestion" of the image; enter the specular, specularizable, and dialecticable suggestion. The accent that the young Lacan puts on the ego's originary alienation, far from contradicting the philosophical model of consciousness inherited from Descartes and Hegel, fully reinstates it and, in fact, has no other reason than its preservation.

Does this situation change after the "turning" of the 1950's, under the auspices of speech and language, and the beginning of the well-known "return to Freud"? It would seem so, since the dialectical speech that, in 1936, Lacan expected to relieve symptoms and "complete the personality" is exactly the same speech that he then criticizes under the name of "empty speech," opposing it to "true" or "full speech." The "Rome Discourse," his manifesto of the new theory of analysis, begins with precisely that observation. Implicitly contradicting his previous position, Lacan proclaims that in order to de-alienate the subject, it is not sufficient to return his own image to him. On the contrary, that recognition in the mirror ends only in "his capture in an objectification—no less imaginary than before—of his static state or of his 'statue,' in a renewed status of his alienation" (*Ecrits: A Selection*, p. 43). This is the principle of " 'empty' speech, where the subject seems to be talking in vain about someone who, even if he were his spitting image, can never become one with the assumption of his desire" (ibid., p. 45). In empty speech, the subject recognizes his ego (that is, his object), but not his desire (that is, himself, as non-object).

Hence the *prise de conscience* (since that is what is at stake in recognition in the mirror) is no longer the objective of the cure. This is so true that the theme of "full speech" is introduced through the example of the first cathartic cures under hypnosis, in which, as Lacan justly emphasizes, the *prise de conscience* was completely lacking. In fact, how is it possible to assimilate the "putting into words" of the traumatic experience with conscious recollection, as Josef Breuer and Freud did, when "in the hypnotic state verbalization is dissociated from the *prise de conscience*" (ibid., p. 46)? In reality, Lacan continues, the subject has remembered nothing, no real event, not even an image:

> He has simply recounted the event. But I would say . . . that he has made it pass into the *verbe* or, more precisely, into the *epos* by which he brings back into present time the origins of his own person. And he does this in a language that allows his discourse to be understood by his contemporaries, and which furthermore presupposes their present discourse. Thus it happens that the recitation of the *epos* may include a discourse of earlier days in its own archaic, even foreign language, or may even pursue its course in the present tense with all the animation of the actor; but it is like an indirect discourse, isolated in quotation marks within the thread of the narration, and, if the discourse is played out, it is on a stage implying the presence not only of the chorus, but also of spectators.
>
> Hypnotic recollection is, no doubt, a reproduction of the past, but it is above all a spoken representation—and as such implies all sorts of presences. It stands in the same relation to the waking recollection . . . as the drama in which the original myths of the City State are produced before its assembled citizens stands in relation to history. (ibid., pp. 46–47; translation modified)

Must we then conclude that "full speech," like the hypnotic "talking cure," is a presentative, mimetic speech, and that Lacan now believes in a sort of pure repetition of the unconscious, to the detriment of any *prise de conscience* of a self? Not in the least. In fact, two pages later, we come upon an unrepealable condemnation of hypnosis: "I . . . repudiate any reliance on these states ['hypnosis or even narcosis'] . . . whether to explain the symptom or to cure it" (ibid., p. 49). Why is this? After all, Lacan had just used the example of hypnotized speech to demonstrate the effectiveness of "full speech."

In reality, however, there was never any question in his mind of attributing the disappearance of the symptoms to hypnosis; rather, he considered this to be due solely to the pure "speech addressed to the other" (ibid., p. 48). Note the precautions, in this regard, with which Lacan envelops himself at the moment he describes the hypnotic talking cure: the hysterical *epos*, he says, is admittedly a "drama," "played out" and rehearsed in "the present tense" with "all the animation of the actor," but it is suspended in the isolating quotation marks of an epic recitation, and, most importantly, is executed on a "stage," "before [the] assembled citizens." In other words, what matters is not that the hysterics mimetically identify with their role, speaking "under the name of the other" (as Plato would have said), but only that they speak *to* the others, having their fiction recognized in a public place and thus sealing their truth in the pact of speech. In other words, what matters is that they *put themselves in representation*, taking a pose before the other and thus posing themselves before themselves, in a "distanciated" identification, to use Brecht's term. In short, what matters is their *not being hypnotized*.

Here, once again, we find Lacan's original presuppositions, still just as disastrous for the hypothesis of a "hypnotic" unconscious. The subject's truth resides entirely in the fact of being spoken, that is, in a performative autoenunciation or representation (no matter how fictive and deceptive this utterance might be in relation to reality— that is, from a constative point of view); and this autorepresentation presupposes an autoexteriorization, a self-exhibition in the "place of the Other," where one has oneself recognized in speech. The problem, however, is that this recognition no longer has anything to do with a *prise de conscience*, if by that we mean self-recognition. Lacan now maintains that recognition of oneself in an other is the very principle of *méconnaissance* and imaginary resistance, whose hypnotic and suggestive traits he also emphasizes (*Ecrits*, pp. 377, 439). This assimilation of the specular *prise de conscience* with hypnosis is very significant; it testifies to a sort of retreat toward the front on the part of Lacan: the subject's truth is no longer his identification in (and even less *with*) the imaginary other in which he represents himself; his truth is now his nonidentification in a symbolic "big Other," who represents the subject only by absenting him.

Why is this? Essentially, because the subject who is to be recognized in speech is no longer the imaginary ego but the subject of *desire*; and Lacan, under the influence of Alexandre Kojève's commentary on Hegel, conceives of this desire as the pure non-self-identity of a subject defined by his radical negativity. This means that this "desire" has nothing to do with the Freudian *Wunsch*, or even with the Hegelian *Begierde*,[10] for in Hegel *Begierde* remains the desire of a *Selbst*, a self-consciousness, whereas Kojève, in his anthropologizing and para-Heideggerian reading of Hegel, turns desire into the essence of a humanity dedicated to negating nature—that is, the "real," the self-identical "given being"—which this humanity *is not* and which it can never be: there is no identity between the real and the rational because the real is impossible for man. Kojève says, in effect, that man can be what he is (i.e., a self-consciousness) only by transcending, and transcending himself in, every object, without ever being able to pose himself as a self that is identical to himself. Therefore (as Sartre repeats), he is what he is not and he is not what he is, because the condition of relationship with self is distance from self. It follows that his desire, insofar as it is conflated with that perpetual ek-static transcendence, is not the desire of any particular thing but rather a "Desire of Desire," or again, a "Desire of the Desire of the other." This is Kojève's reformulation of Hegel's "desire of recognition": desire can be human only by negating itself as animal desire or need, and it must therefore be directed toward

a non-natural object, toward something that goes beyond the given reality. Now, the only thing that goes beyond the given reality is Desire itself. For Desire taken as Desire—i.e., before its satisfaction—is but a revealed nothingness, an unreal emptiness. Desire, being the revelation of an emptiness, the presence of the absence of a reality, is something essentially different from the desired thing, something other than a thing, than a static and given real being that stays eternally identical to itself.[11]

All these traits are to be found in Lacan. "Man's desire," he repeats, "is the desire of the other" (*Seminar of Lacan: Book I*, p. 146; *Four Fundamental Concepts*, p. 115)—that is, the desire of no object, the desire of nothing (*Seminar of Lacan: Book II*, p. 223), and, finally, the desire of death (ibid., pp. 230–33). By the same token, we understand why no specular alter ego "can [ever] become one with the assumption of his desire": the subject-desire, who is to be recognized, is no longer a substantial "ego." Desiring the desire of the other, he admittedly desires "himself," but only as pure desire—that is, as never being "himself," as not "identical to himself," as always "beyond" himself. Therefore, if he "recognizes himself" in an other desire, it is only because the other "reveals" his own nothingness by "revealing"—*nothing*. Therefore, the analyst, who is the operator of this revelation, must be an "empty mirror" (ibid., p. 246)—that is, a pure desire.

In contrast, the specular image does reveal *something* to the subject, namely, an ego-object, and as a result he cannot recognize himself (or have himself recognized) in the image as a subject, a transcendence toward nothing, and "being-toward-death" (*Séminaire VII*, p. 357). On the contrary, that image can be nothing but an alibi of the subject, not only because the image (re)presents him at a distance from himself but because it causes him to appear there, where he is not: here (*da*) "before" himself; and not over there (*illic, fort*). The specular image or representation of self is an alibi of that radical alibi of the subject as a "creature of distance"[12] and absolute "Elsewhere" (*Ecrits: A Selection*, p. 193).

Nonetheless, the subject must manifest himself *somewhere* if, as Lacan says, he is to accede to his truth. In fact, Lacan strongly insists that desire is a desire of recognition (ibid., p. 58; *Ecrits*, p. 343); this is the sign of his attachment to the idea of transcendent representation, understood as the only possible form of manifestation. Desire must have a *da*, because it desires to have itself recognized, that is, exhibit itself outside, in the light of a public place. But where is this place, if desire is always "elsewhere"? On what scene (or stage) will it represent itself, if the place "in which the recognition of desire is bound up with the desire for recognition" is always "beyond" (*Ecrits: A Selection*, p. 172)? Lacan would say, where else but at that "Other scene" or "Other place," the place of speech and the signifier, since desire represents itself there not in presence but *in absence*?

In fact, this is precisely Kojève's lesson concerning Hegel: Language, as the manifestation of a subject who poses himself by negating the real, performs the amazing feat of making be what is not.[13] By naming the rose, language abolishes it as a real rose, making it the "*absente de tous bouquets*"; and in that ideal rose, language manifests the negativity of a subject who is the rose's fading "being." In other words, language presents the absence of a subject who speaks himself in language by "nihilating" all reality, his own included. Thus, as Lacan translates, language is the *da* of that *fort*:

The symbol manifests itself first of all as the murder of the thing, and this death constitutes in the subject the eternalization of his desire. (ibid., p. 104)

This is why the subject, in "true" speech, does not have himself recognized as a meaning that would exist prior to the speech addressed to the Other. Truly "full" and "symbolic" speech occurs when the subject quite literally institutes himself in a speech pact that does not represent or constate some thing that would predate its enunciation. This speech presents—one could even say *performs*—the "nothing" that the subject is. "You are my wife," and thus I receive my own message in an inverted form: "I am your husband"—which I *was not* before uttering those words. Nothing changes, in that respect, when the theme of "full speech" gives way in Lacan to that of the "autonomy" of the signifier. If Lacan finds it so important to emphasize, by way of Ferdinand de Saussure and structural linguistics, that the signifier represents nothing—neither referent nor signified—it is because he wants to establish that it does represent (i.e., manifest) the "nothing" that the subject is:

The signifier represents a subject . . . (not a signified); for another signifier (which means: not for another subject). ("Radiophonie," p. 65)

As this last, famous quotation clearly demonstrates, Lacan continues to define the subject in terms of representation. Admittedly, there is no longer any question of intersubjective recognition but only of a "discourse of the Other," in which the subject has himself represented by a signifier to another signifier, without ever being able to grasp himself as the elusive "signified" of that perpetual "*signifiance*." The fact remains that the signifier represents nothing but the subject, who never stops speaking himself in the signifier while absenting himself in it, in some strange subjective *alētheia*—or, better yet, that "signifier" is nothing but the subject "himself," incapable of relating to himself (of being conscious of himself) except by separating from himself, absenting himself in the representation that manifests him outside, as the non-being transcendence that he "is": always elsewhere than where he is, always *alibi*. In short, that structure of referral of the signifier, identified by Lacan with the structure of the unconscious, truly is the structure of the *cogito*, as Lacan himself clearly says—an empty *cogito*, admittedly (the *cogito* of a consciousness that appears to itself only in disappearing), but a *cogito* all the same, always and forever defined in terms of autorepresentation, not the blind *cogito* of a hypnotized person or a dreamer, the unrepresentative *cogito* of an unconscious "other scene."

Let us verify this one last time with the ultimate avatar of Lacanian theory, namely, the "*objet petit a*" as it functions in hypnosis and analysis.

By "*objet a*," we know that Lacan means the object of fantasy, understood as the "object cause of desire." If it is necessary to say "object *cause* of desire" and not simply "object of desire," it is because, for the hyper-Kojèvian that Lacan continues to be, desire, strictly speaking, can have no object. Once again, desire is the pure transcendence of a subject who desires himself in negating / passing-beyond the object that he wants *not to be*; thus it goes without saying that he can desire himself only in (and as) a non-object, in the no less pure negativity of an other subject—that is, in his *desire*. Desire, Lacan repeats, after Kojève, is the "desire of desire" (*Ecrits*, p. 852), the desire to be desired by the Other, and not the desire to be the *object* of the Other's desire, a formula that defines instead what Lacan calls the "deceit of love" (ibid., p. 853), specifically that of transference love (*Four Fundamental Concepts*, p. 268). By identifying himself as "lovable," the subject of desire actually identifies himself as an object, whereas he is nothing—nothing but "lack-of-being" (*Ecrits: A Selection*, p. 164), as Sartre also said,[14] "want-to-be" (ibid., p. 259), and ek-sistence without essence. More succinctly, he identifies himself, he who is perpetual non-self-identity and radical inquietude of the negative.

The problem, however, is that the subject of desire must simultaneously be "something," precisely in order to be it "in the mode of not being it," as Sartre put it. Here again, we find the request for transcendent manifestation, proper to the thought of representation: the *fort* of ek-static transcendence must have a corresponding *da* in which it can manifest itself *as it is not*, as the alibi and nonidentity that it "is." As we have seen, the signifier has initially been given the role of presenting this absence, and we also know that this is especially true for the "signifier of signifiers" (ibid., p. 265), the phallic signifier. Lacan tells us that this is the "signifier of a lack in the Other," with which the subject can identify only on the condition of the "Law" of castration, which commands him not to identify with it. But, starting in the 1960's, Lacan gives the *objet a* of fantasy the function of manifesting the subject of desire, as if he is not completely satisfied with that first "linguistic" solution. In the signifier, he admits, I simply cannot identify myself, because nothing responds to the question of what the Other "wants," and thus of what I am for him. *Ché vuoi?* How do you want me? There is nothing but an immense silence from the Other, since he answers me only by referring me to a signifier that represents me to another signifier, and so on. In the fantasy, on the contrary, I really do get an answer, an answer as certain as it is enigmatic; and it is the undisclosable object that I myself am in the scenario that fascinates and "fixes" my desire. The *objet a* is that singular object that I put in the place of the lack in the Other (ibid., pp. 320–21), and with which I identify to "prop" and "cause" my desire, which, in itself, is a desire of nothing.

For all that, is it simply a matter of a "stopgap" object, an object destined to falsely fill the gaping wound of castration (i.e., of desire, i.e., of the subject)? No. As described by Lacan, that object has this original trait: it is not solely an imaginary object, the prop of a simply specular identification. If it were, it would not have the ambiguous function that Lacan gives it: that of "imaging" the unimaginable disappearance of the subject in the signifier. In fact, the subject identifies with that object only insofar as it is lacking in the Other, insofar as it is an "organ" (*Four Fundamental Concepts*, p. 196 ff.) or piece of the body from which the body separates itself in order to constitute itself in its corporeal unity: breast, feces, phallus, voice, or gaze. The result, according to Lacan, is that this "profoundly lost object" does not enter the specular image (*Ecrits: A Selection*, p. 316) unless as an incomplete part, a heterogeneous "stain," or a hole whose edge that object is—that is, as a disturbed, enigmatic image in which the subject henceforth identifies himself, but without being able to recognize himself in it. The subject *sees* himself without seeing *himself* in it, and Lacan illustrates this structure by way of his own version of Sartre's famous analysis of the phenomenon of the gaze. In the gaze, I do not see myself in a mirror, as the other sees me (i.e., as he "loves me" or "wants me"). On the contrary, I see myself as the Other gazes at me, seeking my gaze (i.e., my desire) beyond the visible eye (the object) that I am for him. In short, I see myself in the gaze as I cannot see myself, as the lacking and "fundamentally lost" object of the desire of the Other: *as non-object*, that is, *as a subject of desire*. The scopic *objet a* (which Lacan significantly says is the fantasy object par excellence) thus has the remarkable property of making appear, in imaginary space, precisely what escapes in principle from every specular identification and objectification. There, in that nonspecular image—namely, the gaze (or painting, or stain) that "gazes at me" (or "concerns me")[15] before I see it—I am present in my absence; I identify myself in my nonidentity, in my perpetual distance from myself: *ego sum alibi*.

Such is, according to Lacan, the objective of the analytic cure, and the principle of its radical difference from hypnosis: to bring the subject to that nonspecular *cogito* through which his non-self-identity is finally revealed to him. Transference love, Lacan explains in the last lecture of his eleventh *Seminar*, consists of an identification "centred on the Ideal point, capital I, placed somewhere in the Other, from which the Other sees me, in the form I like to be seen" (*Four Fundamental Concepts*, p. 268): the subject sees himself in that point as "lovable" (ibid., p. 243), as the object capable of fulfilling the desire of the Other. In contrast, the *objet a* is situated in that

> other point where the subject sees himself caused as a lack . . . and where *a* fills the gap constituted by the inaugural division of the subject. . . . It is at this point of lack that the subject has to recognize himself. (ibid., p. 270)

If, however, these two points are conflated, we obtain the phenomena characteristic of hypnosis. Put an "object in the place of the ego-ideal,"[16] says Freud in *Group Psychology*, and you get the driving force behind the fascination of groups hypnotized by their *Führer*. Put the gaze of the analyst (or almost any shiny object) in the place of the subject's ego-ideal, Lacan adds, and you get the formula for that zenith of specular identification: hypnosis.

> To define hypnosis as the confusion, at one point, of the ideal signifier in which the subject is mapped with the *a*, is the most assured structural definition that has been advanced. (ibid., p. 273).

This is also the definition of bad (fascist) analysis, characterized by "identification with the analyst" (ibid., p. 271). Lacan continues:

> Now, as everyone knows, it was by distinguishing itself from hypnosis that analysis became established. For the fundamental mainspring of the analytic operation is the maintenance of the distance between the I—identification— and the *a*. . . . [The analyst] isolates the *a*, places it at the greatest possible distance from the I that he, the analyst, is called upon by the subject to embody. It is from this idealization that the analyst has to fall in order to

be the support of the separating *a*, in so far as his desire allows him, in an upside-down hypnosis, to embody the hypnotized patient. This crossing of the plane of identification is possible. (ibid., p. 273)

Therefore, the true analysis, in conformity with its name, is one that dissolves and separates. It separates itself from hypnosis by separating the point in which the subject sees himself as the object that *fulfills* the desire of the Other from the point in which he sees himself as the object that the Other *lacks* (that "fallen" object which hypnotizes the analyst). In sum, the analyst "breaks" the identification by separating the subject from his specular object (i.e., "himself"). In that ungraspable separation, which confuses the imaginary fascination, the subject can finally see himself dis-appear, appear before himself as the non-object or "nothing" that he is. There, the analyst says, you are there, in those bleeding eyes that fall from me "like scales" (*Séminaire XII*, p. 140) and that, as blind as they may be, "*gaze at you*": in them you may see the truth of your desire to see (*voir*) and to know (*savoir*), which is also mine.

"Upside-down hypnosis," Lacan says, meaning that the subject, after the "crossing of the phantasy," can no longer see *himself*—that is, identify himself—in the gaze of the Other. An upside-down *cogito*? So it seems, since Lacan earlier characterized the scopic *objet a* as the "underside of consciousness" (*Four Fundamental Concepts*, p. 83), explicitly opposing it to the "I see myself seeing myself" of the *cogito* (ibid., p. 80). In fact, the "crossing of the phantasy" is equivalent to an upside-down *cogito*, since the subject identifies himself in it as non-self-identity, becoming conscious of the "underside of consciousness" that he himself is. And yet, however reversed that *cogito* is, it is nonetheless a *cogito*, if only because it requires a gaze, an "object" that it itself is, at a distance from itself (i.e., a self-representation). That gaze is perhaps blind, but at the very least the subject *sees* himself in it as incapable of seeing. In that opaque mirror, the subject reflects his reflection, and specularizes his unspecularizable negativity; he becomes conscious of the impossibility of his consciousness becoming conscious of itself, except by becoming conscious of an object that it *is not*. But never does this subject lose consciousness. However much he faints (or fades) into the object that represents him in his absence, he faints only in knowing it— and without fainting, therefore.

This is a far cry from the blind *cogito* presented by the young Lacan in the "suggestion" of the image, and equally far from the enigma of the unconscious that Freud called "hypnosis." Indeed, as I hope you have seen, the hypnosis that Lacan claimed as the diametric opposite of analysis is really nothing but an alibi-hypnosis: a specular, specularizable, representable hypnosis, a hypnosis kept at a distance precisely so that one can become conscious of it. It is the hypnosis of consciousness, placed on the scene to exhibit one's own night and nightmares, not that completely other hypnosis which seizes us "before" any consciousness, where there is nothing to see (*voir*) and nothing to know (*savoir*). Where is that, you ask? Right here, not *elsewhere*: in that "other scene" of the unconscious which haunts the scene of consciousness before consciousness is even aware of it. "Psyche is extended; knows nothing about it."

Translated by Douglas Brick

Notes

Notes

Unless otherwise noted, all excerpts from Freud's works are quoted from James Strachey, ed., *The Standard Edition of the Complete Psychological Works of Sigmund Freud*, 24 vols. (London: Hogarth Press, 1953–74). *The Standard Edition* is subsequently referred to as *SE*.

The Primal Band

This paper was originally presented in May 1980, at the conference "Journées Confrontation: Le lien social et l'être psychanalyste," and later printed in *Le Lien social*, ed. René Major (Paris: Editions Confrontation, 1981). It should be noted that this conference took place in the context of the institutional chaos provoked by the dissolution of the *Ecole freudienne de Paris*, announced by Jacques Lacan in January 1980. The epigraph comes from Ludwig Binswanger, *Erinnerungen an Sigmund Freud* (Bern: Francke, 1956), cited in Jacques Lacan, *Ecrits* (Paris: Le Seuil, 1966), p. 487.

1. François Roustang, *Dire Mastery: Discipleship from Freud to Lacan*, trans. Ned Lukacher (Baltimore, Md.: Johns Hopkins University Press, 1982).

2. *Group Psychology*, *SE* 18: 97.

3. Ibid., p. 121.

4. Ibid., p. 127.

5. Roustang, *Dire Mastery*, p. 17: "If one compares Freud's analyses of the Church and the army in *Group Psychology and the Analysis of the Ego* to his project for a psychoanalytic society in *On the History of the Psychoanalytic Movement*, one is forced to notice a strange relationship between the two. . . . It is as if Freud, who radically criticized the foundations of two societies typical of our culture, was unable to find another model on which to base a society composed of supporters of a practice, a technique, and a theory aimed at dismantling some of the structures essential to the functioning of Western civilization." See also Lacan, *Ecrits*, pp. 474–75.

6. *Group Psychology*, *SE* 18: 69.

7. Following recent practice, Freud's *Besetzung* is here translated as "in-

vestment" except in direct quotations from *SE*, where it is usually "cathexis"—Trans.

8. "Project for a Scientific Psychology," *SE* 1: 368.

9. Freud's *Trieb* (French *pulsion*) will generally be translated as "drive," except when quoting directly from *SE*, where it is usually "instinct"—Trans.

10. *Group Psychology*, *SE* 18: 87.

11. Hannah Arendt, *The Origins of Totalitarianism* (San Diego: Harcourt, Brace, Jovanovich, 1973), chap. 10, "A Classless Society."

12. Philippe Lacoue-Labarthe and Jean-Luc Nancy, "La Panique politique," in *Cahiers Confrontation*, no. 2 (Paris: Aubier, 1979), pp. 42–43.

13. This passage plays heavily on the ambiguity inherent in the French *Moi*, which means "I," "me," and is also the French translation of Freud's *das Ich* (literally "the I"), our "ego." The original French is: "Moi-l'Auto-analyste-qui-m'auto-institue-comme-Moi-la-psychanalyse, Moi-les-psych-analystes, Moi-qui-lègue-mon-Moi-à-ceux-qui-se-réclament-de-Moi, Moi-la-Cause-freudienne"—Trans.

14. *Group Psychology*, *SE* 18: 96.

15. Ibid., p. 102. Strachey's translation of *nahestehende Fremde*, "strangers with whom they have to do," is here altered to "close strangers"—Trans.

16. *Inhibitions, Symptoms and Anxiety*, *SE* 20: 130.

17. *Beyond the Pleasure Principle*, *SE* 18: 52.

18. Ibid., p. 54.

19. *Group Psychology*, *SE* 18: 105.

20. Translating *à même* as "with" loses the play of *même* (literally, "same") with *autre* ("other")—Trans.

21. *Group Psychology*, *SE* 18: 107.

The Freudian Subject

This text was originally delivered as a lecture in June 1986 at the Psychoanalytic Institute in Paris, as part of a seminar on "The Subject in Psychoanalysis" conducted by Dr. Paulette Wilgowicz and Dr. Jean Gillibert. The Freud epigraph is from *Civilization and Its Discontents*, *SE* 21: 131–32.

1. Mikkel Borch-Jacobsen, *The Freudian Subject*, trans. Catherine Porter (Stanford: Stanford University Press, 1988).

2. Philippe Lacoue-Labarthe and Jean-Luc Nancy, *Le Titre de la lettre* (Paris: Galilée, 1973).

3. Jacques Lacan, *Ecrits: A Selection*, trans. Alan Sheridan (New York: Norton, 1977), p. 1.

4. Michel Henry makes this point in his admirable and highly important *Généalogie de la psychanalyse* (Paris: Presses Universitaires de France, 1985).

5. Jacques Lacan, "Radiophonie," *Scilicet* 2 / 3 (Paris: Le Seuil, 1970), p. 65.

6. Sigmund Freud and C. G. Jung, *The Freud / Jung Letters*, ed. William McGuire, trans. Ralph Manheim (Princeton, N.J.: Princeton University Press, 1974), p. 278.

7. *On Narcissism: An Introduction*, SE 14: 90.

8. *Group Psychology*, SE 18: 105.

9. "Findings, Ideas, Problems," *SE* 23: 299.

10. *Group Psychology*, SE 18: 69.

11. Claude Lefort, "L'Image du corps et le totalitarisme," in *L'Invention démocratique* (Paris: Fayard, 1981).

12. Serge Moscovici, *L'Age des foules* (Paris: Fayard, 1981).

13. Jacques Lacan, *Ecrits* (Paris: Le Seuil, 1966), pp. 474–75: "For our purposes, we must begin with the remark—never made, to our knowledge—that Freud started the I[nternational] A[ssociation of] P[sychoanalysis] on its path ten years before he became interested, in *Group Psychology and the Analysis of the Ego*, in the church and the army, in the mechanisms through which an organic group participates in the crowd, an exploration whose clear partiality can be justified by the basic discovery of the identification of each individual's ego with a shared ideal image, whose mirage is supported by the personality of the chief. This was a sensational discovery, made before the fascist organizations rendered it patently obvious. *Had he been made aware earlier of its effects* [emphasis added], Freud probably would have wondered about the field left open to dominance by the function of the boss or caïd in any organization," etc. This remark gives rise in turn to several others: (1) Freud's "basic discovery" in *Group Psychology* is not at all that egos are united in the same *identification* with the ego's Ideal-Chief, because he states, on the contrary, that they mutually identify because of their shared *love* for the "Object" that is set up "in place of" the Ego ideal. In fact, Lacan's "remark" supposes a reinterpretation of Freud's thesis, a reinterpretation probably dictated by implicit reflection on the fascist phenomenon. (2) Freud's "sensational discovery" "anticipates" the fascist mass organizations (as Georges Bataille was to note as early as 1933; cf. his *Oeuvres complètes* I [Paris: Gallimard, 1970,] p. 356) only because it broadly confirms a description of "crowd psychology," such as Gustave Le Bon's, that fascist ideologues, led by Hitler and Mussolini, were to exploit deliberately (cf. R. A. Nye, *The Origins of Crowd Psychology: Gustave Le Bon and the Crisis of Mass Democracy in the Third Republic* [London: Sage, 1975], pp. 178–79; see also Moscovici, *L'Age*, pp. 92–95). (3) "Made aware of its effects" in 1921, Freud felt absolutely no need to reorganize the analytical community on another model—and for good reason: as Lacan himself noted in the earlier version of his text (published as an appendix to *Ecrits*, p. 487), Freud stressed

his own function as Chief-Father all the more for never once doubting the basic "inadequacies" of his "band" of disciples. The masses need a leader— isn't that what all the great "leaders" of this century have contended, publicly or privately, from Lenin to Mao by way of Mussolini or Tito? And isn't this what Lacan himself is also saying, in his own way, when he heaps contempt on those attending his seminar, or when he signs contributions to *Scilicet* with his name alone? In fact, neither Freud nor Lacan did anything at all to deal with what Lacan called "the obscenity of the social tie" or to substitute another one for it, one "cleansed of any group needs" ("L'Etourdit," in *Scilicet* 4 [1973], p. 31).

14. "Why War?" *SE* 22: 212.

15. *Group Psychology*, *SE* 18: 123: "He, at the very beginning of the history of mankind, was the 'superman' whom Nietzsche only expected from the future. Even to-day the members of a group stand in need of the illusion that they are equally and justly loved by their leader (Führer), but the leader himself need love no one else; he may be of a masterful nature, absolutely narcissistic, self-confident and independent."

16. *Totem and Taboo*, *SE* 13: 143. Translation slightly modified.

17. Ibid.

18. Ibid.; cf. also *Civilization and Its Discontents*, *SE* 21: 132: "This remorse was the result of the primordial ambivalence of feeling toward the father. His sons hated him, but they loved him, too. After their hatred had been satisfied by their act of aggression, their love came to the fore in their remorse for the deed. . . . Now, I think we can at last grasp two things perfectly clearly: the part played by love in the origin of conscience and the fatal inevitability of the sense of guilt."

19. *Totem and Taboo*, *SE* 13: 142. See also *Moses and Monotheism*, *SE* 23: 82: "They not only feared and hated their father but also honoured him as a model, and . . . each of them wished to take his place in reality. We can . . . understand the cannibalistic act as an attempt to ensure identification with him by incorporating a piece of him."

20. *Totem and Taboo*, *SE* 13: 143.

21. First of all in *Totem and Taboo*, where Freud, as if alarmed by his own paradox, had the father's murder followed by a fratricidal struggle— which brought Freud back to his point of departure and thus constrained him to fall back on the hypothesis (a far more classical one, which the hypothesis of "retrospective obedience" was intended to avoid) of a "social contract" among the rival brothers. See also *Group Psychology*, *SE* 18: 135: "None of the group of victors could take his place, or, if one of them did, the battles began afresh, until they understood that they must all renounce their father's heritage"; and *Moses and Monotheism*, *SE* 23: 82: "It must be supposed that after the parricide a considerable time elapsed during which

the brothers disputed with one another for their father's heritage, which each of them wanted for himself alone."

22. "Thoughts for the Times on War and Death," *SE* 14: 295: "What came into existence beside the dead body of the loved one was not only the doctrine of the soul, the belief in immortality and a powerful source of man's sense of guilt, but also the earliest ethical commandments. The first and most important prohibition made by the awakening conscience was 'Thou shalt not kill.' It was acquired in relation to dead people who were loved, as a reaction against the satisfaction of the hatred hidden behind the grief for them." Therefore, the important thing in arousing the moral conscience is not that the corpse be that of a father or even that it actually have been murdered. The only important thing is that "primaeval man" be confronted with a *dead person with whom he identifies* in the ambivalent mode of devouring "love," for "then, in his pain, he [is] forced to learn that one can die, too, oneself, and his whole being revolt[s] against the admission; for each of these loved ones was, after all, *a part of his own beloved self*" (ibid., p. 293; emphasis added).

23. Ibid., p. 294: "Man could no longer keep death at a distance because he had tasted it in his pain about the dead; but he was nevertheless unwilling to acknowledge it, for he could not conceive himself as dead."

Hypnosis in Psychoanalysis

This paper was originally presented as a lecture on January 24, 1985, at the invitation of the Société Française de Médecine Psychosomatique, and was subsequently published in Mikkel Borch-Jacobsen, Léon Chertok, et al., *Hypnose et psychanalyse* (Paris: Dunod, 1987).

1. *Introductory Lectures to Psychoanalysis*, *SE* 16: 292.

2. "Advice to Physicians on Psychoanalytic Treatment," *SE* 12: 118.

3. Jacques Lacan, *The Four Fundamental Concepts of Psychoanalysis*, trans. Alan Sheridan (New York: Norton, 1977), p. 273.

4. *An Autobiographical Study*, *SE* 20: 17.

5. "The Unconscious," *SE* 14: 168.

6. *The Ego and the Id*, *SE* 19: 13.

7. Mikkel Borch-Jacobsen, *The Freudian Subject*, trans. Catherine Porter (Stanford: Stanford University Press, 1988).

8. *Group Psychology*, *SE* 18: 114–15.   9. Ibid., p. 125.

10. Ibid., p. 89.   11. Ibid., p. 117.

12. *Résurgence de l'hypnose. Une Bataille de deux cent ans*, ed. Léon Chertok et al. (Paris: Desclée de Brouwer, 1984).

13. Sigmund Freud, *The Origins of Psychoanalysis* (New York: Basic Books, 1977), letter 2, p. 53.

14. Plato, *Republic* 392c–398b. Insofar as I shall be making use, in what follows, of Platonic terminology, I should recall that Plato distinguishes three modes of poetic enunciation, depending on whether the poet "speaks in his own name without seeking to make us believe that it is someone other than he who is speaking" (this is "pure narrative," *haple diegesis*); "makes a speech under the name of an other" (dramatic *mimesis*); or, finally, uses a combination of both registers (which is the "mixed narrative" characteristic of the epic).

15. Josef Breuer and Sigmund Freud, *Studies on Hysteria*, SE 2: 6.

16. *An Autobiographical Study*, SE 20: 21.

17. Jacques Lacan, *Ecrits: A Selection*, trans. Alan Sheridan (New York: Norton, 1977), p. 46.

18. Ibid., p. 48.

19. Ibid., p. 47.

20. "Preface to the Translation of Bernheim's *Suggestion*," SE 1: 77.

21. Octave Mannoni, *Un Commencement qui n'en finit pas* (Paris: Le Seuil, 1980), pp. 49–50.

22. Roger Gentis, unpublished lecture on the "New Therapies," Strasbourg, April 1984.

23. Breuer and Freud, *Studies on Hysteria*, SE 2: 303.

24. Ibid., p. 304.

25. "Fragment of an Analysis of a Case of Hysteria," SE 7: 116.

26. Ibid., p. 117.

27. *The Question of Lay Analysis*, SE 20: 226–27.

28. François Roustang, *Dire Mastery: Discipleship from Freud to Lacan*, trans. Ned Lukacher (Baltimore, Md.: Johns Hopkins University Press, 1982), chap. 4.

29. *An Autobiographical Study*, SE 20: 42.

30. *Beyond the Pleasure Principle*, SE 17: 18.

31. *An Autobiographical Study*, SE 20: 42–43.

32. *Introductory Lectures*, SE 16: 453.

33. *Beyond the Pleasure Principle*, SE 18: 18.

34. Ibid.

35. "The Dynamics of Transference," SE 12: 107–8.

36. Lacan, *Four Fundamental Concepts*, p. 146.

37. *Inhibitions, Symptoms and Anxiety*, SE 20: 18: "It must be that after the ego's resistance has been removed the power of the compulsion to repeat—the attraction exerted by the unconscious prototypes upon the repressed instinctual process—has still to be overcome. There is nothing to be said against describing this factor as the *resistance of the unconscious*."

38. *Beyond the Pleasure Principle*, SE 18: 19–20.

39. Ibid.

40. *Group Psychology*, SE 18: 107.

Analytic Speech

This lecture was delivered in February 1987, at Stanford University, Stanford, California, as part of the conference "The Ends of Rhetoric," organized by John Bender and David E. Wellbery.

1. Martin Heidegger, *Unterwegs zur Sprache* (Pfullingen: Neske, 1959), p. 206.

2. Paul Ricoeur, *La Métaphore vive* (Paris: Le Seuil, 1975).

3. Roland Barthes, "L'Ancienne Rhétorique," *Communications* 16 (1970): 194–95; Gérard Genette, "La Rhétorique restreinte," *Communications* 16 (1970): 158–59; Ricoeur, *Métaphore*, pp. 13–14 and 63–66; Tzvetan Todorov, *Théories du symbole* (Paris: Le Seuil, 1977), chaps. 2 and 3. The quoted term is from Ricoeur, *Métaphore*, p. 14.

4. Genette, "La Rhétorique," p. 158.

5. Barthes, "L'Ancienne Rhétorique," p. 174.

6. G. A. Kennedy, *Classical Rhetoric and Its Christian and Secular Tradition from Ancient to Modern Times* (Chapel Hill: University of North Carolina Press, 1980), pp. 4–6.

7. V. Florescu, *La retorica nel suo sviluppo storico* (Bologna: Il Mulino, 1971). On that (very classical) opposition between the "art of persuasion" and the "art of speaking well," compare also C. Perelman and L. Olbrechts-Tyteca, *Rhétorique et philosophie* (Paris: Presses Universitaires de France, 1952), pp. 15–16; A. Kibédi Varga, *Rhétorique et litérature* (Paris: Didier, 1970), p. 20; and, not forgetting Immanuel Kant, *The Critique of Judgment*, trans. James Creed Meredith (Oxford: Clarendon Press, 1952), p. 192: "Rhetoric, so far as this is taken to mean the art of persuasion, i.e., the art of deluding by means of a fair semblance (as *ars oratoria*), and not merely excellence of speech (eloquence and style), is a dialectic, which borrows from poetry only so much as is necessary to win over men's minds to the side of the speaker before they have weighed the matter, and rob their verdict of its freedom."

8. Emile Benveniste, "Remarques sur la fonction du langage dans la découverte freudienne," in his *Eléments de linguistique générale* (Paris: Gallimard, 1966), pp. 75–87; Roman Jakobson, "Two Aspects of Language and Two Types of Aphasia Disturbances," in his *Fundamentals of Language* (The Hague: Mouton, 1956); Jacques Lacan, "The Agency of the Letter in the Unconscious," in his *Ecrits: A Selection*, trans. Alan Sheridan (New York: Norton, 1977), pp. 146–78.

9. Jean-François Lyotard, *Discours, figure* (Paris: Klincksieck, 1971), especially the chapters "Le Travail du rêve ne pense pas" and "Connivences du désir avec le figural"; Todorov, *Théories*, chap. 8 ("La Rhétorique de Freud"); Genette, "La Rhétorique," p. 162, n. 1; Nicolas Abraham and Maria Torok, *L'Ecorce et le noyau* (Paris: Aubier-Flammarion, 1978), the chapter "L'Ecorce et le noyau."

10. "Psychical (or Mental) Treatment," *SE* 7: 283.

11. Ibid.

12. Ibid.

13. Plato, *Menexenus* 234c–235a.

14. Friedrich Nietzsche, *Course of Rhetoric*, § 3, quoted by Philippe Lacoue-Labarthe, *Le Sujet de la philosophie* (Paris: Aubier-Flammarion, 1979), p. 48 (English translation by Douglas Brick).

15. "Psychical Treatment," *SE* 7: 292.

16. Ibid., p. 293.

17. Ibid., p. 294.

18. Ibid., p. 293.

19. Ibid., pp. 293–95.

20. Ibid., p. 296.

21. "Preface to the Translation of Bernheim's *Suggestion*," *SE* 1: 82.

22. "Psychical Treatment," *SE* 7: 296.

23. *Totem and Taboo, SE* 13, chap. 3 ("Animism, Magic and the Omnipotence of Thoughts").

24. Plato, *Phaedrus* 261a. *Collected Dialogues*, ed. Edith Hamilton and Huntington Cairns, trans. R. Hackforth (Princeton, N.J.: Princeton University Press, 1961), p. 506 (translation altered).

25. Aristotle, *Rhetoric*, Book 2, 1377b–1391b, trans. W. Rhys Robert (New York: Modern Library, 1954).

26. *Beyond the Pleasure Principle, SE* 17: 18.

27. Plato, *Phaedrus* 266e–267c, 270b–272d.

28. "Remembering, Repeating and Working Through," *SE* 12: 148–49.

29. *Group Psychology, SE* 17: 115.

30. "On Psychotherapy," *SE* 7: 258: "A factor dependent on the psychical disposition of the patient contributes, without any intention on our part, to the effect of every therapeutic process initiated by a physician. . . . We have learned to use the word 'suggestion' for this phenomenon . . . it is a disadvantage, however, to leave the mental factor in our treatment so completely in the patient's hands. Thus it is impossible to keep a check on it, to administer it in doses or to intensify it. Is it not then a justifiable endeavor on the part of the physician to seek to obtain command of this factor, to use it with a purpose, and to direct and strengthen it? This and nothing else is what *scientific* psychotherapy proposes" (emphasis added).

31. *Group Psychology, SE* 17: 88–90.

32. Jacques Lacan, *Ecrits* (Paris: Le Seuil, 1966), p. 106 (psychoanalytic dialogue discussed in relation to the "failure of verbal dialectic" in the *Republic*); p. 128 (in relation to the exclusion of rhetoric in *Gorgias*); p. 192 (in relation to *Parmenides*); p. 292 (in relation to "the dialectic of consciousness-of-self, such as it is realized from Socrates to Hegel"); and p. 852 (in relation to "Socrates, precursor to the analyst"). See also Maurice Blanchot,

"La parole analytique," in his *L'Entretien infini* (Paris: Gallimard, 1969), pp. 343–44 (psychoanalytic dialogue discussed in relation to the substitution of "dialectic" for the "magic" of hypnosis).

33. Plato, *Phaedrus* 277b.

34. See, among a thousand other passages, "Intervention sur le transfert," in Lacan, *Ecrits*, pp. 215–26.

35. "Remembering, Repeating and Working Through," *SE* 12: 156: "From a theoretical point of view one may correlate it [analytic treatment] with the 'abreacting' of the quotas of affect strangulated by repression—an abreaction without which hypnotic treatment remained ineffective."

36. "The Unconscious," *SE* 14: 166: "It is of course only as something conscious that we know it [the unconscious], after it has undergone transformation or translation into something conscious."

37. *Beyond the Pleasure Principle*, *SE* 17: 60.

38. Lacan, *Ecrits: A Selection*, pp. 121, 123.

39. "Metaphor of the Subject" is the title of the *Annexe II* of Lacan's *Ecrits*, which is devoted to a discussion of the works of C. Perelman's *Traité de l'argumentation* [Paris: Presses Universitaires de France, 1958], vol. 2.

40. *An Autobiographical Study*, *SE* 20: 42.

41. *Group Psychology*, *SE* 18: 77, 80.

42. Ibid., p. 107. Freud takes identification with the symptom to be a model for collective hysteria: "One ego has perceived a significant analogy with another upon one point—in our example upon openness to a similar emotion; an identification is thereupon constructed on this point, and, under the influence of the pathogenic situation, is displaced onto the symptom which the one ego has produced" (ibid.).

43. Ibid.

44. Ibid., p. 105.

45. For a fuller discussion, see Mikkel Borch-Jacobsen, *The Freudian Subject*, trans. Catherine Porter (Stanford: Stanford University Press, 1988), pp. 127–239.

46. Plato, *Phaedrus* 260d.

Talking Cure

This lecture was delivered at Brown University in April 1988, as part of the conference "Who Cares for Lacan? Psychoanalysis and the Cure," organized by Pierre Saint-Amand.

1. Maurice Blanchot, "La Parole analytique," in his *L'Entretien infini* (Paris: Gallimard, 1969), p. 343. [My translation—Trans.]

2. "Psychical (or Mental) Treatment," *SE* 7: 283.

3. *The Question of Lay Analysis*, *SE* 20: 187–88.

4. Blanchot, *L'Entretien infini*, pp. 343–44.

5. The short titles in parentheses refer to the following works by Jacques Lacan:

> *Ecrits* (Paris: Le Seuil, 1966).
> *Ecrits: A Selection*, trans. Alan Sheridan (New York: Norton, 1977).
> *The Four Fundamental Concepts of Psychoanalysis*, trans. Alan Sheridan (New York: Norton, 1977).
> *Le Séminaire III* (Paris: Le Seuil, 1981).
> *The Seminar of Jacques Lacan: Book I. Freud's Papers on Technique, 1953–1954*, trans. John Forrester (New York: Norton, 1988).
> *The Seminar of Jacques Lacan: Book II. The Ego in Freud's Theory and in the Technique of Psychoanalysis, 1954–1955*, trans. Sylvana Tomaselli (New York: Norton, 1988).

6. Quoted by François Roustang in his *Lacan, de l'équivoque à l'impasse* (Paris: Minuit, 1986), p. 21; and also by Léon Chertok in Mikkel Borch-Jacobsen, Léon Chertok, et al., *Hypnose et psychanalyse* (Paris: Dunod, 1987), p. 11. [*Truquage* is roughly equivalent to the English "trickery"—Trans.]

7. On the question of affective "immanence" and representational "transcendence," see the work of Michel Henry, especially *The Essence of Manifestation*, trans. Girard Etzkorn (The Hague: Martinus Nijhoff, 1973). Here Henry notes, in particular, the internal relation between the Hegelian concept of "recognition" and the ontological primacy accorded to transcendence (pp. 709–10).

8. G. W. F. Hegel, *Phenomenology of Spirit*, trans. A. V. Miller (Oxford: Clarendon Press, 1977), p. 43.

9. "Remembering, Repeating and Working Through," *SE* 12: 156: "From a theoretical point of view one may correlate it [working through] with the 'abreacting' of the quotas of affect strangulated by repression—an abreaction without which hypnotic treatment remained ineffective."

10. Claude Lévi-Strauss, *Introduction to the Work of Marcel Mauss*, trans. Felicity Baker (London: Routledge and Keagan Paul, 1987), p. 18.

11. Alexandre Kojève, *Introduction to the Reading of Hegel*, trans. James H. Nichols (New York: Basic Books, 1969), p. 6.

12. Ibid., p. 5.

13. Hegel, *Phenomenology of Spirit*, p. 66.

14. G. W. F. Hegel, *Hegel and the Human Spirit: A Translation of the Jena Lectures on the Philosophy of the Spirit (1805–6) with Commentary*, ed. and trans. Leo Rauch (Detroit: Wayne State University Press, 1983), pp. 88–95: "Language . . . gives {the thing} a name and expresses this as the being of the object. [We might ask, for example,] What *is* this? We answer, It *is* a lion, a donkey, etc.—[namely] it *is*. Thus it is not merely something yellow, having

feet, etc., something on its own, [existing] independently. Rather, it is a *name*, a sound made by my voice, something entirely different from what it is in being looked at—and this [as named] is its true *being*. . . . By means of the name, however, the object has been born out of the I [and has emerged] as *being (seyend)*. This is the primal creativity exercised by Spirit. Adam gave a name to all things. This is the sovereign right [of Spirit], its primal taking-possession of all nature—or the creation of nature out of Spirit [itself]. [Consider] *Logos*, reason, the essence of the thing and of speech, of *object (Sache)* and *talk (Sage)*, the category—[in respect to all of these,] man speaks to the thing as *his* (and lives in a spiritual Nature, in this world [of Spirit]) {this parenthesis is Hegel's marginal note, added by the editor as a footnote}. And this is the *being* of the object. Spirit relates itself to itself: it says to the donkey, You are an inner [subjective] entity, and that Inner is I; your being is a sound which I have arbitrarily invented." [All words in brackets [] are Leo Rauch's; those in braces {} are mine—Trans.]

   15. Kojève, *Introduction to Hegel*, pp. 140–41.
   16. John L. Austin, *How to Do Things with Words* (Cambridge: Harvard University Press, 1962). It appears that Lacan had no knowledge of Austin's works before their posthumous publication, but it is interesting to imagine what might have been the destiny of Lacan's theory of language (and of "structuralism" in general) if such had been the case. On this point, see: Daniel Bougnoux, *Le Fantôme de la psychanalyse* (Toulouse: Ombres / Presses Universitaires du Mirail, 1991), p. 117 ff., which outlines a comparison between "full speech" and "performative utterances" that certainly deserves to be prolonged and verified in detail.
   17. *Truc* and *machin* are roughly equivalent to the English "whatsit" and "thingumajig"—Trans.
   18. Lévi-Strauss, *Introduction to Mauss*, pp. 55–63: "These types of symbols occur to represent an indeterminate value of signification, in itself devoid of meaning and thus susceptible of receiving any meaning at all; their sole function is to fill a gap between the signifier and the signified, or, more exactly, to signal the fact that in such a circumstance, on such an occasion, or in one of their manifestations, a relationship of non-equivalence becomes established between signifier and signified, to the detriment of the prior complementary relationship. . . . Notions of the *mana* type . . . represent nothing more or less than that *floating* signifier which is the disability of all finite thought."
   19. Claude Lévi-Strauss, "The Sorcerer and His Magic" and "The Effectiveness of Symbols," in his *Structural Anthropology*, trans. Claire Jacobson and Brooke Grundfest Schoepf (New York: Basic Books, 1963).
   20. Ibid., p. 198.   21. Ibid., p. 179 ff.
   22. Ibid., p. 201 ff.   23. Ibid., p. 204.

24. Jacques Lacan, "Le Mythe individuel du névrosé ou Poésie et vérité dans la névrose," *Ornicar?* 17 / 18 (1978).

25. Passage quoted and (masterfully) analyzed in Roustang, *Lacan*, pp. 42–43.

26. Lévi-Strauss, *Structural Anthropology*, pp. 197–98: "But no such thing happens to our sick when the causes of their diseases have been explained to them in terms of secretions, germs, or viruses. We shall perhaps be accused of paradox if we answer that the reason lies in the fact that microbes exist and monsters do not. And yet, the relationship between germ and disease is external to the mind of the patient, for it is a cause-and-effect relationship; whereas the relationship between monster and disease is internal to his mind. . . . It is a relationship between symbol and thing symbolized . . . between sign and meaning [*signifiant à signifié*]." But Lévi-Strauss's paradox is obviously untenable: it is only from *our* point of view that the "monsters do not" exist, not at all from that of the "native." Lévi-Strauss himself remarks this just a few lines earlier: "The sick woman believes in the myth and belongs to a society which believes in it" (p. 197)—just as we believe, let it be added, in viruses. What, then, is the difference between the viruses and the monsters, between the ("real"?) science and the ("mythic," "fictive") symbol?

27. Marcel Mauss had already noted: "Every symbolic act [is not] efficacious by nature. . . . The number of those which are valuable for magic is singularly small" ("Esquisse d'une théorie générale de la magie," in *Sociologie et Anthropologie* [Paris: Presses Universitaires de France, 1950], pp. 43–44; passage translated by Douglas Brick).

28. Lévi-Strauss, *Structural Anthropology*, p. 204: "The myth *form* takes precedence over the *content* of the narrative."

29. Luc de Heusch, "Possession et chamanisme" and "La Folie des dieux et la raison des hommes," in his *Pourquoi l'épouser?* (Paris: Gallimard, 1971), pp. 226–44 and 245–86. See also Jean Pouillon, "Malade et médecin: Le Même et / ou l'autre? (Remarques ethnologiques)," in his *Fétiches sans fétichisme* (Paris: Maspéro, 1975), pp. 77–103.

30. Especially in the Siberian field; on this point, see Evelyne Lot-Falck, "Psychopathes et chamans yakoutes," *Echanges et communications (Mélanges offerts à Claude Lévi-Strauss pour son 60e anniversaire)*, (Paris and The Hague: Mouton, 1970), and Roberte Hamayon, "Soigner le mort pour guérir le vif," *Nouvelle Revue de Psychanalyse* 17 (Spring 1977): 55–72. In the American Indian field, the shaman's inaugural "crisis" is frequently replaced by the absorption of toxic substances, such as tobacco juice (cf. Lucien Sebag, "Le Chamanisme ayoréo," *L'Homme*, 1–2 [1965]: 106–13).

31. Lévi-Strauss, *Structural Anthropology*, p. 187.

32. Ibid., p. 197.

33. Plato, *Republic* 392c–398b.

34. On the extraordinary epidemic of cases of "double" or "multiple" personality in the nineteenth century, see Henri Frederic Ellenberger, *The Discovery of the Unconscious* (New York: Basic Books, 1970). To be consulted with equal profit is the abundant literature devoted to the subject: Etienne Eugène Azam, *Hypnotisme, double conscience et altération de la personnalité*, preface by Jean-Martin Charcot (Paris, 1887); Alfred Binet, *Les Altérations de la personnalité* (Paris, 1892); Théodule Ribot, *Les Maladies de la personnalité* (Paris, 1888); Max Dessoir, *Das Doppel-Ich* (Leipzig, 1892); and, certainly not to be forgotten, the famous tandem of the theory of double personality, Henri Bourru and Prosper Burot, *Variations de la personnalité* (Paris, 1888).

35. Josef Breuer and Sigmund Freud, *Studies on Hysteria*, SE 2: 6.

36. Plato, *Republic* 393a.

37. "Future Prospects of Psycho-analytic Therapy," *SE* 11: 139–51.

38. Lévi-Strauss, *Structural Anthropology*, p. 204.

Mimetic Efficacity

The present article is the text of a speech given at a colloquium at Cerisy entitled "Autour de l'hypnose" in September 1989. [The title would normally be translated "Concerning Hypnosis," but the author here plays on the more literal meaning of *autour*, "around" or "about"—Trans.]

1. Léon Chertok and Isabelle Stengers, *Le Coeur et la raison. L'Hypnose en question, de Lavoisier à Lacan* (Paris: Payot, 1989), pp. 202–3.

2. See Alberto Konicheckis, "'Oh! cruelle destinée.' Considérations sur la référence à l'hypnose et à la suggestion en psychanalyse," *Psychanalyse à l'Université* 54 (April 1989): 39–67; Jacques Gagey, "Note sur la tentation de la suggestion dans la cure," in Mikkel Borch-Jacobsen, Léon Chertok, et al. *Hypnose et psychanalyse* (Paris: Dunod, 1987), pp. 69–71; and Jacqueline Rousseau-Dujardin, "A propos de 'La parole analytique' de Mikkel Borch-Jacobsen," *Psychanalystes* 29 (December 1988): 21–25.

3. Claude Lévi-Strauss, *Introduction to the Work of Marcel Mauss*, trans. Felicity Baker (London: Routledge and Kegan Paul, 1987), p. 14.

4. Charles Brockden Brown, *Edgar Huntly or, Memoirs of a Sleep-Walker* (Kent, Ohio: Kent State University Press, 1984). On the difference between "trance" and "ecstasy," see Gilbert Rouget, *La Musique et la transe* (Paris: Gallimard, 1980), p. 26 ff.

5. Georges Bataille, *L'Expérience intérieure* in his *Oeuvres complètes* (Paris: Gallimard, 1973), 5: 21: "You have to *live* the experience. . . . It is only from within, lived to the point of trance, that it appears, uniting what thought must discursively separate."

6. See Léon Chertok, "L'Hypnose animale," *Psychiatrie animale*, ed.

Brion and Ey (Paris: Desclée de Brouwer, 1964); Albert Demaret, "De l'hypnose animale à l'hypnose humaine," in *Résurgence de l'hypnose, Une Bataille de deux cent ans,* ed. Léon Chertok et al. (Paris: Desclée de Brouwer, 1984).

7. Luc de Heusch, "Possession et chamanisme" and "La Folie des dieux et la raison des hommes," in his *Pourquoi l'épouser?* (Paris: Gallimard, 1971).

8. The French terms *mal, maladie,* and *malade* (used adjectively) have generally been translated as "ill," "illness," and "ill," respectively. *Malade* (used nominatively), however, has generally been translated as "patient," but some effort has been made to signal its relatedness in the more important cases by retaining the French in parentheses—Trans.

9. Roberte Hamayon, "Soigner le mort pour guérir le vif," *Nouvelle Revue de Psychanalyse* 17 (Spring 1977): 58.

10. Jean Pouillon, "Malade et médecin: Le Même et / ou l'autre? (Remarques ethnologiques)," in his *Fétiches sans fétichisme* (Paris: Maspéro, 1975), p. 81. See also (with regard to Siberian shamanism) Hamayon, "Soigner le mort," p. 56.

11. The common trait contained in spiritual aggression and "mimetic violence" is revealed quite unadornedly in the ideology of sorcery, since it regularly attributes the sorcerer's action to envy and jealousy: "A sorcerer attacks a man when he is pushed to it by hate, envy, jealousy, and cupidity" (E. E. Evans-Pritchard, *Sorcellerie, oracle et magie chez les Azandé* [Paris: Gallimard, 1972], p. 137; see also Marie-Cécile and Edmond Ortigues, *Oedipe africain* [Paris: Union Générale d'Edition], p. 271).

12. de Heusch, *Pourquoi l'épouser?,* p. 249.

13. On this subject, see the classic studies by Michel Leiris, *La Possession et ses aspects théâtraux chez les Ethiopiens de Gondar* (Paris: Le Sycomore, 1980) and H. Jeanmaire, *Dionysos. Histoire du culte de Bacchus* (Paris: Payot, 1951).

14. de Heusch, *Pourquoi l'épouser?,* p. 257.

15. Ibid., p. 259.

16. Rouget, *La Musique et la transe,* p. 61.

17. Henri Junod, *Moeurs et coutumes des Bantous. La Vie d'une tribu sud-africaine,* vol. 2: *Vie mentale* (Paris: Payot, 1936), pp. 436–37. (This trait is not retained by de Heusch in his summary of Thongan ritual.)

18. Ibid., p. 450.

19. Claude Lévi-Strauss, "The Effectiveness of Symbols," in his *Structural Anthropology,* trans. Claire Jacobson and Brooke Grundfest Schoepf (New York: Basic Books, 1963); hereafter *SA.* [In this text, I translate *efficacité symbolique* as "symbolic efficacity" rather than using Jacobson and Schoepf's "effectiveness of symbols," in order to avoid an unwieldy paraphrase—Trans.]

20. Lévi-Strauss, *Introduction to Mauss,* pp. 55, 63–64.

21. Jacques Lacan, *Ecrits: A Selection*, trans. Alan Sheridan (New York: Norton, 1977), pp. 46–47.

22. de Heusch, *Pourquoi l'épouser?*, p. 260.

23. Ibid., p. 281.

24. Ludwig Wittgenstein, *Remarks on Frazer's Golden Bough*, trans. A. C. Miles (Atlantic Highlands, N.J.: Humanities Press, 1979), p. 14.

25. See de Heusch, *Pourquoi lépouser?*, pp. 266–67, and Pouillon, *Fétiches*, pp. 82–87.

26. de Heusch, *Pourquoi l'épouser?*, pp. 274–75.

27. See Evelyne Lot-Falck, "Psychopathes et chamans yakoutes," *Echanges et communications (Mélanges offerts à Claude Lévi-Strauss pour son 60e anniversaire)*, (Paris and The Hague: Mouton, 1970); Hamayon, "Soigner le mort," pp. 68–69.

28. See Lucien Sebag, "Le Chamanisme ayoréo," *L'Homme* 1–2 (1965): 106–13. Sebag notes that for the Ayoréos, every cured psychopath can become a shaman if he wants to, and without resorting to the absorption of tobacco juice: "If the mental patient is compared to the shaman, it is because the former presents the negative face of the phenomena that, in the personage of the latter, are given in a positive form. The voluntary mastery of his illness suffices to cause the individual to go from neurosis to shamanistic power. The same forces are at work in both cases, but they have changed their sign" (p. 112).

29. de Heusch, *Pourquoi l'épouser?*, p. 281.

30. Michel Foucault, *Madness and Civilization: A History of Insanity in the Age of Reason*, trans. Richard Howard (New York: Random House, Vintage Books, 1973), pp. 3–37, especially pp. 9–10.

31. Ibid., pp. 255–56.

32. Pierre Janet, *De l'angoisse à l'extase* (Paris: Alcan, 1926): "My soul is not mine, for God has seized it completely" (p. 66), and "It comes all by itself, it's a sort of possession" (p. 94).

33. Idem, *L'Automatisme psychologique* (Paris: Alcan, 1889), particularly p. 12.

34. Jean-Martin Charcot, *Leçons sur les maladies du système nerveux* (Paris: Delahaye, 1887), 3: 337 (with regard to the cataleptic state).

35. Charles Richet, *L'Homme et l'intélligence* (Paris: Alcan, 1894), 157.

36. Charcot, *Leçons* (Paris: Delahaye, 1880), 1: 359.

37. See Armand Marie-Jacques de Chastenet de Puységur, *Mémoires pour servir à l'histoire et à l'établissement du magnétisme animal* (Toulouse: Privat, 1986); Justinus Kerner, *Die Seherin von Prevorst* (Stuttgart-Tübingen: 1829); Despine, *De l'emploi du magnétisme animal et des eaux minérales dans le traitement des maladies nerveuses, suivi d'une observation très curieuse de guérison de névropathie* (Paris: 1840).

38. *Group Psychology, SE* 18: 89.
39. "On Psychotherapy," *SE* 7: 259.
40. Henri-Frederic Ellenberger, *The Discovery of the Unconscious* (New York: Basic Books, 1970); Léon Chertok and Raymond de Saussure, *La Naissance du psychanalyste* (Paris: Payot, 1973); Franklin Rausky, *Mesmer ou la révolution thérapeutique* (Paris: Payot, 1977).
41. Michel Foucault, *Maladie mentale et personnalité* (Paris: Payot, 1977), p. 71. See also idem, *Madness and Civilization*, pp. 55–57.
42. Michel de Certeau, *La Possession de Loudun* (Paris: Julliard, 1970), chapter entitled "Le Théâtre des possédées."
43. Gérard Wajeman, "L'Hystérie de Morzine," *Ornicar?* 3.
44. Lot-Falck notes, in "Psychopathes et chamans," that the Yakoute *ojun* sometimes falls back into one of the two illnesses that he was supposed to have successively traversed to become a shaman, the *mänärijär* (or possession by spirits) and the *irär* (or dispossession of the soul).
45. On sorcery in rural Mayenne, see Jeanne Favret-Saada, *Les Mots, la mort, les sorts* (Paris: Gallimard, 1977). Also worthy of mention is the tarantulism of Southern Italy, studied by Ernesto de Martino, *La Terre de remords*, Fr. trans. Claude Poncet (Paris: Gallimard, 1966).
46. *The Interpretation of Dreams, SE* 4:101–2.
47. Octave Mannoni, *Un Commencement qui n'en finit pas. Transfert, interprétation, théorie* (Paris: Presses Universitaires de France, 1971), p. 95.
48. Rausky, *Mesmer*, p. 185. Georges Lapassade, "Les Somnambules de Buzancy," in Puységur, *Mémoires*, p. xvi: "Since Mesmer, the magnetizer has replaced the exorcist, and the fluid, the possessive demons."
49. Lacan, *Ecrits: A Selection*, p. 49: "I . . . repudiate any reliance on these states [hypnosis or even narcosis]—and as deliberately as Freud forbade himself recourse to them after a certain time—whether to explain the symptom or to cure it."

The Unconscious, Nonetheless

This essay was developed from a lecture given at the Collège International de Philosophie in November 1987, at the invitation of Dr. René Major. The present English version is somewhat shorter than the French.
1. Michel Henry, *La Généalogie de la psychanalyse* (Paris: Presses Universitaires de France, 1985); henceforth *GP*. Other references in the text are to idem, *The Essence of Manifestation*, trans. Girard Etzkorn (The Hague: Martinus Nijhoff, 1973); henceforth *EM*.
2. Jacques Lacan, *Ecrits: A Selection*, trans. Alan Sheridan (New York: Norton, 1977), p. 1.
3. Idem, *The Four Fundamental Concepts of Psychoanalysis*, trans. Alan Sheridan (London: Norton, 1981), p. 36.

4. Ibid., pp. 35–36, 43–47, etc.

5. Lacan, *Ecrits: A Selection*, p. 166.

6. Edmund Husserl, *The Crisis of European Sciences and Transcendental Phenomenology*, trans. David Carr (Evanston, Ill.: Northwestern University Press, 1970), p. 188.

7. Idem, *Ideas: General Introduction to Pure Phenomenology*, trans. W. R. Boyce Gibson (New York: Macmillan, 1931), p. 143.

8. Georges Bataille, "The Solar Anus" and "Rotten Sun," in *Visions of Excess*, ed. Allan Stoekl (Minneapolis: University of Minnesota Press, 1985); on "life," "intimacy," "immanence," and "transcendence," see his *Théorie de la religion*, in idem, *Oeuvres complètes* (Paris: Gallimard, 1976), vol. 7. These references to Bataille should not cause us to forget that "the interior experience," contrary to the one that Henry speaks of, is first of all that of an "ecstasy" and "communication." Indeed, "we must *live* the experience," and "grasp its sense from within," but that "within" is "a place of communication" (*L'Expérience intérieure*, in ibid., 5: 20–21), that is, an "outside," an "ecstasy": "The interior movements are no object, nor are they subject since they are the subject losing itself. . . . In the end the necessity of getting out of oneself becomes imperious" (ibid., p. 137).

9. Edmund Husserl, *Cartesian Meditations: An Introduction to Phenomenology*, trans. Dorion Cairns (The Hague: Martinus Nijhoff, 1969), p. 33.

10. Critique of phenomenological light and Husserlian theoretism, critique of Heidegger's ek-stasy and "openness" of Being—all these themes cannot help but invoke Emmanuel Lévinas, and, to tell the truth, one is astonished that he is never quoted by Henry. But this is undoubtedly because Henry's paths could not be less Lévinasian. The privilege Lévinas gives to Descartes's *Third Meditation*—that is, via the idea of a divine infinity, to a nonphenomenological relation to the other that, in Henry, remains constantly and profoundly closed to the ego—already testifies to this. On this point, see Bernard Forthomme, "L'Epreuve affective de l'autre," *Revue de Métaphysique et de Morale*, 91st year, no. 1 (Jan–Mar 1986): 90–114.

11. René Descartes, *Discourse on Method, and the Meditations*, trans. F. E. Sutcliffe (New York: Penguin Books, 1968), p. 107.

12. This is what Jean-Luc Nancy ("*Larvatus pro Deo*," in his *Ego sum* [Paris: Aubier-Flammarion, 1979]) was still doing—as part of a reading of the *cogito*, whose intention and goals are, nonetheless, not far from those of Henry.

13. Husserl, *Cartesian Meditations*, p. 35. But Husserl knew, pertinently, that the transcendental reflexion inherent in the *epochê* (the *Ichspaltung*, he says himself) "alters" the original experience by making "an object out of what was previously a subjective process but not objective" (ibid., p. 34). This is the whole problem (an immense one in Husserl) of the retention and capacity of the "living present" to unify the different egos required by

the reduction (a problem that Henry solves rather abruptly by invoking the "*self*-impressing of *self*" by the *Ur-Impression*, *GP*, p. 188).

14. Martin Heidegger, "European Nihilism," in his *Nietzsche*, vol. 4, trans. Frank Capuzzi (San Francisco: Harper and Row, 1982); idem, "Die Zeit des Weltbildes," in his *Holzwege* (Frankfurt: Vittorio Klostermann, 1977).

15. Jacques Derrida, "Cogito and the History of Madness," *Writing and Difference*, trans. Alan Bass (Chicago: University of Chicago Press, 1978), p. 55: "It [the act of the *cogito*] is no longer a question of objective, representative knowledge"; and again, "[Descartes] seeks to reassure himself, . . . to identify the act of the Cogito with a reasonable reason. And he does so as soon as he *proffers* and *reflects* the Cogito. That is to say, he must temporalize the Cogito, which itself is valid only during the instant of intuition" (ibid., p. 58).

16. Lacan, *Four Fundamental Concepts*, p. 141; see especially idem, *L'identification* (stenographic copy of unpublished seminar), lectures of November 15 and 22, 1961.

17. Nancy, *Ego sum*, p. 121 ff.

18. Compare, among many others, this passage from Lacan's *Four Fundamental Concepts*, p. 221: "Of course, every representation requires a subject, but this subject is never a pure subject. . . . There is no subject without, somewhere, *aphanisis* of the subject."

19. Descartes, *Discourse on Method*, pp. 106–7; translation modified.

20. "Sein ist das *transcendens* schlechthin," in Martin Heidegger, *Sein und Zeit* (Tübingen: Niemeyer, 8th ed. 1957), p. 38 (quoted by Henry following the *Letter on Humanism*, *GP*, p. 111).

21. Bataille, *Théorie de la religion*, pp. 293–94.

22. "Instincts and Their Vicissitudes," *SE* 14: 122.

23. "The Unconscious," *SE* 14: 177.

24. "Instincts and Their Vicissitudes," *SE* 14: 121–22. On this equivocation, which has caused a great deal of ink to flow, one should consult James Strachey's introductory notice for this essay in *SE* 14; Paul Ricoeur, *Freud and Philosophy: An Essay on Interpretation*, trans. Denis Savage (New Haven: Yale University Press, 1970), pp. 136–37, n. 57; and Michel Tort, "A propos du concept freudien de 'représentant' (*Repräsentanz*)," *Cahiers pour l'analyse*, no. 5 (Paris: Le Seuil, 1966).

25. "The Unconscious," *SE* 14: 166. "How are we to arrive at a knowledge of the unconscious? It is of course only as something conscious that we know it, after it has undergone transformation [*Umsetzung*] or translation [*Ubersetzung*] into something conscious. Psycho-analytic work shows us every day that translation of this kind is possible."

26. This is the translation proposed by Ricoeur for the Freudian *Repräsentanz* (see his *Freud and Philosophy*, p. 135ff.), but it would be valid only

for "affective representative"—an expression that Freud never uses, and for good reason.

27. "The Unconscious," *SE* 14: 177.

28. Tort, "A propos du concept," p. 45: "It is no accident that this internal exteriority, the excitation coming from the body, is perceived by Freud as radically internal: in the end, it is so internal only by being perceived as being able at each moment to erupt in the 'internal' par excellence, that is, the psyche."

29. "The Unconscious," *SE* 14: 186.

30. "Would be," for so far Henry's book has hardly found any response from the psychoanalysts. (Already in 1965, Lacan, reacting against the theses of *The Essence of Manifestation*, felt the need to silence even the *name* of Michel Henry. I thank Claude Morali for having brought this malicious episode, confined to p. 870 of Jacques Lacan's *Ecrits* [Paris: Le Seuil, 1966], to my attention.) One notable exception to this cold-shoulder strategy: François Roustang, "A Philosophy for Psychoanalysis?" trans. Terry Thomas, *Stanford Literature Review* 6.2 (1989).

31. *The Ego and the Id, SE* 19: 17.

32. Ibid., p. 18.

33. "The Dynamics of Transference," *SE* 12: 97–108.

34. *Beyond the Pleasure Principle, SE* 18: 18.

35. "Remembering, Repeating and Working Through," *SE* 12: 153.

36. *An Autobiographical Study, SE* 20: 42.

37. "Remembering, Repeating and Working Through," *SE* 12: 152.

38. "Acting" is my translation of *agir*, which is Borch-Jacobsen's translation of Freud's *Agieren*, usually translated in English as "acting out," and in French as *mise en acte*. In this regard, see Jean Laplanche and Jean-Bertrand Pontalis, "Acting Out," in their *The Language of Psycho-Analysis*, trans. Donald Nicholson-Smith (New York: Norton, 1973). In the French *Oeuvres complètes* of Freud (Paris: Presses Universitaires de France, 1988–) Jean Laplanche has himself recently opted for the term *agir*—Trans.

39. "Remembering, Repeating and Working Through," *SE* 12: 150–51.

40. "The Dynamics of Transference," *SE* 12: 107–8.

41. *The Ego and the Id, SE* 19: 50–51.

42. *Beyond the Pleasure Principle, SE* 18: 22.

43. *An Autobiographical Study, SE* 20: 42.

44. "Preface to the Translation of Bernheim's *Suggestion*," *SE* 1: 77.

45. "Point of otherness" is the translation adopted by Catherine Porter for *point d'autrui* in Mikkel Borch-Jacobsen, *The Freudian Subject* (Stanford: Stanford University Press, 1988), p. 26ff. *Point d'autrui* also means "no other," and thus it is the point where otherness ceases to be other, the point where I become the other who does not exist—Trans.

46. Josef Breuer and Sigmund Freud, *Studies on Hysteria, SE* 2: 304.

47. *An Autobiographical Study, SE* 20: 43.
48. "The Uncanny," *SE* 17: 236.
49. "Findings, Ideas and Problems," *SE* 23: 300.
50. "Formulations on the Two Principles of Mental Functioning," *SE* 12: 220.
51. *Group Psychology, SE* 18: 105.
52. *The Ego and the Id, SE* 19: 28–30.
53. A formulation of the superego according to Sigmund Freud and William C. Bullit, in his *Thomas Woodrow Wilson: Twenty-Eighth President of the United States—A Psychological Study* (Boston: Houghton Mifflin, 1967), p. 42.

The Alibis of the Subject

This lecture was delivered in October 1990 at the conference "Speculations," organized in London by Sonu Shamdasani and Michael Münchow under the auspices of the Freud Museum.

1. *The Ego and the Id, SE* 19: 13.
2. "Findings, Ideas and Problems," *SE* 23: 300.
3. *Group Psychology, SE* 18: 115: "Hypnosis would solve the riddle of the libidinal constitution of groups for us straight away, if it were not that it itself exhibits some features which are not met by the rational explanation we have hitherto given of it as a state of being in love with the directly sexual trends excluded. There is still a great deal in it which we must recognize as unexplained and mysterious."
4. The short titles in parentheses refer to the following works by Jacques Lacan:

Ecrits (Paris: Le Seuil, 1966).
"Radiophonie," *Scilicet* 2 / 3 (1970).
Ecrits: A Selection, trans. Alan Sheridan (New York: Norton, 1977).
The Four Fundamental Concepts of Psychoanalysis, trans. Alan Sheridan (New York: Norton, 1977).
Les Complexes familiaux dans la formation de l'individu (Paris: Navarin Editeur, 1984).
Le Séminaire, livre VII: L'Éthique de la psychanalyse (Paris: Editions du Seuil, 1986).
The Seminar of Jacques Lacan: Book I. Freud's Papers on Technique, 1953–1954, trans. John Forrester (New York: Norton, 1988).
The Seminar of Jacques Lacan: Book II. The Ego in Freud's Theory and in the Technique of Psychoanalysis, 1954–1955, trans. Sylvana Tomaselli (New York: Norton, 1988).
Le Séminaire XII: L'Envers de la psychanalyse (Paris: Le Seuil, 1991).

5. On the relationship between Alexandre Kojève and Lacan, see Elisabeth Roudinesco, *La Bataille de cent ans: Histoire de la psychanalyse en France* (Paris: Le Seuil, 1986), p. 149 ff.; and Philippe Van Haute, "Lacan en Kojève: Het imaginaire en de dialectiek van de meester en de slaaf," *Tijdschrift voor Filosofie* 48 (1986): 391–415. On the relationship between Sartre and Lacan, see idem, *Psychoanalyse en filosofie, Het imaginaire en het symbolische in het werk van Jacques Lacan* (Louvain: Peeters, 1989), chap. 3 (particularly pp. 122–28).

6. On this question, see the important developments made by Michel Henry in *The Essence of Manifestation*, trans. Gerard Etzkorn (The Hague: Martinus Nijhoff, 1973), Bk. 1, Sec. 1; and idem, *La Généalogie de la psychanalyse* (Paris: Presses Universitaires de France, 1985). See also Manfred Frank, *Die Unhintergehbarkeit von Individualität* (Frankfurt: Suhrkamp, 1986), the chapter entitled "Subjectivity as Self-Consciousness or as Consciousness of Consciousness."

7. René Descartes, *Philosophical Writings of Descartes*, trans. John Cottingham, Robert Stoothoff, and Dugald Murdoch (Cambridge: Cambridge University Press, 1984), 2: 17.

8. G. W. F. Hegel, *Phenomenology of Spirit*, trans. A. V. Miller, (Oxford: Clarendon Press, 1977), p. 110.

9. *Group Psychology*, SE 18: 107: "Identification is the original form of emotional tie [*Gefühlsbindung*] with an object."

10. Both these terms are currently translated in French as *désir*—Trans.

11. Alexandre Kojève, *Introduction to the Reading of Hegel*, trans. James H. Nichols (Ithaca, N.Y.: Cornell University Press, 1969), p. 13.

12. Martin Heidegger, *The Metaphysical Foundations of Logic*, trans. Michael Heim (Bloomington: Indiana University Press, 1984), p. 221.

13. Kojève, *Introduction to Hegel*, p. 141.

14. Jean-Paul Sartre, *Being and Nothingness*, trans. Hazel Barnes (New York: Philosophical Library, 1956), p. 88: "Desire is a lack of being. It is haunted in its inmost being by the being of which it is desire. Thus it bears witness to the existence of lack in the being of human reality."

15. *Qui me regarde* means either "which gazes at me" or "which concerns me"—Trans.

16. *Group Psychology*, SE 18: 113–16.

Library of Congress Cataloging-in-Publication Data

Borch-Jacobsen, Mikkel.
  [Lien affectif. English]
  The emotional tie : psychoanalysis, mimesis, and affect / Mikkel
Borch-Jacobsen.
    p. cm.
  ISBN 0-8047-2035-5 (cl.)—ISBN 0-8047-2037-1 (pbk.)
    1. Psychoanalysis—Philosophy.   2. Identification (Psychology).
  I. Title.
  [DNLM: 1. Hypnosis.   2. Psychoanalytic Theory.   3. Psychotherapy.
WM 460 B726L]
RC509.B6713   1993
150.19′5—dc20
DNLM/DLC
for Library of Congress   92-20356
                                                    CIP

∞ This book is printed on acid-free paper.